Rory MacLean

was born in Vancouver. He has lived in Berlin, Italy, the Hebrides and Clapham Junction. His first book, *Stalin's Nose*, won the *Yorkshire Post* Best First Work prize and was shortlisted for the Thomas Cook Award. *The Oatmeal Ark* and *Under the Dragon* followed, the latter winning an Arts Council Writers' Award and also being shortlisted for the Thomas Cook. He is a regular contributor to BBC Radio 4 and has a soft spot for mermaids.

From the reviews of *Next Exit Magic Kingdom*:

'MacLean pulls off Florida's Mickey Mouse mask and exposes the real face underneath . . . A real "pack it in your suitcase and spill suntan lotion all over it as you sip a rum punch" sort of read'
LUCY GILMORE, *Independent on Sunday*

'Whether tracking alligators, communing with spirits or looking for the Tree of Life in the Garden of Eden, his eye and ear are always sharp, and the weird and wonderful people of Florida don't let him down . . . entertaining and insightful'
ANTHONY SATTIN, *Sunday Times*

'Welcome to Florida, home of Noah's Ark! . . . Some travel books make you want to "go there" with the writer. This one makes you pleased he's done it for you'
NEIL MULLARKEY, *Observer*

'Bizarre!' *Glasgow Evening News*

'A minor triumph of the travel writer's art . . . a sharp, funny, engaging and rather brave attempt to pin down the essence of a very strange, yet strangely magnetic place'
SEAN THOMAS, amazon.co.uk

Further reviews overleaf

Also by Rory MacLean

Stalin's Nose: Across the Face of Europe
The Oatmeal Ark: From the Western Isles to an Inland Sea
Under the Dragon: Travels in a Betrayed Land

Next Exit
Magic Kingdom

Florida Accidentally

Rory MacLean

Flamingo

An Imprint of HarperCollins*Publishers*

To David

Flamingo
An Imprint of HarperCollins*Publishers*
77–85 Fulham Palace Road,
Hammersmith, London W6 8JB

The HarperCollins website address is:
www.**fire**and**water**.com

Published by Flamingo 2001
9 8 7 6 5 4 3 2 1

First published in Great Britain by
HarperCollins*Publishers* 2000

Copyright © Rory MacLean 2000

The Author asserts the moral right to
be identified as the author of this work

ISBN 0 00 655228 5

Set in Simoncini Garamond and News Gothic

Printed and bound in Great Britain by
Omnia Books Limited, Glasgow

Contents

Apalachicola River

Sawdust

Bristol

Ta

Apalachicola

AIR CONDITIONING
INVENTED HERE

NOAH'S ARK
BUILT HERE
(GARDEN OF
EDEN TOO)

Next Exit Magic Kingdom

A Journey around the Sunshine State,
Florida USA.

------ Route taken

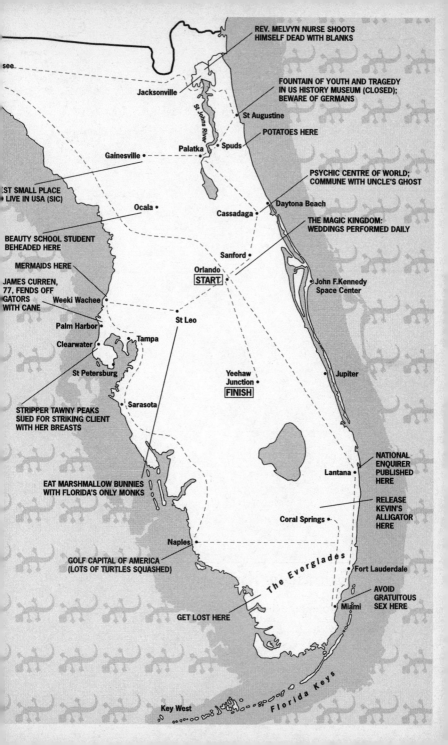

REV. MELVYN NURSE SHOOTS HIMSELF DEAD WITH BLANKS

FOUNTAIN OF YOUTH AND TRAGEDY IN US HISTORY MUSEUM (CLOSED); BEWARE OF GERMANS

Jacksonville

St Johns River

St Augustine

POTATOES HERE

Palatka • Spuds

Gainesville •

PSYCHIC CENTRE OF WORLD; COMMUNE WITH UNCLE'S GHOST

...EST SMALL PLACE ...LIVE IN USA (SIC)

Ocala •

Cassadaga •

Daytona Beach

THE MAGIC KINGDOM: WEDDINGS PERFORMED DAILY

BEAUTY SCHOOL STUDENT BEHEADED HERE

Sanford •

MERMAIDS HERE

Orlando START

JAMES CURREN, 77, FENDS OFF GATORS WITH CANE

John F. Kennedy Space Center

Weeki Wachee •

Palm Harbor •

St Leo •

Clearwater • • Tampa

St Petersburg

Yeehaw Junction • FINISH

Jupiter •

STRIPPER TAWNY PEAKS SUED FOR STRIKING CLIENT WITH HER BREASTS

• Sarasota

NATIONAL ENQUIRER PUBLISHED HERE

EAT MARSHMALLOW BUNNIES WITH FLORIDA'S ONLY MONKS

Lantana •

RELEASE KEVIN'S ALLIGATOR HERE

Coral Springs •

Naples •

GOLF CAPITAL OF AMERICA (LOTS OF TURTLES SQUASHED)

The Everglades

Fort Lauderdale

AVOID GRATUITOUS SEX HERE

GET LOST HERE

Miami •

Florida Keys

Key West

1

Stumble onto the Beach

Chance of a Lifetime! Sunsational Orlando
Fly-drives from £199
Just Do It!

DAILY MAIL

Yetminster, Friday 24th – I went to Florida because the *Daily Mail* was delivered to my door by mistake. If my usual paper had turned up I'd be in Germany now.

I threw on some clothes, sprinted up the High Street and joined the early-morning scrum at Oak House Stores. A snarl of dripping umbrellas and muddy dogs in the doorway. Dorothy, at the head of the queue, said she was sorry we had missed the garden-club talk on training ramblers. She took the last copy of the *Telegraph*. Frances, the vicar's wife, has dyed her hair leek-green. She bought the last *Independent*. I watched *The Times* and the *Western Gazette* go with Evershot loaves and bantam eggs. When I reached the counter all the other papers had been sold. Dawn laughed and winked and leaned towards me to say, 'Call it the luck of the draw.' I was stuck with the *Mail*.

It's not yet a year since we settled in the village, unpacking our knapsacks and swapping our old Escort for a new lawn-mower. Our puppy inherited Winston's collar and lead. The Burmese basket was stowed in my father's steamer trunk. Katrin's passport expired. We scrubbed the walls of distemper, painted the bedroom cameo white and planted lavender by the front door. We dug in the garden until putting down roots gave me itchy feet.

My most prized possession is the ability to travel, and I soon realised that it was time to make another journey. I considered the options, weighed up the alternatives and settled on a destination. At the time it seemed rational to return to the country where my first book had begun, one project evolving out of another, so I started my research. But unlike my experience with previous books, nothing seemed to work out. The road may be no stranger, yet the E30 Hanover autobahn didn't welcome me back like an old friend.

For four months I've been preparing to write a book about Germany. I've mapped out a journey along the old trade routes that used to wind across the country and have today been severed by motorways. I've ploughed through dense tomes called *Über Alles* and *Made in Germany: The Corporate Identity of a Nation*. Annotated maps of the Black Forest are pinned to my study wall. The 'Romantic Fairy-tale Trail' unfolds across my floor. I've written two dozen letters in bungled German – a language which I don't speak – to various august organisations – which don't respond. Only one walking club has agreed to help me, and their chief guide – Herr Schlinzig – thinks that I am a woman. Katrin is too busy making baskets for Dorset Arts Week to travel with me. Both Corinna and the Kellers are away on holiday. And yesterday it started snowing in Düsseldorf.

I don't lack tenacity. I can handle disappointment. But waste drives me mad. With each passing week I became more and more determined not to squander the time I'd already invested in the trip, even if Luck seemed unwilling to join me on it. So I was resolved not to waste the *Mail* either. I flicked to the Travel pages to find a cheap flight to Hamburg. I looked down column after column but couldn't find one. Next I tried for Berlin. No joy. Frankfurt? Not a sausage. There wasn't a single flight to Germany advertised on any of the *Mail's* fifteen travel pages. It started me thinking.

I phoned my friend David.

'If no one wants to visit Germany,' I said to him, 'who'll be interested in reading a book about the place?'

'Germany?' said David. 'Oh God, you don't want to write about Germany.'

He hadn't mentioned this before.

'Any book will be just *laden* with themes, like looking for bits of clothing left over from the Holocaust.'

This wasn't particularly helpful.

'So where *is* everyone going, then?' he asked.

I glanced back at the paper. The travel advertisements were both big and small, in colour and black and white, on page after page, and all to the same destination: 'Sunsational Fun. Fly-drive Gatorland. Jacksonville Hotline.'

'Florida,' I replied. 'All the ads are for Florida.'

'Florida's perfect,' he said without hesitation.

'Perfect for what?'

'For you. Have you been there?'

'Never. I don't know anything about it.'

'*Perfect*,' he said again, this time with feeling. 'You don't go with any expectations. You just go.'

'David, be sensible,' I said, alarm bells ringing in my head. David lets ideas run away with him, and I was wary of being trampled underfoot. 'My room's knee-deep with brochures on Schleswig-Holstein. All the maps have lines drawn on them. I could walk the medieval trade routes with my eyes closed. I can tell you all about German plans for European integration, but I don't even know what the capital of Florida is.'

'Miami,' he said, as cool as a cucumber. 'Or Tallahassee.'

'"Make your Disney dreams come true,"' I read aloud from the *Mail*, hoping to tether his galloping enthusiasm. 'I don't *have* any Disney dreams.'

'Listen, the more organising you do beforehand, the more baggage you take with you. It limits you. I tell you, Florida's got legs.'

'But I hate beaches. I keep out of the sun. I'm like Woody Allen – I don't tan, I stroke.'

'At least you speak the language.'

'And I don't know what to write about.'

'Just talk to people, tell the truth and don't try to be clever. The book will write itself. And it'll get you out of bloody Dorset.'

'I like Dorset,' I told him, but then I hesitated. The idea was mad, barking mad, but Florida suddenly *felt* right.

Over the months I'd been banging my head against a brick Berlin Wall. My contacts disappeared and my itineraries seized up. I buckled down, persevered and got a headache. '*Du bist auf dem Holzweg*,' Herr Schlinzig might have told me, though I wouldn't have understood him. You're following a wooden path. On the wrong track.

'I suppose it would be a cheaper trip,' I said, admitting to myself that Germany's appeal was waning faster than a European Currency Unit. Any trip there would be heavy with history, causality and potato dumplings. In Florida on the other hand I could travel lightly, without expectations, by chance. 'A fly-drive package to Orlando probably costs the same as a bus ride from Hamburg to Bremen.'

At that very moment – and I promise this is true – it stopped raining, and the sweeping arc of a rainbow appeared above Knighton Hill. I told David.

'It's a sign,' he cried, quite manic now. 'It'll be such a gas. You'll have fun. You'll get laid.'

'I don't want to get laid, David. I'm married.'

'I wish *I* was going to Florida,' he said. And who would have said that about Germany?

I don't know *anything* about Florida. So I went downstairs and rummaged through the old newspapers in the utility room. I found one article on HIV-positive gays partying to death in Miami. I also remembered reading another piece about American college kids congregating on Panama City Beach for casual sex every Easter. But I couldn't find it. The section had been used for the puppy to pee on. Probably a good thing, too. Then I e-mailed my brother in Canada. He's reliable and level-headed. I needed an objective opinion: Tampa or Tübingen? He replied within five minutes.

'I believe Florida is the best place for your next book. This way you can expose the blue-hair-rinse scandal and I can come down and visit you in your Ernest-Hemingway-novel-on-the-beach and share martinis.'

So I told Katrin.

'*I* want to go to Florida,' she said, her summer-breeze demeanour turning chilly. '*I* want to lie on the beach.'

She hadn't offered to come with me to Flensburg. Missing out on sunbathing by the Baltic hadn't been too great a sacrifice for her.

'I'm not going to lie on the beach,' I told her. 'I'll be working.'

'Well you can go off, then, and leave me at Surfside.'

My mother took it in her stride. 'Darling, before you go – wherever you go – do you mind going up into the attic and getting down the silver?'

But my mother-in-law was another matter. She *is* German, and during the planning of the trip I had quipped, 'After I've written a book about the real Germany, my mother-in-law will never speak to me again. It's the price one pays for literature.'

Now that I was considering not writing about Germany, it was Katrin's turn to joke.

'Your mother-in-law really *will* never speak to you again,' she said.

Katrin's day hadn't got off to a good start. I'd brought her the wrong paper, spent half an hour arguing with David on the phone, and still hadn't taken the puppy out for its walk. In protest the dog had chewed two inches off its new willow basket.

Katrin banged the pots and pans as she put them away. 'You have to decide between Florida or Germany right now,' she told me, dumping the cutlery into the drawer.

'Why now?' I asked.

'Because I arranged to call Herr Schlinzig this morning.'

'Herr Schlinzig?'

'The guide who thinks you're a woman. You're due to meet him on Monday in Lübeck. And then go walking together. Remember?'

I'd never spoken to Schlinzig. He'd written a nice letter to me, in German. It had taken me almost two hours to read. So Katrin had made all the calls to him. His English was as bad as my German. And I was about to spend a week wandering the old *Salzstraße* with him, repeating over and over my stock German phrases: Will it still be snowing tomorrow? Shall we have *bratwurst* for lunch again today? Are there many themes in German society?

Katrin wanted an answer. She might feel cheated out of the beach. She might be willing to accept temporary desertion. But she would not tolerate thoughtlessness or indecision.

'Germany or Florida?' she asked again, her fingers hovering over the telephone.

I didn't answer her. I was distracted. I had just remembered a footnote torn out of a newspaper, alongside an article on the cost of Bavarian agricultural reform. It was about last-minute flights.

I sat Katrin down, restrained her from calling the Fatherland, and pelted upstairs to look for the article. I found it, charged back down to the kitchen and rang the Last Chance Holiday Shop.

'Anything going to Florida,' I asked, breathless. 'Tomorrow?'

At 35,000 feet, Saturday 25th – Decided to do some preparation. For my previous books I'd spent up to half a year reading, planning, cobbling together a sort of loose-limbed hypothesis of how the journey might evolve. This time nothing was set in stone. I hoped that by travelling in an open manner, without a fixed design, the act of making would be influenced by chance and change, would lead me somewhere that I did not necessarily expect to be. Like Orlando. So I began my research. I opened the in-flight magazine.

I hadn't slept before leaving for Gatwick. All night I'd heard noises, mysterious thumpings somewhere in the house.

'Thumpings in your head, more likely,' said Katrin.

Her humour hadn't improved, though she had helped me to pack my bag: shorts, t-shirts, laptop, Factor 15.

'Every time I begin to drift off,' she complained around midnight, 'you start crackling like a lightning conductor beside me.'

I got up. Went downstairs. Checked the puppy. Checked the safety locks on the windows. Came back to bed. Tried to think of films and TV series set in Florida: *Key Largo*, *Miami Vice*, *Scarface*. Had none of them on video. Tossed. Turned. Woke Katrin, again. Got up, again. Went back downstairs and turned on the television. Chance will direct me, I thought. Serendipity will dish me out a sign. I tuned in to a rerun of *Holiday*. Somebody named Monty Don – who, according to the *Daily-Mail*-which-changed-my-life, is a 'rugged outdoor type' – became a stunt man for a day at Universal Studios Florida. He was thrown into the deep end with a fibreglass Great White shark. Decided to skip Universal Studios. Turned off the TV. Left home early.

I reached Gatwick and walked into a party. Barney the purple dinosaur was working the queues. Pluto signed autographs. There are 116 direct flights a week from the UK to Orlando but, judging from the crowd in the South Terminal, that's not enough. The passengers all wore baseball caps and shades, as if West Palm had come to West Sussex. Some of them carried golf clubs, others snorkels and scuba tanks. A woman in shorts asked me if I'd met the Blues Brothers yet. I hadn't, so she gave me a Mickey Mouse balloon. A surfer from Southend flexed his biceps and longed for Key West. The check-in clerk's designer black cap read 'FLA, USA'. My droopy, bleached sunhat was not going to cut much ice on Boynton Beach. I found the puppy's teething ring in my pocket.

I called Rachel, my agent, just before boarding. 'You know that book I was going to write on Germany.'

'Was?' said Rachel, quick off the mark. 'What do you mean "was"?'

I explained about the *Daily Mail* and how, since my decision to go to Florida all those minutes ago, things had begun to slip into place. The preparations had been effortless: finding a flight, booking a car, packing my swimming trunks. There was no need for a phrase book, visa or permit. I hadn't even bothered to bring a map. Researching Germany had left me anxious and shorter of hair. In contrast, America was a breeze.

'You know that feeling when you arrive in a new city and sense that you should turn left,' I enthused, 'but you don't listen to yourself and instead rely on signposts or bad advice?'

Rachel didn't respond.

'You get lost, wander around, only to return hours later to the original spot and realise that the instinct to turn left was right.'

Still she said nothing.

'That's how I feel now.'

I reasoned that a measure of Florida chill-out would suit me fine. Then I mentioned the rainbow to her.

'Sorry if I'm a little slow,' she said. I was patient with her. It was early, and her son Milo was crying for his first feed. 'Are you saying you've dropped four months' preparation and decided to fly to Orlando simply because a rainbow happened to appear outside your window?'

'Yup,' I replied. For me Germany was history.

Rachel sighed. 'Have fun,' she said. 'And don't get shot.'

We're still climbing, now passing over Dorset. I can make out the Isle of Purbeck and the curve of Chesil Beach. There's a flash of light away to the north – the weather vane of St Andrew's Yetminster, or an aircraft flying to Bonn?

'Sit back, relax and let us bring America to you,' oozes a cabin attendant. On offer is a hot brunch of chicken nuggets, potato smiles and Lime Slime dessert. I pass up on a Southern Star cocktail. The movie – after reruns of *Cheers* and *Frasier* – stars Jack Nicholson and a dog.

On the in-flight magazine's world map I trace our course west: the Great Circle Route across the North Atlantic, landfall over rocky Newfoundland, south down the eastern seaboard. I follow the line beyond my destination to the Caribbean, with its ten thousand coral islands, and South

America. The spine of the Andes winds down the continent's back like a Quechua Indian's braid. To the west stretches the broad blue Pacific, its scattered atolls stepping-stones for fleet-footed Polynesian giants. Its waters lap against New Zealand's green glaciers and plunging fjords. The Daintree rainforest rises behind the Great Barrier Reef. Asia dips its fingers into the Indonesian archipelago. There are hot green curries to taste in Bangkok's street kitchens and cloves to smell in the spice bazaars of Kerala. In Sri Lanka dawn breaks over Adam's Peak, casting a shadow across the clouds. Desert-dry feet walk on fox-brown Bessarabian carpets. The spring tide scours the beach in Zanzibar. At the full moon visitors to Victoria Falls lift their eyes to catch sight of a luminous lunar rainbow. But I'm not travelling so far. Like two million Britons every year, I am heading to Florida, a sort of limp penis dangling off the body of America.

It hits me now, here in the aircraft, somewhere beyond Land's End. Is this any way to start a book, lacking in sleep, without a route, flying in the wrong direction? As a rule travel books recount rare journeys that have a rational purpose. They tell heroic stories about paddling up the Congo in search of pre-historic lakes, or crossing the Atlantic in leather boats. Maybe I should be following the trail of, say, Ponce de León, the explorer who looked for the secret of eternal life in Florida?

(My research is paying off. I found that gem in the in-flight magazine. Also some amazing facts about the International Banana Museum.)

Maybe I should visit towns with German place names, as a sort of homage to the months of research.

(Next stop Frink, Fla.?)

Or try to navigate through the Florida Keys with a road map of the Black Forest.

(I just found one in my carry-on bag. Turn right at the Bodensee. Looks like a bayou to me.)

Or is it enough simply to be open to chance and to learn to accept it? At any moment the fellow in the next seat may turn to me and ask, 'Excuse me, sir, but you don't happen to know the undiscovered yet fascinating town of Waldo?'

(I have my doubts, especially as he's fallen asleep under a copy of *Golf Illustrated*.)

Over a quivering bowl of Lime Slime I realise that I'm scared. I have no security blanket of notes to wrap around my anxiety. No string of colourful local contacts. No hilarious synopsis or signed contract. All I'm carrying to Florida is a full load of ignorance. My itchy feet begin to shake with a nervous twitch.

I try to get a grip. Remind myself that I'm driven forward not by theory but by events, by curiosity, by a desire to understand. I steel myself. Decide just to jump in the car, hit the road and stop at the first friendly place that takes my fancy.

'Say, this *is* a pretty town,' I'll say to a local character.

'Hands up, asshole, and give me your wallet.'

Jonathan Raban once wrote, 'When the true and sincere traveller pulls the front door shut and turns the key in the lock, he casts himself adrift in the world. For the foreseeable future, he'll be a creature of chance and accident.'

That is what I am doing. Heading out into the unknown. Filled with anticipation. Asking myself, 'What the hell am I doing here? I should be in Glückstadt.'

2

'Wo ist Arcadia, Herr Sheriff?'

Randall James Baker, forty-five, shot his friend Robert Callihan, forty-seven, in the head while attempting to blast the button off the top of his new baseball cap.

ORLANDO SENTINEL

Orlando, Saturday 25th *(still)* – America. A vast stars-and-stripes sails above the airport terminal building. The immigration officers carry guns.

'Have you ever been or are you now involved in espionage or sabotage; or in terrorist activities; or genocide; or between 1933 and 1945 were you involved, in any way, in persecutions associated with Nazi Germany or its allies? (Tick Yes or No.)'

In the arrivals hall filling out landing papers. The I-94W *Non Immigrant Visa Waiver Arrival Form* seems more suited to German border control. It also asks if I have a communicable disease.

'You travelling by yourself, Rory?' asks Deloris, the US immigration officer. I know her name is Deloris because she wears a name badge ('Hi! I'm Deloris! Obey Me!'). Bleached blonde bob, copper-brown arms and a pistol; a Barbie doll with attitude.

Behind her the President smiles in Kodacolor.

'I'm a creature of chance,' I tell her. Kookily. Casting myself adrift. Then add in a reasoned tone, 'My wife wanted to stay at home with the puppy.'

Deloris doesn't high-five me. She doesn't yell, 'Are you going to have a good time or what?' Instead she says, 'That right?' She's unmoved, even when I show her the teething ring. If I fell to my knees and confessed to being a closet fascist, spying for Libya and dishing out communicable diseases in my spare time, she would have taken it in her stride. She knows my type. Class C2 (Chance, Creature of): 90-Day Stay Granted. She stamps both the I-94W and my passport.

'You have a good time, you hear,' she tells me. And doesn't wink.

At the Alamo car rental counter Fran hands me the keys to a new, metallic-green Chevy Cavalier and asks, 'D'y'all know where you're headin'?'

'No,' I admit.

'Disney World? Wet'n Wild? Buc'neer Bay?' She wants to direct me onto the appropriate airport exit road. 'MGM Studios? Marineland?'

I shake my head. The other passengers have collected their cars and high-tailed it out of the airport. Some of them may already be queuing for the *Terminator 2* simulator ride.

'How 'bout Monkey Jungle?'

'Where are the theme parks?' I ask her.

'To the south, mostly.'

'Then I'll head north.' I look at her free Alamo map and poke my finger at the central section of the state. 'I'll go up around here.'

Fran is in her early twenties, fresh-faced and full-bodied – that is, fat. A victim of snack abuse. Not a stranger to Burger King Smoothies. 'Get Ready for Unlimited Smileage' billows across her ample chest. On Sundays she probably bakes Rice Krispies Treats and scoffs half of them before they cool. But now she looks at me like a sensible schoolmistress.

'You know anything 'bout Florida, Rory?' she asks me, focusing her lax, Have-a-Nice-Day gaze.

'Sure,' I reply. 'I know that flamingos and melanoma are big here, that there are lots of Cubans and fashion victims. And that I don't need Wellington boots.'

'So you haven't been here before?'

'No.'

'Are you familiar with the term "rednecks"?'

'Of course.' I'd seen the cigarette ads.

'Up here' – she pokes at my random destination – 'they don't get many visitors. It's a closed society, you understand. Tourists tend to stick to the coasts.'

'So there are really *two* Floridas?' I say, excited, thinking that my luck is in. This might be my purpose: to explore the parallel Floridas of tourists and residents.

'I guess,' says Fran with a lazy shrug.

Then again, it might not be.

'Do you remember a TV programme called *The Andy Griffith Show*?' she asks.

I do. I grew up with it in Canada. Like the Andy Hardy films and *Leave it to Beaver*, it was the American equivalent of the Ealing comedies. Both portrayed a cosy, ideal world which never existed. A deputy sheriff might take an afternoon off to compete in the county singing competition. And so reform a local mischief-maker. Or a handful of villagers would stand up against state bureaucracy to save a branch-line railway. And win. The comedies epitomised the values of the day: optimism, neighbourliness and faith in abiding goodness. They were amiable, enchanting, fake folk art.

'It ain't like that any more.'

'There are no more Good Humor ice-cream vans ringing their bells in Happy Valley?' I ask. Unlike the programme itself, which runs and runs on cable TV.

'Nope.'

'Oh.'

'So how 'bout Gatorland?'

I'm tired after the flight and the sleepless last night at home. But I don't want to spend the next month in Gatorland.

'Are you telling me,' I ask, 'that if I drive into a small town the locals might not be too helpful.' Maybe Fran just doesn't like my sunhat.

'Might not be.'

She hands me the Alamo Guide to Safe Travel. It advises travellers to keep their car doors locked and their windows up when driving. If lost, the guide suggests, do not pull over on the side of the road and study your map. Instead, drive to a well-lit, populated, public place. It also recommends to 'be sure to check inside and underneath your car' before hopping behind the wheel. Not a rousing endorsement of Southern hospitality.

'It ain't for nothin' that Florida's got Old Sparky.'

'Old Sparky?'

'The electric chair.'

I'm surprised that the guide doesn't add, 'Try not to speak to anyone at all, except law enforcement officials, and hurry home as soon as your wallet is empty.'

'Look, if you really don't want the parks, then why not go up to Saint Augustine?' Fran advises, handing me the map. 'It's a bit touristy but it's nice and – well – kinda European. There's the Bavarian Bierkeller up there.'

I smile in a lax sort of way. 'Thanks.'

'Drive happy,' she says.

Step outside the terminal building. It's hot. Oven hot. Start to sweat.

'Steamier than the devil's bedroom today,' says a car jockey who directs me across the molten lot.

I take off my jacket, jumper and shirt. I start the Cavalier and turn on the air-conditioning. I dump my carry-on in the boot. I put up the windows. There's a one-touch button on the dash which locks the car's four doors. All that's missing is a .357 Magnum in the glovebox.

I toss Fran's crumpled map onto the back seat, put the car into Drive and wait.

Five seconds. Ten seconds. A minute.

Nothing happens.

No prophetic stranger knocks on the window and tells me to head to Okeechobee. No Southern Sibyl in flowing white robes appears beyond the bonnet holding a sign which reads, 'Turn right for Pensacola, sugar.' No inspiration comes to me. I simply drive out of the car park and take the wrong exit and end up at the air-freight terminal. I make a U-turn and nearly slam into a Datsun which shoots out of nowhere. I collect myself, drive west for twenty minutes, then turn around and head right back to my starting point. I may not know where I'm going, but at least the petrol is cheap.

At a 'populated, public place' I get out of the car and smooth out the map on the ground. Should I throw three *I Ching* coins onto it? Or roll a pair of dice? Or try to divine the future by counting through forty-nine yarrow stalks? The procedures do not suit a critical mind used to scientific method and objective analysis. Florida is a peninsula, all but surrounded by water, almost an island. For the foreseeable future my only confines will be its coasts and the state line to the north. But I have no idea where to begin. In a moment of weakness I think of Alpine villages, hear Bavarian cowbells, imagine buxom waitresses clutching foaming beersteins. Then I smell burning skin. I look down and watch my forearms turn red. I need to make a decision. I have to get out of the sun.

Close my eyes and throw a pencil at the map. The tip punctures Saint Johns County. I call a motel chain's toll-free number and ask an operator to find me a room near the pencil's tear. She books me one in Daytona. I climb back in the car, lock the doors and drive north up I-4.

I'm *en route* without a route, following my instincts, totally knackered. Turn on the car radio. On WKIS 740 AM the German band Kraftwerk chants, '*Fahren, fahren, fahren auf den Autobahn*'. Retune and Chuck Berry sings 'No Particular Place to Go'. Robert Lynd, the essayist, once wrote, 'It is only in literature that coincidences seem unnatural.' Maybe he had a loose grasp on the laws of probability.

Windscreens glint along the Interstate. Arrow-straight roads run away to the ocean. The land is flat and ugly but the azure sky goes on forever. There's a squashed armadillo on the roadside. I realise that the Dartford Marshes are more attractive.

Pull into a shopping mall and buy a notebook, ten gallons of Winn-Dixie Sodium Free Spring Water and three pounds of glossy Yankee Macintosh apples. Add a six-pack of blueberry muffins to my basket. Almost everything on the shelves seems loaded with Nutrasweet.

At the checkout I start yawning. I think this place is called Sanford, but I'm not sure. I ask how far it is to Daytona.

'Say what?' says the ebony teenager behind the till ('Hi! I'm Latasha. Your Cashier Today').

'Daytona,' I repeat, slowly, suddenly light-headed.

'*Day*tona,' she says, mimicking my pronunciation, and enters into a conversation with the Latino bag-packer. 'About two hours,' they decide. 'For you.'

'Two hours?' I hear myself say. I might not last two minutes. 'Can you point me in the direction of the nearest motel?'

'I just *love* your accent,' gushes Latasha.

The Budget Inn on Highway 17-92 'overlooks beautiful Lake Ada'. But from the reception desk I can only see Gibson's

Truck World. I negotiate ten dollars off the rate, take a room and fall into the pool. A five-year-old child in a bikini displays herself on a sunbed. Two other kids argue over small change by the Coke machine. I float on my back gazing up into the endless evening sky. I lock myself out of my room and – dripping wet – call the manager for help. He throws his shoulder against the door. It opens.

'You didn't have your Wheaties this morning.' Wheaties – the Breakfast of Champions.

I turn up the Coolerator and call Katrin.

'The puppy's started eating slugs,' she says, 'because she can't find her teething ring.'

I tell her it was almost seized by the US Government.

'Are you all right?' she asks.

'Sure,' I reassure her. Having a good time. No worries.

'So where are you driving tomorrow?' she asks.

'North,' I say, and my voice goes tight. Am I worried? Yes. Anxious? Yup. Charged? Absolutely. 'Somewhere . . . north.'

I'm adrift in Florida.

At 3 a.m. a black man wakes me, standing outside my door, yelling into his mobile phone, 'Tell me where you are, you bad-ass bitch. Tell me your room number. I'm coming to git you.'

Next door I hear laughter, then a woman calling, 'I'm here, Lionel.'

Minutes later the sound of their lovemaking shakes the shared wall.

'That feels good, honey,' moans the woman. 'I feel so good.'

Feeling good. Looking good. Good Humor. Drive happy. The cheap wall lamps begin to shiver and the woman cries out.

'Baby, that's bad,' roars Lionel.

I eat three muffins. The solitary footsteps of a Pizza Hut delivery man squeak on the balcony. Tyres lick on pavement. Police sirens sound like car alarms. I fall asleep in my air-con cocoon to the muffled drone of distant televisions.

Sanford, Sunday 26th – I pack and check out of the motel. It's too early for waffles at Mel's Family Diner. Or a quick-lube at Gibson's Truck World. Lionel and his friend are asleep, still feeling good. Pizza boxes lie open like giant cardboard molluscs beached on the parking lot.

I turn left onto the highway, rested now, at ease, letting the day take me where it will.

In the cool morning a blonde in a metallic cherry convertible drags on a Marlboro Light, her brown left leg tucked up beneath her. A pink furry pig dangles above the dashboard. Oreo cookie vans, thundering sixteen-wheelers and low-slung black Corvettes drive alongside me. There are Trailways buses and chopper motorcycles, gas-guzzling rustbuckets and stretch limos. A Highway Patrol car slices up the fast lane. A biker stripped to the waist is making for the beach. Sunday-best families ride to church and RVs head for KOA campgrounds. A U-haul rental van with out-of-state plates lumbers by, towing the family car. This is a restless, mobile society: Daytona Beach 53 miles, Saint Augustine 105 miles, Los Angeles 2,661 miles.

I drift north, cutting between industrial parks and fields of high grass, McDonald's drive-ins and the backsides of housing estates with clothes lines and above-ground swimming pools. Cross a river as thick and brown as gravy. Ranks of orange groves march off to American breakfast tables. I see no Good Humor vans.

Twenty minutes beyond Sanford, I pass a sign: 'Next Exit Cassadaga Spiritualist Camp (a Historical District since

1992)'. Curiosity catches hold of me in a brace of shakes. Kersmack! I'd planned to go further towards the pencil tear, equating distance driven with distance travelled, but swing off the Interstate instead. At Junction 54. As if I've been thrown a lifeline. It's lucky I don't have an accident.

'Psychic Center of the World', reads the awning of the old Cassadaga Hotel. 'Astral Projections and Past Life Regenerations our Speciality.'

I park outside the Oracle Office and wind down a grey, sandy lane overhung with canopies of green towards Spirit Pond. Magnolia leaves blow down the sleepy side-roads like tarot cards, snapping in the breeze. Five mediums are on duty at the Spiritualist Therapy Center. Crystal angels and lush potplants hang above broad verandahs. Silvery chimes ring from every balcony and branch.

Screen doors don't slam in Cassadaga. They sigh shut.

As I walk, a purple haze of superannuated hippies emerges from the faded clapboard houses, their neon flares flapping above O'Neill sandals. A ponytailed Philemon and a coltish Baucis appear hand-in-hand, wearing matching embroidered waistcoats. Rip van Winkle lifts himself up from his porch swing, then leaps over his holistic herb bed.

'The dream workshop was *so* far out,' I overhear, catching up with the peppy geriatrics. 'Andre touched Jupiter.'

I imagine them pitching tepees behind the termite-infested walls, sitting cross-legged around incense burners, chanting mantras to the earth spirits. They might gaze into crystal balls and read the runes. They may even divine where I should go in Florida.

'Hollywood's bug for the kabbalistic texts is fantabulous.'

The heady residents converge on the Colby Memorial Temple, meeting, greeting, touching. I fall into line behind them, feel for my notebook and follow Rip's kaleidoscopic bandanna into the mock-Moorish auditorium.

The 'camp' was founded by George Colby, a trance medium and 'the Seer of Spiritualism'. He came to Florida in 1875, 'led through the wilderness by his spirit guide Seneca who instructed him to organise a psychic center on the site'. The first believers to follow him lived in tents until cottages were built. Under the hanging beards of Spanish moss they practised the gift of mediumship, affirmed the continuity of existence 'after the change called death' and lived in 'the fellowship of kindred spirits'. The Ladies' Auxiliary arranged card parties and an annual masquerade ball.

Inside, a verger hands me a turquoise Spiritualist Hymnal. I find a place on a packed pew. The Reverend Jerry Frederich, the camp pastor, leads the congregation in an enthusiastic rendition of 'Beautiful Isle of Somewhere'. The tune is Christian and familiar. The words are childish and vague.

'Land of the true,
where we live a-new,
Beautiful Isle of Somewhere.'

'We believe that the phenomena of nature, both physical and spiritual, are the expression of Infinite Intelligence,' Frederich then intones, his head bowed in prayer. 'We affirm that communication with the so-called dead is a fact, scientifically proven by the phenomena of Spiritualism.'

Two hundred regular worshippers and curious passers-by gather for the Sunday service under the temple's lazy ceiling fans. A white-haired matron in a flowery straw hat kneels beside a bean-slender student in a long, black Lycra dress. The camp's aged residents mix with dozens of youngsters in clean jeans and tasselled thunderbird jackets.

The electronic organ swells, ebbs and flows. Jerry lifts his arms towards the heavens:

'Do not stand at my grave and weep.
I am not there. I do not sleep.'

Three candles are lit on the stage, symbolising body, mind and spirit. There are dozens of flowers and an American flag. No Christian cross. I try to catch the eye of the slender student to share the joke, but instead of looking my way she too bursts into song:

'I am a thousand winds that blow,
I am the diamond glints on snow.
I am the sunlight on ripened grain,
I am the gentle autumn rain.'

The congregation joins her in her devotions, singing with heartfelt fervour. Strangers embrace. Rip links arms with Philemon. I pinch myself.

'When you awaken in the morning's hush
I am the swift uplifting rush
Of quiet birds in circled flight.
I am the soft stars that shine at night.
Do not stand at my grave and cry,
I am not there; I did not die.'

Over ten million self-proclaimed Spiritualists live in the USA.

'Dolly Cargill, Woody Henderson, Connie Pearson and Doc

Schmidt,' chants Jerry, remembering family and friends who have 'passed over to the Higher Side of Life'. His thin grey hair has been slicked into a tragic seventies quiff. It might even be tinted with Grecian Formula. 'Mimi Sourant and all the loved ones of Eleanor Goodwin; dear ones whose continuing existence we commemorate.' There's a button missing from his acrylic blazer. 'We affirm that the doorway to reformation is never closed against any human soul, here or hereafter.'

'Hallelujah!'

Then Jerry invites us to be healed.

'Two particles, once separated, will always be linked, and will always search for that link.'

Pew by pew we step to the back of the hall and sit on a line of stools, as if at a barbershop for the spirit. We are to *anticipate* being healed, to *concentrate* on the power the Great Unseen Healing Force within us, to breathe deeply and to 'let go and let God'.

I smirk, anticipating a promise of instant enlightenment, and follow a smiling Cuban with a plump, babbling infant. She settles herself on a stool, closes her eyes, and the child falls quiet. The resident healers stand behind us, laying their hands on our shoulders, foreheads, stomachs. They chant blessings, channel energies and call for health and happiness:

'I ask the Great Unseen Healing Force
To remove all obstructions
From my mind and body
And to restore me to perfect health.
I ask this in all sincerity and honesty,
and I will do my part.'

'Take care of this person . . .' whispers my healer, a bright-eyed sexagenarian in Hopi string tie. 'Keep him well, and keep those who he loves well.' I am surprised by the softness of his hands.

Another hymn follows, then prayers and announcements. An upcoming workshop on 'the Alchemy of Humor'. Monday evening's Mediums Night (Mini-readings $15). Arrangements for next weekend's Gala Day. Jerry reminds the congregation of the 'Healing Hotline'.

'In an attempt to offer more healing opportunities,' he says with homespun sincerity, 'we have established an absentee network of caring individuals who will generate immediate spiritual power to help you in times of emergencies.'

He gives out the Hotline's telephone number. The man sitting next to me scribbles it onto a matchbook. And the absurdity of my being here, of having stumbled off the Interstate onto New Age touchy-feely Florida, makes me want to laugh out loud. The ceremony is trite and tacky, the Oprah Winfrey Show in polyester. I would hotfoot it out of town, make tracks for the map's pencil tear, were it not for the congregation's profound, dazzling devotion. They bow their heads, cultivate humility and reach for the elusive realm of existence shimmering beyond the test tube.

'My first premonition was the most frightening,' says Mario, a big man pushing sixty, squat and broad with an athletic gait. He looks more like a Miami Dolphins linebacker than a clairvoyant.

'What happened?' I ask, sceptical.

'I was sitting with my class, in a circle for the energy, when I saw this beautiful head of red hair. You know, that real rich red that some women have? It was like watching through a screen door, seeing this girl walk down the drive to her car, all dressed up like she was going to a party. Her name came to me, so I asked the class, "Does anybody here know a redhead named Georgia?"'

Tight black curls frame a jowled face, a face which tells that he – in common with all the other mediums – has not lived a pampered life. Like most of the congregation he exudes an air of pain suffered, of having endured abuse, divorce or death.

'One of the other students did, so I told her what I'd seen. "But Georgia's alive," she said to me. "I'm going out with her Friday night." So I thought nothing more about it. Then the next weekend the student came in and said, "Georgia was killed in a car accident on Friday, and the last person to see her alive was her mother. She watched her walking away to her car through the screen door."'

After the service I'd waited outside the Temple. Mario had walked up to me and introduced himself. He explained that he was a student medium. I couldn't imagine anyone who looked less spiritual.

'It started for me with a crystal ball,' he explains, holding out broad hands that look more suited to catching a football.

We are walking up Stevens Street, past overgrown front yards, garden gnomes and concrete monks. There are no fences between the houses, but winged mythical beasts guard the occasional rusting gate.

'Like I said, I'm a building engineer. I'm always analysing things, looking for explanations. Two years ago I had this crazy idea to buy a crystal ball. I just couldn't get it out of my head. One day I walked out of the office and started driving up I-95, even though there was one of these metaphysical shops at the end of my street. I just drove and drove and ended up here in the bookstore, asking about a crystal ball. I talked to Sally the manager about the things I'd been feeling and she told me that the Educational Program was beginning that Saturday. I signed up there and then.'

'Did you buy the crystal ball?'

'Never did. But it taught me about opening myself up to chance.'

'That's similar to how I came to be here,' I tell him, my suspicions eased by the coincidence. 'Although for me it was by getting the wrong newspaper. Three days ago I was preparing to fly to Germany.'

'I should have said it,' responds Mario. 'I felt that you came here on a whim. You trusted an instinct, got focus and followed it.'

Every resident of Cassadaga is either a Spiritualist or a medium. They lounge in faded armchairs, beside signs which read 'Dr. R. Warren Hoover, Spiritualist Counsellor and Teacher', and 'Rev. Virginia Robbins-Bolek: Medium, Counsellor, Healer'. They recall Zen recipes and intimate chats with angels. Silver baubles trim their balconies. More than the odd shutter has gone missing.

We climb the steps of the broad-eaved Andrew Jackson Davis building and sit together on a bench on the verandah. People come and go, clutching copies of magazines called *Fate* and *Shaman's Drum*, signing up for the Medicine Wheel Pipe Ceremony and waiting for the Sunday Afternoon Message Service. Bluejays and red-cockaded woodpeckers fly between the banana trees and pines.

'Once I started the course, everything developed real fast,' explains Mario. 'I was getting messages for people and names of relatives on the Other Side. Like now I'm seeing, maybe, your uncle.'

'*My* uncle?' I say, startled, wary again.

'Your mother's brother. You take after your mother's side of the family, don't you?'

'I do, but . . .' I hesitate, doubting his motives, not expecting to be drawn into a daylight séance. 'How can you tell he's a maternal relative?'

'Because he's on the left-hand-side of my vision.' Mario gazes into the middle distance, maybe into a parallel world, maybe at my uncle, who died eight years ago. 'For me, it's mother's family on the left, father's on the right. I learnt that real early on. I see him being very physical,' he divines. 'Was he a sporty man?'

I shake my head. A bad guess. I'm relieved. Causality prevails. Yet I also feel a twinge of disappointment.

'A gardener, then,' says Mario. 'Did he work in the garden?'

My uncle had loved his garden. Every weekend through winter's mud and summer's droughts he had wheeled himself around it, planting, pruning, battling against ground elder and multiple sclerosis.

Then Mario says my uncle's name.

'But how does it work?' I ask, fascinated now. Divination seems to be out of context here, in the hot sun, down the road from the Kennedy Space Center, far from damp northern Europe where my uncle lived. 'Where do you start?'

'I go down into this big, black hole and open myself up. The spirits appear above me, as if they're on a circular balcony, and start shouting at me, calling out names and messages. I had to learn to focus in on them one at a time.'

Focus.

Mario spends the week at home in Boca Raton, an affluent city a jet-ski ride north of Miami. He walks five miles along the beach every day and looks forward to weekends at Cassadaga.

'How does your wife react to your . . . insight?' I ask him. I imagine it could be hell arguing with a medium. Questions would be answered before they were posed. 'Especially your being able to see the future?'

'I don't tell her. But she doesn't complain about my coming to the camp, not since I sold the business.'

'Your engineering company?'

'One of the very first messages I got was to sell it. So I did, and for a good price. My wife thought I was nuts, until a couple of months later when the industry collapsed. I couldn't have got out at a better time. I told you, I'm always looking for explanations. The way I think of it is that every life is like a video. You can rewind it or play it or run it fast forward.

All you got to do is learn to tap into the video and then to interpret it. Anybody can do it. It's just something that's there. Like your uncle. He's wearing a white shirt. A bright white shirt. Does that mean anything to you?'

In Cassadaga people stare. Call in at the bookstore or drop by the Sunshine Exchange and conversation stops. Mediums focus in on the newcomer. Then on his or her aura. Finally on any spirit guide standing by their side.

As Mario leads the way into the Afternoon Message Service I feel torn. I want to resist any conjurer's hocus-pocus. I'm reluctant to let go of the mundane certainty that life ends and the dead commune only with worms and daisies. But I also want to believe in an alluring ideal. I want to catch hold of that which has been lost. I want him to see my uncle again.

The aim of the Message Service is 'to demonstrate the continuity of life in a public setting'. Two dozen people wait at refectory tables, sipping on Styrofoam cups of coffee. After a moment Reverend Jerry steps up to the microphone. His blue angel tie is clipped into place with a unicorn pin. 'Can everyone hear me?' he asks.

The response is muted, self-conscious.

'I can't hear you,' he says.

'Yes,' we reply together, laughing at our nervousness, a little bolder.

'You've got to speak up; the voice vibration excites the Spirit.' He looks up and down the tables for a moment, glances over our faces, then stops and stares. 'You, sir, what's your name?'

'Bill,' says a stocky man with a shy smile.

'There's a gentleman standing right behind you, Bill.'

Bill glances over his shoulder. There is no one behind him.

'He would have been maybe forty-five when he moved on. He went kinda sudden, you know. His name is Ch . . . Chas, Charles . . .'

'Chips?'

'Chips. Do you know a Chips?'

'Chips was my father.'

'Was Chips a sailor?'

'He was in the Marines.'

'Then why is he showing me a submarine being squeezed by water? I just don't ... Oh, I get it. Are you under a lot of pressure in your life, Bill?'

Bill nods. It's why he has come here.

'Then Chips is saying just hang in there,' relays Jerry. 'He's real proud of what you're doing, and it's gonna work out, so just hang in there.'

A safe, easy assumption. An artful dodge. I suspect sharp practice.

Bill drops his gaze and smiles a shy smile. The vulnerable-looking white-haired matron beside me turns the pages of her dream book. Her flowery hat lies on the table between us. Over her shoulder I read, 'I walked through the wilderness of this world and kept looking for Mother.'

Jerry scans the tables again, his eyes coming to rest on a young family. He asks them to shout out their names.

'I'm seeing a roll-top desk,' says Jerry. 'You been doing some studying?'

The husband responds with a single, sharp shake of the head. He has a dark olive complexion. His pelt of matted, shoulder-length hair is combed back over his crown. His temples are blade-shaved.

'No?' says Jerry. 'Then you should be. Spirit is real strong on this. You sow the seed and the new plant will grow. It'll put a lot of peace on your mind and your Significant Other's mind. You know what I'm talking about?'

His wife, the Significant Other, understands. Both she and their child have a delicate appearance. With long blonde hair and pale, forlorn eyes, they are mirrors of each other but for their ages. There seems to be nothing of the husband in the child. Suddenly I picture him beating them.

'You know, when you're calm, you have a very beautiful aura,' Jerry tells the man, a firmness in his voice. 'You're a wonderful person to be with. But when you get all het up and mad, even your wife doesn't recognise you. You get what I'm saying?'

The readings aren't conversations, but they are exchanges. There may be trickery in them, yet a little of the husband's anger seems to dissipate. He begins to glow under the medium's short-lived attention.

'You've just got to try to stay calm. And to study. Settle on studying.'

Donna Bohrer, a roly-poly stormtrooper of the Higher Side of Life, follows Reverend Jerry. The audience applauds her, then sits up straight, excited, hoping like children at a birthday party to be picked next.

Donna rolls her shoulders and cracks her knuckles. She takes four deep breaths and reaches out for the vibration. She chooses a thirtysomething at the back of the hall.

'The lady there in the cream blouse. What's your name, please?'

'Hazel,' says the woman.

'Hazel honey, I'm seeing Baskin-Robbins. Does that mean something to you?'

The vision means nothing to Hazel, so Donna gets tough with the hereafter.

'What's Baskin-Robbins got to do with anything?' she snaps at the ether. She likes the rough and tumble of communion. 'Come on, speak up.' Then she listens. 'OK, stop it. You're scaring the puddin' out of me. Boy, he's cranky today.' The spirit-rapper fixes her eyes back on Hazel.

'Honey, he's saying you've been like in an ice-cream parlour with thirty-one flavours, tasting a bit of this one, then that one, until you've tried them all. But you get discouraged too easily, and now you've *got* to choose. You've been thinking of changing your job, and . . .' Donna hesitates. 'What?'

she asks, pausing again. 'And you should join the public sector. No, not the public sector, the military. The air force. He's certain that you should join the air force. Working with your hands is good for you. You should operate computers. That's what Spirit just came in and said.'

After Donna resumes her seat, Reverend Patti Aubery walks up to the front of the hall. She is pushing fifty, a tall, bony skeleton wrapped in a slack sack of skin that has seen too much sun.

'I guess it's got to be you,' she says to me.

'Be receptive,' the Cassadaga Annual Program advises. 'Do not go for a consultation with a closed mind.' I try to remain detached and objective. I remind myself that I am an observer. Then Patti's shining, alight eyes catch me like a rabbit in the headlamps of an oncoming car.

'What's your name?' she asks.

I tell her.

'Do you roar?'

'Sometimes,' I reply.

'I don't think so,' she says, then stares. 'You have a very welcoming presence,' she tells me. 'People are drawn to you, and then they tell you about themselves. You are a good listener and you draw them out.'

'It's part of what I do,' I say, but she doesn't seem to hear me.

'You know, you have a great gift, to give joy.' I blink in the headlights, wanting to remind myself of that next time my car breaks down on the M3. 'I say that again: to give *joy* to people.'

Then she pauses. 'Now I'll tell you something that will really surprise you,' she says. 'Do you know what you are going to do one day? You are going to write a book.'

On medieval German trade routes?

'A book about this place.'

I have a late lunch at the Lost in Time Café. A Spirit Burger with a mug of Celestial Seasoning Red Zinger tea. The tag on the bag quotes Carl Jung: 'Synchronistic events draw the observer into what is happening and make him an accessory to them.'

I knew that I would write a book, but no one else in Florida did. I hadn't told Mario. My droopy sunhat doesn't read, 'Travel Writer (No German Spoken)'. But Patti had looked into me and seen even more than the book.

'You hear things in your head and it surprises you,' she told me. 'You say, "Wow, did I think that?" And you did, but you know that it isn't you alone.'

I knew this too, of course. We all filter and interpret stories overheard. But it was unnerving to be told it by a stranger. Patti had left me with an odd sense of public intimacy, as if we'd canoodled in the aisle of Westminster Abbey.

And now Jung pops up in my tea. The waitress brings me ice to pour into my mug and make Iced Zinger. Maybe I should have ordered a Coke. I bite into my burger. Provolone drips onto my lap. The couple at the next table are down from Ocala for the day.

'So, you gonna get a spiritual reading or what?' asks the woman.

'They can't tell nothing,' says her husband, more interested in his Tuna Curry Melt than astral projection.

'They could tell us when we're going to Tennessee.'

'We already know when we're going to Tennessee.'

'We do?'

The wish to communicate with the dead is as old as life. Spiritualism has long been practised in Africa, the Caribbean and by Native North Americans. In the Old Testament Saul visits the witch – or seer – of Endor. Mental mediumship was common during the witch trials of the Middle Ages. Ouija boards and table-turning were popular Victorian parlour games. Today's New Age movement, with its psychic fairs and pseudo-shamanistic singles groups, fills the same need. Death comes too soon, and our rational, secular age prescribes no soothing tonic.

I want to be sceptical of Mario and Patti's readings. I try to explain away their insights as fraud and lucky guesses. But it isn't the case. In Cassadaga I see the widow comforted. I see the bereaved consoled. Like them, I have lost family and friends. I long to see my uncle, to sit with him again in the fading light after a day's gardening, to share stories and glasses of Austrian *Tannenzapfenschnapps*. After all, it was his example of fighting against disease, and for life, which formed my ideal of strength and dignity.

I hadn't expected to find faith in flaky Florida.

My body restored, I wander back towards the lake. Cicadas and tree frogs sing in the baking heat. Native dream-catchers are half-price at Sydney's Telepathic Corner. After the morning rush, the healers have hung 'Closed' signs on their front doors. 'Sorry, no more psychic journeys today.' The career-track clairvoyants have shut up their weekend cottages and headed back to day jobs in Orlando or Jacksonville. The town's winding lanes look all but deserted to me. But to the mediums they must appear crowded: extinct Timucuan hunters bumping into frontier homesteaders, long-dead property developers stepping on the toes of hit-and-run fatalities. I try to imagine all of Cassadaga's departed – plus my uncle – idling away the lazy Southern afternoon beside me.

'Sometimes it's like Miami Beach here,' says Steve Adkins, startling me out of my reverie. At first I think he is talking about the ephemeral crowd. 'But Sunday afternoons are always quiet.'

Steve has the look of an intrepid Victorian explorer, without the sideboards and pith helmet. Only his sallow, pitted skin betrays him as a former heavy drinker. Another reformed soul.

He introduces himself as Mario's teacher and asks me if I'm staying in town. I tell him I can't afford the hotel.

'I wish I'd known. You could have stayed in Harmony Hall. We rent out Room 8 to visiting lecturers or Spiritualists.'

'But I'm neither.'

'It doesn't really matter,' he shrugs, 'so long as no one's already in it.'

I had asked Mario to guide me to my next destination. Maybe my uncle would speak through him and say, 'I-4 West to Highway 27, then turn left at Frostproof.' Maybe I was to watch out for a man wearing a white shirt. But Mario opened my Alamo map only to point out tourist attractions and danger spots. 'You'll love Busch Gardens,' he said, 'but avoid Liberty City unless you want to get ram-robbed.' Nothing else came to him, so, with the good fortune of Steve's offer, I decide to spend the night in Cassadaga.

Steve and I shuffle off in search of the Harmony Hall keyholder, no urgency in our passage. Steve is Camp Vice-President as well as a jobbing electrician, and every second passer-by stops him to discuss either *feng shui* or fuses.

'Walk across this town and you run into half the world,' he says, shaking hands with a couple in wrap-around sunglasses. 'This guy's here from England,' he tells them. 'He's going spend a couple of days in Room 8.'

'That's great,' says the man.

'Just don't put him in Room 13, now,' jokes his partner. 'The ectoplasm hasn't been scraped off the walls yet.'

We call at the houses of various mediums, but none of them – or their spirit guides – seems to know where the key has been left. I do not understand how a clairvoyant can unlock the secrets of the afterlife yet mislay a door key. After an hour it turns up in the bookstore, in a small drawer behind the Tranquil Moments Incense. The drawer is labelled 'Keys'.

On the way to Harmony Hall, Steve calls up to an effeminate-looking man slouched in a cane armchair on his verandah. 'How you getting on this afternoon, Warren?'

'I'm trying to muster up enough energy to water these orchids.'

We climb the steps to share the shade with Dr R. Warren Hoover and June M. Mahoney. Warren's upper arm is tattooed with his name – in hieroglyphs. June is a Southern dragon pushing eighty. Both are dressed in white kaftans and smoking Virginia Slims. Rosencrantz and Mystic Meg.

'Rory here is going to be your neighbour,' Steve tells them.

'Well, neighbour,' warns June, in a flame-scorched drawl, 'you all better lock your door tight, 'cause it's wild here at night.'

'Cosmic karma?' I ask. I wouldn't want to get on the wrong side of her incantations.

'College kids,' she says, sharp and peppery. 'Warren here just became our first victim of crime.'

'Last night I heard a commotion and came out to see it gone,' he says, gesturing up at the bare branches of a big oak.

'It?' I ask.

'Stolen,' stresses June. 'Swiped.'

'I called the sheriff's office,' Warren explains, 'and said, "I'd like to report a missing UFO."

'"A missing what?" the deputy said to me.

'"A flying saucer."

'"And what did this flying saucer look like?" asks the deputy.

'"Oh the usual," I told him. "Coloured lights around the rim and a big white beacon on the base for astral projection."

' Then the deputy asked me, "Are you calling from Cassadaga?" And when I said that I was, he sort of sighed and said, "I'll send somebody around to see you in the morning."'

'College kids hacked it right off that tree,' flares June,

clinging onto a precarious branch herself. 'It's the sort of thing that happens when the moon moves into Virgo.'

Cassadaga, Monday 27th – The night passed without incident. The bed didn't levitate and the plumbing didn't tremble with celestial vibrations. Only the late-night snores and conversation from the room above interrupted my sleep. A couple seemed to drift between dead slumber and fitful discussions. They didn't disturb me – at least, less than the discovery the next morning that the widow upstairs lives alone.

Spend Monday exploring both sides of town. 'Camp Approved Mediums on Streets to the *Right* Only', warns a sign. But the left-hand side of Cassadaga doesn't seem to be possessed by demons, only by rusting Buicks. A 'Let There Be Light' mobile of old headlamps hangs in one front yard. In a vacant lot a cat dozes on a '53 Roadmaster, beneath the notice 'Two hidden video cameras scan this area 24 hours a day'.

The Purple Rose Metaphysical Stuff Store stocks birthstone earrings by B.joyful Enterprises and books called *Why Die?* and *Soul Traveller.* The *Angelspeake Guide* ('How to Talk with Your Angels') is a big seller, as is the Now & Zen Alarm Clock. It's a metronome in a pyramid made by a firm called 'Cultural Artefacts of the Spiritual Renaissance'. A snip at $99.95.

Over a hummus burrito at the Sunflower Deli, I scribble these pages and leaf through *New Horizons*, a listings magazine that offers 'Spiritual Insights for New Age Florida'. If the fancy takes me, I can 'Travel Inter-Dimensionally Beyond the Christ Grid' with the Sacred Mercaba Ascension

Technique (an Ancient Mystery School), or stock up on vials of *vibhuti* holy ash, created from thin air by Indian guru Sai Baba. Customers are discouraged from swallowing the ash.

At the next table a pensioner eats a Cactus Chilli. His long, icing-white hair and goatee beard make him look like a shaggy vanilla cupcake. He asks me to pass the ketchup, then introduces himself as George the flying-saucer maker.

'Did you build the one that was stolen?' I ask in disbelief.

'It was a real beaut,' he sighs, shaking his head. 'These days I even have to chain down my pyramids.'

The Healing Hotline. UFOs. Now pyramids. I want to keep myself open to the irrational fullness of life, to submit myself to chance and accident; but it's beginning to jumble my judgement. How do I sort the wheat from the cupcakes?

'Are you the writer from England?' he asks.

I nod. Patti's reading has made the rounds.

'During the Second World War I flew Forts out of Molesworth, dropping 22,000-pound Earthquake bombs on Germany. Kaaa-booom!'

'I'm sorry?' I say, spilling hummus on my chin.

'To knock out a factory with those babies, you didn't need to make a direct hit. You just had to hit the right town.'

I had learnt that it takes six years' training to become a certified medium, and another two to four years to become a Spiritualist minister. But George is neither. Instead of a third eye he has a ludicrous cherry carbuncle on his forehead. He is a former pilot of US 8th Air Force.

'Then I ferried B-24s across to Karachi.' He smokes between mouthfuls of chilli. 'We'd take them out to Bermuda, then via those islands off Africa . . .'

'The Azores?'

'Via the Azores to Cairo. We didn't have no set schedule, so I'd always take a few days off there. Go out to Giza and rent a camel. It was there I first became interested in pyramids.'

George assembles pyramids to order, big and small, out

of plastic to cover a bedside glass or from aluminium sheeting to put over tanks of drinking water. He tells me that man is a spiritual being, even while encased in flesh, so needs to drink pure, ionised water.

'I make aliens too,' he adds. 'Life-size.'

'Life-size?'

'That's right.'

'George?' I ask.

'Yeah?'

'How big is an alien?'

Before he can enlighten me, a young travelling salesman steps in off the street. Short-sleeved shirt. Clip-on tie. Pudding-bowl haircut. Single gold earring. His girlfriend, chewing gum and carrying a cardboard box, pushes the door closed behind them. It clicks shut. Her shoulders are burnt lobster-red from a weekend on the beach. Bonnie and Clyde.

'You the owner?' asks the boy, cocky but nervous.

The woman who made my burrito nods.

'I'm a subcontractor to a wholesale company and we're selling Talking Picture Frames.' He takes an ugly plastic frame from the girl's cardboard box and speaks into it. 'Hi, Mom. Happy Mothers' Day. I love you.' He presses a button and plays back the recording. 'Cool, huh?'

'This is a health-food restaurant,' says the woman.

'In K-Mart these Talking Pictures go for $24.99,' he continues, ignoring her. 'The deal here is I'm selling them for ten bucks.'

'This is a health-food restaurant,' she repeats. There are no nicknacks on her shelves.

'You know, you have some really cute stuff here,' he says. 'You could do well with these, with Mothers' Day coming up. I've only got three left.'

It is obvious that the boy is lying. His manner is too tense. His story too transparent. It surprises me when the owner takes the frames.

'Ten dollars?' she asks.

'I'll do three for twenty-five dollars,' he rushes, toying with his keyring. 'It's a steal.'

Another sham. At least he doesn't pull out a machine gun and start shooting. Or drop a 22,000-pound incendiary bomb.

'Hey, do you have any diet soda?'

I finish my lunch and head back to the right side of the street.

Cassadaga, Tuesday 28th – Tuesday morning and I've had enough of wind chimes. I'm feeling touched, though not by angels. There are bats in my belfry.

Up early and ready to leave by 7 a.m. Decide to take one last look at the Spirit Lake. To sit for a moment beside it, to listen to the waves, not to *chi*-surf with early-bird diviners. I step out of Harmony Hall.

June Mahoney, the Southern dragon, paces back and forth across her verandah, spitting fire.

'Been stood up by that Warren. He always takes me for breakfast. Always,' she fumes. 'Kids today do crazy things.' Warren is sixty years old.

'But you've got food in the house, don't you?'

'I don't keep food, 'cause I don't wanna get fat.' June is fiercely thin. Her face is oblong, with cut-glass features. 'He up and forgot me. Now you're going off too. I don't know what I'm gonna do.'

'Where does he take you for breakfast?' I ask. The Sunflower Deli won't be open for two more hours. 'DeLand?' DeLand is a sixteen-mile drive. 'Deltona?' Twenty miles. I want to leave Palookaville behind me.

'Oh no, honey. He just drives me to the Feed Store. It's about four blocks away.'

I offer to take her.

'Have you had your breakfast?' she asks.

'It's too early for me to eat. But I'll have a cup of tea.'

'Tea? I don't know if they've got tea.'

At the Feed Store, citrus farmers and mystics sit side by side eating eggs 'easy over'. Cattlemen and Capricorns tuck into their hash browns. There are bottomless cups of coffee, root-beer floats and no tea.

June knocks open the door with her cane, complains to strangers, tells the wait staff that Warren has stood her up. 'And now somebody's gone and taken my regular table. What are *you* kids doing here?'

Philemon rocks back and forth in his chair, abandoned to laughter. His wife Baucis, squat and frisky, lays her head in her hands and giggles like a schoolgirl. They hoot, shake and split their sides. Every day of their married life begins by telling each other silly rude jokes.

'What did Linda Lovelace wear on her wedding night?' asks Philemon, still sporting his embroidered waistcoat.

'How is a G-spot like a Pop Tart?' responds Baucis.

As they laugh I imagine them making love on June's usual table. A wrinkled cherub and a geriatric baby hippo cuddling, capering and coming at the wrong time. In my mind's eye plates of cherry pie and sourdough pancakes crash onto the linoleum. Their bodies' soft skin would be stuck together by maple syrup and laughter.

'We thought it would be fun to have breakfast out for a change. Hi, I'm Dick,' says Philemon to me, regaining composure, stretching out a warm paw. 'Who are you?'

I am introduced as the writer.

'So you're the one researching Cassadaga,' says Baucis – or Hilly – lifting her hands towards me as if for a sticky embrace. I wonder if anyone keeps secrets in camp.

'That's *wonderful*,' enthuses Dick, enunciating each syllable, meaning 'full of wonder'. 'You're here for the week, then.'

I look at my watch. 'I'd planned to leave this morning . . .'

'You can head off now, honey,' says June. 'These two'll run me back. That Warren,' she spits at them. 'I'm gonna wring his neck.'

'. . . but I just can't seem to get away.'

'Lot of folks find that,' smiles Dick. He has a child's direct gaze. 'I've been trying to leave for twenty years.'

'He just can't project himself to no place better,' chortles Hilly.

Dick takes hold his wife's nose and twists it. Like a play-school tearaway. Then he asks me, 'Have you seen the library yet?'

I take a deep breath. Consider my plans. Think of Jung again. 'The irrational fullness of life,' he once wrote, 'has taught me never to discard anything, even when it goes against all our theories (so short-lived at best) or otherwise admits of no immediate explanation.'

'No,' I tell Dick, 'I haven't.'

'Then *that's* why you're here,' he declares, letting go of Hilly and slapping the table. 'You can't possibly go till you see the library.'

'Dick, don't you mess with his mental clock,' Hilly chides. 'You heard the man. He has to go.' She turns to me to confess, 'I'm really into this time thing.'

'You gotta catch a plane or something, don't you?' suggests June, providing me with an escape.

'Do you?' asks Dick, leaning forward in his chair, his dreamy eyes glinting. His curly white hair shows its last hint of blond.

'No,' I admit, opening up. Again. 'No plane. I just wanted to get an early start.'

Drive Dick back to Cassadaga. Hilly will bring June the Dragon home after she's had her flame-cooked sausages and home fries.

'We Spiritualists take life as it comes,' rushes Dick, pointing out the direction. 'If there's an opportunity, we grab it. If it doesn't work out, then that's the way it's meant to be. Hilly and I almost never go to the Feed Store for breakfast. So our meeting was ordained.'

Chance and predestination. Accident, necessity and design. The will to choose. Tell him about Germany.

'It's a good thing to follow your instincts,' he tells me. 'You may not know where you're going, or even what you'll write, but for sure you're on the right road.'

'Are you certain about that?' I ask. I'm not. The course of life may be subject to the free decision of man's moral will, and salvation due to divine decree, but it brings little comfort as the road ahead veers off at a sudden, terrifying angle.

'Up there, where the highway goes left, drive straight ahead.'

'Is that a philosophical statement?'

'There are no coincidences.'

The Chevy rocks down a dirt lane and around the back of the camp to reach Summerland House, a white building on a hill overlooking the town. Inside, more than five thousand books on religious and Spiritualist topics have been assembled. Dick worked for two years preparing the library: begging donations, recruiting volunteers, cobbling together a rag-tag Apple Macintosh. His aim is to create a study centre for people seeking information about their spiritual selves. He also plans to go online, once he finds a faster chip to hyperlink the computer's memory: 'We're looking to update ourselves into the cyberworld.'

Glory of the Immortal Life nestles beside Hawthorne's *The Supreme Philosophy of Men*. Schopenhauer shares a shelf with Walt Whitman. From next to Honderich's *How Free Are You?* I pull out a slim volume entitled *Say it with Words*. To me each book represents a life, and like life they appear to be all out of order.

'My biggest forte now is to bring it to the attention of people that they live forever,' trumpets Dick. 'Spiritualism teaches not that a man has a soul, but that man *is* a soul, and has a body.'

For Dick, all those who have passed on live on, and not just in the pages of a book. In Cassadaga life lasts forever. Death is a milestone along a much longer path. In Germany, death certificates are numbered and cross-referenced with birth, school and employment records. Or so I imagine. The sequence of events from cradle to grave is set down in black and white. *Schaffe, schaffe, bau ein Häusli, sterbe.* Work, work, build a little house, die.

'But how do you ever find a specific title?' I ask, looking at the jumbled collection. Determinism and the Dewey decimal system. I wonder if Spiritualist readers simply divine their way to the right book.

'A retired librarian joined the camp last week. She's going to catalogue the texts.'

'That's fortunate,' I say.

'There you go with coincidence again,' he wails. 'Let me tell you a story. Hilly likes to gamble. It's one of her things. Last year we were in Nevada visiting my brother. He's a Methodist preacher there. One morning we decided to get in a little fishing. We jumped into the wagon and started driving. After an hour we reached this turning. It was left to Lake Mead, right to Las Vegas. Hilly suddenly said she could smell toast burning. "Hey, Connie, is that you?" she said. And Connie was there in the car with us.'

'Is Connie dead?' I asked, wanting to be clear on the facts.

'She's moved on.'

'When she was alive, did she burn toast often?'

'*All* the time. You could smell it clear round the camp. So there was Connie in the car telling us to turn right and go to Vegas. I said, "Connie, we can't do that. We've made plans. We got reservations at Lake Mead."

'But Connie said, "Just go."'

'What did you do?' I ask.

'I gave in. How could I win an argument with two women, especially when one of them's in the spirit sphere?'

'You went to Las Vegas?'

'We headed straight to Caesar's Palace and asked for a room. The guy just laughed when I told him we didn't have a reservation. People reserve six months ahead there. "Let's just drive down the strip," said Hilly. We did, and then, bang, right outside the Desert Inn Casino there was a parking space. Have you ever been to Las Vegas?'

I shake my head.

'You *never* get parking spaces on the strip. *Never* happens. "Pull in here," said Hilly. "This is it." So I walked up to the desk and asked for a room and the receptionist was holding a cancellation in his hand. In his *hand*. It had *just* come in. So we took the room, on the thirteenth floor, and Hilly said, "I'm going to the slots."'

Dick bends down to stroke Colby, the camp cat, which is clawing at a stack of pamphlets on concurrence.

'Not a minute later I ran into one of Hilly's old students. "Hey, Terry, what you doing here?" I asked him. He lived over in Big Sur.

'"I need to see Hilly," he said.

'"She's playing the quarter slots," I told him.

'And as we walked toward her she got three white '7's. That's six hundred dollars.'

'In quarters?' I ask.

'Yup. Hilly turned around and Terry said to her, "Didn't you get my messages? I've been trying to reach you for weeks. I've got to speak to you about Connie." And Connie had been one of *his* students. Now, call *that* coincidence.'

I give up looking at my watch. I really am finding it difficult to leave Cassadaga.

Dick hurries ahead up Lake Street, past Medicine Wheel

Park to a modest clapboard house nestling among the pines. There are squirrels in the trees and fresh basil in the well-tended beds.

'Here, taste some,' he says, snapping off leaves. 'And run your hand up the rosemary. *Wonder*ful.' A dozen silvery chimes dangle from eaves and lintels. If a breeze blows up, I'll go mad.

First stop is the bathroom.

'Look at this grand old toilet.'

Dick lifts the lid. Pulls the handle.

'I did all the work myself.'

He leans his head against the wall and strokes the grain.

'And see these fine boards.'

Old pine rubbed down, then lightened with a driftwood wash.

'I looked for these for two years. Finally decided to buy new wood, and on the way to the lumberyard I saw an old house being bulldozed. So I started picking through the rubble and found the boards. The wrecker tried to send me away, but I had a twenty in my wallet and I said to him, "Isn't it about time for your morning break?" He let me take away enough to build the whole bathroom.'

Dick has the ability to transform the ordinary into the remarkable. And vice versa. Cassadaga's residents take the extraordinary in their stride, treating wonders as commonplace. The unexpected never surprises a clairvoyant.

'Call *that* chance.'

In the cluttered living room there are energy crystals, rampant asparagus plants and thirteen Native dream-catcher wheels. On the wall hang college diplomas. Dick is a retired engineer, like Mario. Steve is an electrician. An aptitude for plumbing and wiring strikes me as being at odds with a belief in the incorporeal. Dick shakes his head.

'A lot of us come from an analytical background. All our lives we were taught that if it couldn't be measured, it didn't exist. That got us asking questions. We realised that not everything can be explained.'

'So how does it start?' I ask him. 'Did you see a ghost?'

'My first experience was when I was still a kid,' he nods, while showing me his electric psychograph. 'My grandmother was a hard woman. Nothing sentimental about her. We never got on too great, but when she died I felt sad, and started bawling my eyes out. That's when I heard her voice, as if she were standing right next to me. "Quit being a crybaby, Dickie," she said, "and grow up." I haven't cried since.'

Dick takes the stairs two at a time, not pausing for breath while recounting his neighbour Margaret Ann Schmidt's spiritual awakening.

'Maggie was ten years old when her dad died. Three months later he came to her and told her that she should be a Spiritualist minister.'

Maggie Schmidt was too young to understand. The visitation frightened her. But seven years later she found a letter that her father had written to her on the day before his death. It instructed her to get a reading on her eighteenth birthday. He had enclosed five dollars. She looked in the telephone book to find a medium. When they met, the medium, who was a stranger, asked her if she had brought the letter containing the money. She gave it to him, and he confirmed that she should become a minister.

'I'll Xerox some things that might interest you,' offers Dick. His office is scattered with prisms, Aquarius journals and aura self-portraits. As the photocopier warms up, Dick starts playing four Tibetan crystal basins, a sort of music for salad bowls. The different frequencies of the Hemi-Syncs, when presented separately to the left and right ears, are purported to stimulate lucid dreams. I begin to get a headache.

'This is more fun than Disney World,' he cheers above the humming drone.

Downstairs the screen door slams.

'Haven't you let that poor writer go yet?' shouts Hilly.

'But he's never even *heard* about synchrotherapy,' yells Dick.

'He's got to get on.' Pause. 'He told you.' A longer pause. 'Have you shown him *my* office yet?'

Back downstairs the bed is unmade. Clothes lie where they fell last week. Or last month. I imagine Dick and Hilly sharing bad jokes and making hippo love on the desk top, under the kitchen table, in the home-made bathroom.

Hilly gives me a quartz crystal from Mount Ida for Katrin, even though I haven't mentioned her name.

'It's not magic,' she explains. 'It's a focus point. Whenever there's a problem, she should just focus on it, that's all.' Hilly picks up a clairsentient crystal. 'This is my favourite. I use it when the Space Shuttle takes off. I focus on it and wish the boys a safe flight.'

Dick asks, 'So how old are your kids?'

'I'm sorry?' I say.

'You've got two kids, don't you?'

'No, but we have one puppy.'

'Oh,' he shrugs, then chuckles at himself. 'As long as I don't pollute my powers with thought, my perception is 95 per cent accurate. Otherwise, it's 95 per cent inaccurate.'

He then starts telling me about my Light Beings.

'Dick, let him go,' says Hilly.

'Just stay for our Gala Day,' he pleads. 'There'll be craft booths and mini-readings. And the library will be opened.' Saturday is to be Gala Day. Four days away.

'Sorry,' I say. 'I do have to go.'

'Once you realise that you live forever,' volunteers Dick, 'and that the soul is immortal, then neither death nor Germans will ever scare you again.'

Outside we shake hands. The chimes ring in my ears.

'When you write your book,' Dick calls as I walk away through the airy pines, 'please don't write about haunted houses.'

I make my way back to Harmony Hall. Cream magnolia-blossoms brown on the pavement. Trailing beards of Spanish moss droop low over the road. There are golden lions on doorsteps and plastic snowflakes on the mosquito screens. Dragon June is sitting on her verandah, smoking a Virginia Slim.

'You still here, honey?' she asks.

'I seem to have lost control of my day,' I tell her.

3

The Saint of Palatka

'In these days of crack babies,' Doctor Fleischman said, 'infants may be born weighing a pound or less, only twenty to twenty-two weeks gestational age, but having a heartbeat.'

WSUZ PALATKA

US Highway 17, Wednesday 29th – 'Nothin' and no one good in Palatka,' says the receptionist at the Happy Trails Motor Inn. 'If I was you, I'd drive straight on out of town.'

It had taken me another day to get out of Cassadaga. Dick had felt a vibration from the Higher Side and caught up with me down at Harmony Hall. We'd spent the afternoon discussing Meta-Music and brewing pots of fresh mint tea in the Fogel Healing Park. So it didn't alarm me to be woken before dawn on Wednesday by an almighty crash. At least an even earlier start would get me away before the Feed Store run. But June was already out on her verandah when I took my bag out to the car.

'Did you hear the noise?' I asked her. Hemi-Sync? Rebirthing scream? Mongolian Overtone chanting?

'You bet,' she said, sucking on a coffin nail.

'Was it paranormal?'

'That was plain old mortal, honey,' said June. Apparently Warren had come home late from a séance and driven into his garage door. 'This morning my breakfast may be just a tad late. *Agin.*'

Drove five minutes out of Cassadaga. Reached the junction of Country Roads 4101 and 4139. Became lost. So much for the lucky Mount Ida crystal. Dick had told me not to follow somebody else's signs, which wasn't a problem at the unmarked crossroads. There weren't any signs at all. I drove on a few miles before being offered the choice between US 11, I-4 and US 14/92. None of the highway indicators named their destinations. It was like booking a holiday by flight numbers alone.

Not that it worried me. I could have looked at the map. It lay under the muffin wrappers on the back seat, the pencil tear in Saint Johns County. I left it there unconsulted. I was pleased to be adrift again, free to chance upon my next port of call.

I chose a road. Swung onto it. Drove. Didn't know yet where I was heading. Or even if the compass was true. But I understood that certainty and security never lead to discoveries. The wide world beckons, our days are too few and we can never, ever fit it all in. That is why I cannot accept that journeys are slipshod, haphazard affairs. To do so would be wasteful, unjust, a surrender to the fatalism of the inevitabilities of life. In the same way I cannot believe that my uncle died without reason, that love was lost. For that also would be a failing. Of will. Of faith. Of imagination. I am no New Age Pollyanna, but I accept that Mario saw him, that he spoke to me through Patti. I too need to find a meaning in the pattern of our common actions.

I'm beginning to suspect that I've come to Florida for a reason other than chance. Like the whooping wounded of Cassadaga, I've been drawn here because of fear. Fear of incompleteness, of nothingness, of searching for a better place that will never be found. It's not a matter of travelling to run away. Or even to run towards. Rather a nightmare of running on the spot, filling the black void, getting nowhere, for there is nowhere else. Why try to catch hold of the moment if not to find purpose in the longer journey?

Another crossroads. Another choice. I turned away from Cassadaga with less fear of that unknown, though I did catch myself glancing into the rear-view mirror to see if anyone was riding on the back seat.

Followed the course of the Saint Johns, Florida's longest river, through DeLand and De Leon Springs. Above the clean curve of the highway, billboards touted J.R. Gator's Dockside Food-Spirits-Fun. On 98 Frog FM's Hot Folk Favorites Enya sang 'Anywhere Is': '. . . it's either this or that way, it's one way or the other . . .' A bird dropping slapped onto my windscreen.

At Pierson, self-proclaimed 'Fern Capital of America', the road was lined with mile after mile of black plastic grow-tunnels. Enormous trucks lumbered north filled with delicate ferns for the ornamental flower arrangements of Chicago and New York. *Bienvenuto a Plaza Mexicana*: 'The best tacos in town'. Here were Spanish-speaking churches for migrant workers. Across the road farmers stocked up on hog and cattle panels.

In Satsuma there were trailer parks and run-down retire-ment communities. The Tangerine Terrace offered 'All-U-Can-Eat Catfish Supper $5.95 Fri-Sat-Sun'. I skirted stud farms and grazing land and remembered that, according to Mario, Florida has more cowboys than Texas. But I failed to spot a single Stetson at Don's Pawn ('Guns & Gold Traded'). The elderly clientele seemed more interested in buying used hedge-trimmers. A buzzard circled overhead and vultures picked at roadkill carrion.

I saw no rednecks.

The Veterans' Memorial Bridge swept high over the broad, polluted river and dropped four lanes of highway traffic into the heart of a town called Palatka. Its name sounded so ugly, like an obscure form of tooth decay, that the place took my fancy.

Plaque. Plague. Palatka.

Greyhounds thundered along the road that was once Reid Street, cleaving the town's north side from its south. Ranks of faceless single-storey buildings clung to the highway's edge. Used Pontiacs lay in wait at Bainbridge Motors.

I had wanted a change from fey Cassadaga, and Palatka revealed itself as the town from hell. The poor, symmetrical backstreets suggested crack wars and drive-by killings. I passed a fluorescent red warning sign: State Prisoners Working. Then caught sight of Florida's oldest aluminium diner.

A young black man, dragging his shirt in the grit, stood outside the closed Georgia–Pacific plywood factory shaking his fist and yelling.

I looked at my watch. Wondered if I could make it back in time for last orders at the Lost in Time Café.

Palatka, Thursday 30th – There are 222 million guns in circulation in the United States today.

Five hundred thousand Americans have been shot dead since 1960.

'No one good in Palatka,' the receptionist had said.
I want to prove him wrong.

Every fifth car in town seems to be a police car: Palatka Police,
Putnam County Police, Florida Highway Patrol, Florida State
Troopers. Law enforcement seems to be the big enchilada here,
so a police station strikes me as a reasonable place to start.

The PPD headquarters is an uninviting beige brick building, crouching alongside US 17 at the corner of 11th Street. I
park beneath a sign which reads 'Serving with Pride: Problem
Solving and Dedication'. Walk through the main door. It
slams shut behind me. Two female officers look up from
behind the bulletproof glass.

'I wonder if you can help me,' I say, bending down to
speak through the metal grille, clutching at an instinct. 'I'm
looking for the best person in town. Who's Palatka's Good
Samaritan?'

The women blink at me. Then look at each other. They
have pistols. Wanted posters for spree killers hang on the
wall behind them. In the next office are racks of pump-action
shotguns. Nearly one million American teenagers carry guns
to school every day. And I am asking about goodness.

'Virginia Blue,' says Brenda Holloway, the duty officer, as
casually as if I'd asked for a fishing licence, 'is the saint of
Palatka.'

'Virginia Blue?' I repeat.

'That's right,' confirms the second officer.

Their response is swift and definitive. My question disarms
them faster than any quick-draw Guzzi automatic. They beam
with simple pleasure, and I'm startled by the effect.

'I hail from West Palm,' volunteers Brenda, 'so I can
appreciate what's good in a small town.'

'You can.'

'Yes, sir.'

'Me too,' smiles her partner.

Ten thousand people live in Palatka. Last year the police made more than two thousand arrests. Is Virginia Blue a policewoman awarded a Good Citizen Award? A minister at Morning Star Baptist Church? The Senior Regent of the Moose Lodge?

'Virginia is a hands-on saint: cooks the meals, makes the beds, looks after folks in need. She runs the Caring Center over on Kirby.'

'It's the only homeless shelter in the county.'

'There's a lot of good folks in this town: Wally Stembler, Mr Gauthier, Pat Kinney who helped me when I moved here. But Virginia Blue is something special. She done it all herself. She sings at church too. When she does, her voice fills up the hall.'

Brenda has a map at the ready. She sketches the route for me. The Caring Center is no more than a few hundred yards away towards the river. I ask if I can walk there.

'Walk?'

The women blink at me again. Incredulous. The desk telephone rings. A patrol car's siren wails in from the street. Innocence is lost.

'I'd drive,' advises Brenda, turning back to her work.

The Seminole Indians called this place 'Pilotaikata', meaning crossing or ford; then the army hunted them out, slaughtering them in the Everglades or exiling them to Oklahoma. White settlers and black slaves followed the soldiers, discovering along the Saint Johns's banks half of Florida's original wild-orange acreage. The river carried traders and farmers further inland. Soon schooners from Maine plied the waterway, bringing south loads of ice and returning with fruit, cotton and turpentine syrup. Barge freighters operated on the smaller Ocklawaha, propelled by blacks with poles. But it was the Hart and Lucas lines' sternwheelers which propelled Palatka into its golden age. They ran cruises upriver into the subtropical forest and attracted Florida's first tourists. Thousands came to town to take the popular night-time excursions, where burning pine-knots threw 'a strange but clear light over this exotic, hushed paradise'.

After the defeat of the South in the Civil War, Palatka became a destination for wealthy northerners too, the original 'snowbirds' anxious to escape the bitter winters. Every day throughout the 1880s as many as twenty-two boats steamed up to the docks and twenty-six trains called at the station. Five grand hotels were built in the town. There was sport shooting from the steamers' decks, and Eggleston's Taxidermy did keen business. Will Livingston's streetcar, drawn by a mule, carried visitors up to the Heights and then back down to River Street and the Oyster Saloon. The second-largest cypress mill in the country was established at Wilson's Cove, and ships from as far north as Canada came in to haul away cypress boards.

Then disaster struck. A fire swept through the business district, and the Great Freeze of 1895/96 devastated both tourism and fruit trees. In the same year that paradise froze over the railway reached Miami. Northerners no longer stopped on the Saint Johns but rode the express further south, to where winter sunshine was assured. The through-train sank the riverboats, the cypress mill closed and Palatka began its long, slow decline.

'Sure I'll talk to you, honey,' mumbles Virginia Blue, not looking much like a saint. She covers her mouth with a hand like a clump of black mangrove root. Her dime-store rings flash in the sunlight. 'Just let me get this sandwich out o' my jaw first.'

The Caring Center is a yellow, tin-roofed house. Its window surrounds are painted forest green and criss-crossed with winking fairy lights. At first sight it brings to mind a child's birthday cake, cheery with colourful icing and flickering candles, dropped in the middle of a war zone.

'I was told that there's no good in . . .' I start to say. Virginia raises her hand again to stop me. Swallows a mouthful of baloney. No further explanation seems necessary.

The front parlour is like a hairdresser's stockroom. Boxes of tint, rinse and organic blends are stacked up to the ceiling. There are tubes of L'Oréal Fiery Auburn Liquid Color and back-issues of *Hype Hair*. Shelves groan under the weight of hooded dryers, curling irons and Ginseng Miracle Wonder 8 Oil.

Virginia sits in a threadbare armchair, beside a desk cluttered with rake combs and hairpins.

'I'm the mother o' six children,' she tells me. 'Five living.'

Her face is full and square, her frame solid and stout. Her tired floral dress is picked out with a lace collar. She is sixty-three years old. A big woman.

'I reared my kids by myself. Without one dime child support. All my kids finished high school. All my kids went to college. Today I know where all five o' my kids are. I could be speaking to them in about five minutes.'

Three coiffed and polished chocolate-brown women are draped across the furniture around her. Lori sports a drop-dead bob cut with centre parting. On the second couch Janet toys with her updo. Sabrina, the youngest of the group, wears her hair in a Nubian roll of tight, oiled braids. Beside them big-buttocked Mary, an earnest white balloon in a blue denim dress, pulls at her split ends. The four volunteers appear to be glammed up for a night out, apart from their dowdy working clothes.

'I have a bishop,' Virginia says, holding up her fingers to

count off her children. 'I have an insurance adjuster. I have a contractor. I have a public person in the library in Gaines-ville. I have a lab technician in Ocala.'

She closes her hand into a fist. The polished women whisper between themselves. Virginia's achievement is an exception in Palatka.

'It was not easy. I worked three jobs a day. *Night* and day. When people would be getting up to go to work, I would still be working. Because at that point in time I did laundry, I baked wedding cakes, I did meals. I'd do anything to make an honest dollar to take care of my family. Incidentally, I'm still a licensed caterer . . .'

Her flow is interrupted by a knock at the screen door.

'Yesss?' she says, the word drawn out like stretched elastic.

'Is Mrs Blue in?'

'Yes, she is.'

The door opens an inch. Virginia's gold front tooth flashes in the narrow glare. An apple-cheeked girl, maybe twelve years old, pushes in clutching a crumple of paper. Outside a boy, no older than ten, sits on a bench in the sun with his head in his hands. *'All* guests *must* be cleared by Police Department,' says the sign above the door. Virginia reads the court order and asks the girl to wait. 'I'll be with him in a few minutes, child.'

The door hisses shut.

'You raised your family by yourself?' I ask.

'Uh-huh.' Virginia begins each sentence slowly, as if gather-ing her energy, then races towards the end. 'They called me Momma and Daddy. Momma *and* Daddy. We were deserted by the father.'

'What happened to him?'

'I'll see you later, Kimberly,' she shouts over her shoulder to a leaving volunteer. 'I do *love* that new curl.' She turns back to me. 'He was found dead in the river,' she says, her voice going dull, its music muted. 'In Carolina.'

On the wall above an old piano hang a dated floral tapestry and a reproduction oil of the Arc de Triomphe. There are shelves of beauty-care paperbacks and a well-thumbed copy of the *Home Health Handbook*. Virginia looks at me.

'That's when I knew where he was, when they found him dead in the river. Face down. OK? I didn't grieve over that. Cause he hadn't been with me. He had done me so wrong and left me with a baby.'

The volunteers remain quiet, respectful, distracted only by the odd stray tendril of hair.

'After that I said to myself, "Hey girl, get back to school."'

'While holding down three jobs?'

'I saw an ad in the paper for a position at Food and Nutrition,' she nods. 'I went after it. I knew the one thing that would get me hired.'

'Which was?'

'"May I have the training please?" That's all I said. "The ed-u-cation." They figured that if I was interested in learning then I'd be interested in working. So they sent me to college. And when a job came up at HRS – shooo! – I was right in it. They just slid me right in it. OK?'

'HRS?' I ask.

'Health Rehabilitation Service. You know, welfare. I worked there for twenty some years. I dealt with the sick folk. With the folk that couldn't cook. The folk that need a bath. I'd get called out to hungry people under the trees. I'd go home to make them something to eat. I'd go into homes that were not sanitary. The other workers, when they went into some places, they saw the roaches and started quitting.'

'Because of cockroaches?'

'They were too nice for that. I hope you have a hard stomach?' she asks me.

'Usually.'

'I was the one who went out on cases where people were sick with the worms playing in the flesh. Worms and *lice*. I would have to almost bodily make them go get medical attention.' She rubs a mark off one of her root-thick fingers. 'I saw a lot of things. All of it. And I held on to my job.'

The door swings wide open and a tall, copper-skinned woman sweeps in, carrying six loaves of Wonderbread and a jar of African Pride styling gel. Whip-thin eyebrows curve an inch above her almond-shaped eyes. Her hair, which is crimped and braided, rises in a high ponytail fluffed like a sea anemone's tentacles. 'I come to do them greens,' she says.

Virginia ruffles through the invoices and boxes of castor-oil sheen to find a copy of *Try it Yourself Hair*. The other women sit up in their seats.

'This is what I want,' Virginia informs anemone-top, pointing to a picture in the magazine. 'I want my hair to look like hers.'

The woman stands an arm's length away, her back towards me, poking the picture with a chisel-shaped fingernail. Her creased eyes give her a callous, hostile look. 'I best do those greens first,' she says.

'Lori will help you.' Virginia then explains to me with an unexpected twinkle, 'She's my beautician. *Our* beautician. I'm telling her what I want my hair to look like.' As anemone-top, Lori and the Wonderbread leave the room she cries after them, 'I want to see if you can find that grey mix. Like this, see? The curl's nice.'

Virginia sits poised on the armchair. She is no longer relaxed with the others working in the kitchen.

'All right. OK,' she says, accelerating her story. 'So when I first came down to the Caring Center, it was de-tox.'

'For drugs?'

'Drugs and alcohol. Every day after I got off HRS, I'd rest for about thirty minutes then put on a white uniform and come to work in here. Even though they didn't have no funds to pay me. I told them, "I don't care..."' Her voice lifts like a child's. '"...I'll come to work anyhow." So I came faithful to work from nine at night to two in the morning.'

'Every day?'

'Every day.'

'For no money?'

'No money. All right?' She sneaks a glance towards the kitchen. 'Then I got to thinking that this place should be a homeless shelter. There was starting to be a real need.'

'That's for sure,' says the white balloon. It was the time that welfare cuts closed homes and asylums.

'So I brought in several people and we cleaned the house. I said, "We're going to go twenty-four hours a day." A homeless shelter should be open twenty-four hours. If it's a homeless shelter. Problem was our funds dwindled down. We hardly had enough money to pay the light bill, the water bill, the gas bill and the little mortgage on the place. She can verify it.'

'Yes'um,' nods updo Janet.

'So for six months, you know what I worked for?' asks Virginia, leaning forward, emphasising each word. 'Nothing. I didn't change attitude. I didn't change what I was doing. I just said to myself, "In due time God will take care of this." And He did. They walked up one week and to my surprise handed me a cheque for one hundred dollars.'

'One hundred dollars.'

'It wasn't a salary, but I was grateful. Now I've got a clothes closet for the needy. I've got a full pantry for the hungry. I've got a bread truck delivery to the seniors and the disabled in an apartment complex. I do counselling. I do Christmas baskets for people. Christmas toys, too. And when I got troubles sometimes I play the piano and sing.'

'Mrs Blue don't sleep much at night,' volunteers Janet.

'It doesn't sound like she has the time.'

'I doze in this chair a little bit. I watch TV and go to bed about three o'clock. But I'm awake in an hour or two. I'm not one of those persons that requires eight hours. That's right. I am just here to do what I can.' Virginia shrugs. 'So, sure, there's plenty o' bad in Palatka. But there's also plenty o' good.' She looks back at her girls. 'I guess that's about all.'

Virginia hauls herself up out of the armchair and sways back towards the kitchen, still clutching the hairstyle magazine.

'And when it's time to work,' she says, 'when I say, "We need to do this or we need to do that . . ."'

'Then we do it,' says Nubian Sabrina, speaking for the first time.

'Everybody jumps up. No problem,' adds Janet.

I follow the women into a kitchen jammed full of pots, baking trays and great sacks of flour. Boxes of cookies and Chiquita banana crates are stacked against the walls. There are bags of hamburger rolls and flats of Pepsi. Anemone-top is up to her elbows in a sink full of leaves. Again she doesn't meet my eye.

'There's feelin' good and there's doin' good,' Mary tells me, her broad posterior blocking the narrow doorway. 'Most places in Florida you'll only find the feelin' good.'

'But not here,' says Sabrina.

'Not here.'

Virginia takes her post by the cooker, beneath recipes for pork hocks, meatloaf and creamed chicken ('Serves 26 normal, 18 hungry'). The others begin to scrub potatoes and wash cabbages, taking to the work like a well-drilled platoon.

Sabrina offers me the only chair, confident now that she's at work. I don't sit down.

'My volunteers don't sass me,' Virginia says, pulling a dozen tins of corned beef from her larder.

'No, ma'am.'

'I've only got one little girl who kind of talk back to me. That's my little beautician here. But I don't pay her no attention.'

'I'm going to go off now,' snaps anemone-top, her wet hands dripping onto the curling yellowed linoleum. 'I knows when I'm not wanted.'

'She can't do without me,' baits Virginia.

'She loves Mrs Blue,' whispers Sabrina to me, then drops her eyes.

'Let me tell you,' the beautician declares, addressing us all yet managing to exclude me. 'I'm about the best worker round here.' The others laugh over the chopping boards. 'I know I'm good. I'm always here.'

'Always.'

'And Mrs Blue love me too,' she says, now gentle. 'I just have to be off the chain sometimes.'

Virginia shrieks. Janet drops the Wonderbread. The teasing levity brings to mind a weekend picnic more than a working homeless shelter. The women make me feel welcome, as they would anyone who happens upon the Center. They accept me without surprise or expectation. To them I am just another stranger who appears, stays a while then moves on. Only anemone-top seems to take exception to my being here, a white foreigner asking questions in her poor, rundown town.

'This is the way we get along. Just the way you see us now. We do teamwork.

'We're family,' says Mary.

'Now you best make yourself useful too,' Virginia says to me.

Through the afternoon I do what I can, which isn't much. As the women put the corned beef and cabbage into Dutch-oven roasters, I bake three angelfood cakes (thirty-six egg whites, a bushel of sugar and three cups of flour). When the cakes fail to rise, Virginia asks me to stack clothes boxes, but she carries them with more adeptness than me. I end up sorting through a delivery of tanktops and beach robes, a generous donation of limited use from the Beautification Council of Greater Palatka.

After her chores Sabrina shows me around the Center.

There are seven bedrooms and four bathrooms. The Family Room has space for a mother and her children. A husband too, if he is around. Elsewhere men are separated from women.

'This is where we pig out at,' Sabrina says in the dining room, moving along the clean hallways with familiarity, all traces of her initial shyness dispelled. 'Sometimes we have so many that we have to do two table sittings.'

The walls are painted in soft, pastel colours. The windows are covered with paper blinds, shielding the rooms from the harsh Florida sun, creating a calm, healing atmosphere.

In the parlour 'clients' check in, then idle away the hours down by the river until supper. A young black mother with twins knocks at the door and, after a whispered conversation, carries her children upstairs. She has been burnt out of her home. I collect some clothes for her boys, trying not to wake an exhausted, pockmarked white teenager sleeping against a bundle of trousers. Three lanky schoolgirls with sweet wide eyes and wailing kids on their hips turn up too. They are the children and grandchildren of anemone-top.

At supper thirty people squeeze around the tables. Few pause to speak. All wolf down their food. The volunteers move lightly between the diners, ladling out second servings and topping up glasses of Piggly Wiggly cola.

'I used always to go hungry,' says a myopic drifter trying to eat my angelfood cake. He squints then stabs at the plate. 'But since Monday I've had enough to eat.'

Virginia overhears our conversation. 'Lionel come in the other day asking, "What do you have sweet?" I told him, "Look on the table and see and help yourself."'

'Butterscotch fudge,' he remembers, 'though I could only smell it.'

'He stays alone in the little room out back.'

'I get bad dreams.'

The pockmarked white boy talks to himself throughout the meal. Then sits alone on the back step, slapping his head and whimpering until Sabrina puts an arm around him.

After dinner Virginia counsels a couple who are living in a tent on waste ground behind the School Administration Building. Every time they stop by she takes five dollars from her purse for them to buy gas and maybe find jobs. When they leave, Virginia slumps into her armchair, pushes away the tubes of hair relaxer and turns on the television.

In *NYPD Blue* Simone and Sipowicz investigate a murder.

'Your pal the pimp murdered somebody in the second floor of that hotel,' barks Sipowicz at a hooker on a stretcher, 'and then he blew this guy's buddy's head off.'

'Gerald gone crazy. He done lost his girl and his sense,' cries the actress.

I tell Virginia that I admire the Center's calm industry.

'We all got beat up just last week,' she sighs. 'I got thrown across the table, clothes torn. This crazy man pulled a knife and said to me, "Are you scared?" I told him, "No." He was taken kinda short. "Well why?" he asked. "Because He's takin' care o' me."'

'I tell you what it is,' interjects Mary. She polishes off the left-over cake as anemone-top snips at her split ends. 'It's like you and I have been there.'

'Yeah. I been there,' sighs Virginia.

'And we don't want to see other people have it that rough.'

'So you care for people because you don't want them to go through it too?' I ask.

'That's right,' nods Mary.

'Not for me it ain't,' says Virginia, shaking her head. 'I had to be born with my soft heart. I was the same way when I was a girl.'

On the flickering screen Sipowicz covers a corpse with his jacket.

'Tell me,' I say.

'My mother was not much at home so I did the cooking for my brothers and sisters. As well as for the neighbourhood kids. Then when I had my own children there was a lady across the street with seven boys. Her husband had borrowed a large sum o' money from a minister and skipped town. The poor girl didn't know what to do so I got to feeding her children too.'

'Feeding her seven?'

'Today they still calls me Momma, cause they ate out o' my kitchen.'

'Your old neighbours call you Mother?'

'I have lots o' children in Palatka,' she says, rolling her head back in a sudden fit of laughter.

'That's your predestination,' decides Mary, chuckling too.

'Quit thrashin' about,' snaps anemone-top.

'I started working away from home at eight and one half years,' recalls Virginia, racing through her words again. 'That was my age. Eight and one half. My first job was rubbing this little white lady's foot. She had a foot problem. I cleaned her house too. She got on my nerves because she made me save the dishwater and the tealeaves. Even though she had an abundance o' money.'

Hype Hair falls off her lap. Anemone-top's scissors catch a glint of blue television light.

'Then at thirteen I was living on premises, taking care of a lady that'd had a heart attack. They said a telephone operator had got smart enough to tell her that her husband was cheating on her. So I was putting the hot compresses on her, cooking, working all month until she just told me to get my you-know-what out o' there. That's right. So I walked away. She never gave me one nickel.'

Virginia holds up her fingers again, counting off her jobs.

'Then I was in the potato field when we had the wire baskets that were already heavy before you filled them with the potatoes. We had to pull them into the crocker sacks twice to make a bagful. Which got us six cents. That's one hundred bags a day to get six dollars. The rows o' them were about as long as from here . . .' She gestures away to the west. '. . . to way over across the bridge somewhere.'

Mary lowers her buttocks onto the sofa, cake and cut finished. Then shifts over to let Lori join her. Anemone-top perches on the sofa's arm, scissors at the ready.

'If you asking did I shoot the guy,' Sipowicz tells Simone, 'I already told you: No.'

'I could never pick my jobs,' admits Virginia, 'and I was glad to get every one of them. But without God there is no way I could have kept my strength: to work like I did, to raise my family, to operate this house. There's just no way.'

'It was a kind of rough route,' says Mary.

On the television a new victim has been shot through the ear. Virginia picks up the remote to flip channels.

'Now, what about this hair?' asks anemone-top.

Palatka, Friday 31st – Run errands all morning. Virginia gives me a shopping list and I take Lionel to the oculist. If I'd gone to Germany he would have been another few days without glasses.

Last evening as I'd made to leave the Center, Virginia said to me, 'It don't get dark for another half hour. You'll be fine up 'til then.'

'And after that?'

'It be best if you stay in your motel.'

I told her that I planned to take a walk. Earlier I had watched a group of retired black men fishing for mullet on the shore.

'Palatka used to be a nice little town, at one point,' Virginia said, taking hold of my police map. 'But don't be fooled by the river walk or the beautiful old architecture. This place is worse than New York.' With a felt-tip pen she crossed out block after city block. 'Don't you go to the north side, honey. I wouldn't like anything to happen to you.'

She handed me back my map, with the safe route back to the Happy Trails Inn marked in red.

'We group of ladies used to like to walk out at night, when the air's blowing good. We can't do it now. Unless we got a pistol.'

'Discover Why Palatka Feels So Good!' screams a tangerine billboard above the Chamber of Commerce. 'Win the Minute Maid Bed & Breakfast Here!'

It wasn't my intention to come to the north side. I'd listened to Virginia's advice. But I got lost looking for the Piggly Wiggly discount market. I'm always confusing my left and right.

Drive down Madison Street towards the river, between rows of sunbaked shanties built on stilts with molten tar-paper roofs. Outside the occasional tin-roofed house are carports and beaten-up Chryslers. At the entrance of a dere-lict movie house, half a dozen men slouch in the shade. There is no one else on the street, apart from two sharp-chinned women arguing outside a nameless corner shop. At their feet is a ripped brown paper bag. And broken eggs cooking on the hot pavement.

I remember the Alamo Guide to Safe Travel.

I do not pull over on the side of the road and study my map.

The car rattles along the brick road, over odd lumps of asphalt, then crosses an unmarked border. Madison Street transforms itself from plantation workers' ghetto to steamboat owners' golden mile. Palm and oak trees drape verdant capes around elegant Southern properties. An elderly white man in a rocking chair is served iced tea by his houseboy. His gardener tends to an ornate bird-feeder. Buttercup verandahs and gingerbread fretwork encircle turn-of-the-century mansions. A Revolutionary flag – decorated with a rattlesnake and the motto 'Don't Tread on Me' – dangles over an ochre porch.

I stop at the foot of a manicured lawn.

The elaborate wooden house looks familiar. As do the twee trellises decorating the dormer eave. Then I recognise the building. I saw a photograph of it this morning. On the Center's breakfast table.

'I looked all over the United States for this bed and breakfast,' owner Bland Holland tells me five minutes later, standing in his parlour in front of an arched antique mirror. 'I was real lucky to find it.'

The Minute Maid Bed & Breakfast is featured on fifty million orange-juice containers on sale throughout the country. The house is the grand prize in the corporation's 'Best Breakfast Experience' promotion.

'I'd been travelling for eighty-four days straight and feeling very discouraged,' says Bland, a pallid, square Texan who would have tended towards fat had he not resisted sweets all his life. 'When I flew in from Dallas and rented a little car and drove into Palatka I thought, "I've just wasted a thousand bucks." Then I came closer and turned into this street and realised, "That's the one."'

The 'Queen Anne Victorian' house had been built in 1878 as a wedding present for the daughter of Alexander Putnam, surveyor of northern Florida. But, like Palatka itself, the building fell into disrepair. A century after its construction the porches were held up by scaffolding. A past owner fell through the rotting kitchen floor. Bland saw the potential of the house, undertook its restoration and stocked it with antique furniture. Coca-Cola, the parent company of Minute Maid, then selected it for their campaign. It suited their 'genteel America' promotion. They paid above the odds for the option to offer it as a prize.

'Real, real lucky.'

Bland is as neat as his house, with the creases of his lurid orange 'Enjoy Minute Maid' shirt precisely ironed. He gives me a tour.

'This is the Rose Room, with a balcony that opens onto the front,' he says with a measured twist of the wrist. 'It has a queen-size cherry pediment bed. And here's the Garden Room. I get a lot of men travelling on their own, so I did this one with a little more masculinity.' The room has a marble-top dressing table and a treetop view.

I see the Camellia Room, decorated in mint and mauve floral wallpaper, and the Magnolia Room, with bay window and love seat. Baskets of ferns hang from the second-floor balcony. The aroma of freshly brewed coffee wafts through the house. Downstairs is the pool, fishpond and hot tub. I don't recall seeing a hot tub at the Caring Center.

'Currently we're featured in *Florida Heritage*, and we're getting a few nibbles – because of the Minute Maid stuff – from *Southern Life*.'

He points out the heartpine wainscoting and the open staircase made of curly pine, a wood which is found in only one out of a hundred trees.

'There's also a third floor.' Bland's inflection lifts at the end of each sentence. 'At first I was going to do it half for me and half for two more guest rooms, but I decided I wanted my privacy. I've just finished a forty-three-day straight of guests.' He rolls his eyes. 'You know, I would have gone sturk crazy if I'd had people up there with me.'

I walk back across the manicured lawn to the car. Air conditioners hum around me. Further along the tree-lined road other mansions have private lawns leading to private docks with sailing boats and thrillcraft. The inky river sparkles in the sunlight. I look back up Madison Street, in the direction from which I came, and catch sight of the two women still arguing.

Within the next sixty days one lucky American will snap open their breakfast orange juice and find that they have won the Minute Maid Bed & Breakfast. They can move to Palatka. Or take the alternative prize of $250,000 cash.

Bland does not expect to have to pack his bags.

I had offered to drive Virginia Blue to Gainesville, a college town forty-five miles to the west. Bland told me that *Money Magazine* had voted it the Best Small Place to Live in the USA.

'No it's not,' says Virginia as we turn onto Highway 20.

On the back seat are two cauldrons of soup, eighty rounds of sandwiches, and Sabrina. There are blankets and sleeping bags in the boot. And a box of African Gold beauty products. I should have rented a larger car.

'You seen those refugees in the foreign countries going through a hungry line? That's the way my line is in Gainesville.'

On the weekend Virginia cares for the homeless in neighbouring Alachua County.

'I spent Thanksgiving there feeding the hungry. I thought we were going to come back home that afternoon. We weren't able to, because Thanksgiving night I *still* had hungry people coming through the line. That's some "Best Small Place".'

Her hair has been restyled by anemone-top. The new grey colour suits her white uniform.

'It probably is the Best Small Place to Buy Drugs,' says Sabrina from the back.

'We had a little fellow arrested there two weeks ago for dealing,' says Virginia, her voice at once angry and weary. 'He was fourteen. *Fourteen*. Then on Monday his first cousin got himself shot because he was into the same thing. '

I tell Virginia that I've never seen a handgun in Britain. 'It's illegal to own them there.'

'Wow,' gasps Sabrina, as if I'd said there were no telephones in Europe.

'It's got so now that when my sister calls me from Tampa, the first thing she asks is, "Who you all burying this week?"'

'So what does a gun cost?' I ask.

'A gun?' Sabrina snaps her fingers, her reserve forgotten. She's on familiar territory. 'A gun's free.'

'Ten dollars, maybe,' says Virginia.

'You can buy one off the street.'

'And the drug pusher, if you don't have his money when he come to get it . . .'

'He'll kill you.'

'. . . he'll give you so much time, but if you don't have it . . .'

'He'll kill you.'

'. . . walk up and take you out.'

We drive past cabbage farms and dense stands of cypress and oak. The monotony of the flatwoods is broken by flashes of blue water. Scrub jays and grackles cut between the trees. Virginia tells me she once took a dealer into the house in error.

'I remember that,' Sabrina nods, pulling herself forward and resting her chin on the back of Virginia's seat. 'He didn't tell Mrs Blue what he was into.'

'I try to help people do better. I *want* to see people do better. I've had some come in, get good jobs and within two weeks they're in their own apartment or trailer. But if anybody come into my house wrong, they going to hit the door. They *will* hit the door.'

Virginia gathers herself, swelling with sharp fury, fired by the force of spirit.

'They've been doing their crack and they're high and they're coming in with attitudes towards the people and all. They have to respect my girls,' she spits. 'They have to respect my house. Period.'

On concrete bridges black men stand by their cars, their lines arcing in the water, casting for largemouth bass and speckled perch. There are fishing boats and the odd oil barge on the river. We pass roadside tackle shops and bait stalls. I watch two white anglers in RayBans launch their gleaming, fibreglass *Wet Vett* into the Saint Johns.

'You know, time was my life felt like walking along the top of a real bad old fence,' says Sabrina, so softly that I hardly hear her above the hum of wheels. 'Any old push sent me fallin'.'

I turn to look at her, a fragile Nubian head resting against the seatback.

'This here's an example of somebody who fell right off, then picked herself back up,' says Virginia, turning to set eyes on her too. 'One year ago her sister-in-law called me and said, "Sabrina's got to get out o' my house. You gonna make room for her?" I told her to come by in the morning and talk to me about it. A half hour later she just dropped Sabrina at the door. Kicked her right out o' the house.'

'How old were you?' I ask.

'Nineteen.'

'She walked in wearing a little short dress, with her hair all standing up and the comb this way, like a *bad* girl.'

I remember the two women arguing outside the nameless shop on Madison Street. *Bad* girls.

'I looked at her and I turned my head and I like went into

a little meditation with Him. And He said, just like this, "Take her."'

'You heard a voice?' I ask.

'So I took her.'

Virginia looks forward again, thinks back.

'Sabrina had a problem when she first came here. I spoke with her about it one time. I told her, when I go out I go out clean, and you're going with me. She got to fixing herself up real nice, looking good. She's very helpful to me. She got to be a good, going-church girl. So, she walked herself right into a home. And you see how she look now? I should have taken a picture that first day.' She starts to laugh. 'Before . . . and after.'

'It was the fact that I didn't get along with life then, or at least my past,' says Sabrina. 'I kept on sort of falling off, like I said.'

'Or being pushed,' notes Virginia.

Ahead of us the woods fall back to make room for Gainesville's donut shops and chain motels. Across town 40,000 students occupy the two-thousand-acre University of Florida campus. Outside the Dairy Queen, 4x4s with bullbars park alongside sophomores' scooters. At restaurants named Wingin' It and Takee Outee frat boys chat up Gators football team cheerleaders. Room-mates stop for a Cherry Coke after aerobics class. In 1990 five students were murdered here by a serial killer.

'We work in that area on 5th Avenue at South Main,' explains Virginia. 'My insurance agent says, "You've got to be a brave lady to go down there." But just because folks are down, I don't want them to *feel* that way. We see all kinds, all colours, and everybody look alike. Everybody look alike,' she repeats.

'The Center is one good place I know,' says Sabrina.

'There's a lot o' love.'

'A lot of love.'

'Like they say in the song, "If I can help somebody as I pass along, my living has not been in vain." Go left here, honey.'

We turn off East University and stop near the Saint Francis House. In the park across from the hostel, derelict men and women gather under the trees. A filthy white tramp limps past the car.

'Howdy, Momma,' he calls out to Virginia.

'How can I stay young,' she fusses, pulling at her hair, 'with all these folks calling me Momma?'

Sabrina starts to unload the food but Virginia stays in her seat. Solid and stout. Our eyes linger on her charges, the hungry of the Sunshine State.

'Virginia,' I ask, thinking of making luck and losing it, of strings of events and the body-blow of fate. 'Is it a question of chance?'

'I guess it just has to be ordained of God,' she says, speaking softly now, not looking away from the homeless. 'Bless their hearts.'

'If you could start all over, what would you change?'

'In my life I wouldn't change anything that happened,' she tells me, shaking her head. 'Not one thing.'

'Not even the woman who cheated you?'

'I'm not bitter,' she says. 'I mean, I have a nice home. Anything is in my house that I need: nice stove, nice refrigerator, television in every bedroom.'

Her voice rises as we watch Sabrina pass out the sandwiches.

'I got plenty of shoes. I got double recliners. I got everything in that house that anybody needs. Yet I'm here. I'm here.'

Virginia pulls herself up out of the car and takes hold of a cauldron of soup. Then, almost as an afterthought, she reaches back across the seat towards me.

'There is only one thing that I'd change. One thing I want.'

A cherry pediment bed? A curly pine staircase?

'I want to be the world's greatest lover. That comes from 1st Corinthians, 13th chapter.' Her cheap rings flash in the light. 'Because without love, you're nothing. You're just nothing. So that's me. That's me.'

I leave Virginia Blue with the homeless in Gainesville, near to the spot where the last steamer, *Hiawatha*, was beached, left to rot, then burned.* There are no more night-time cruises through Florida's exotic paradise.

Turn the car around and head away from the Best Small Place to Live in the USA.

---

* Six months later I heard that Virginia had been stabbed and beaten to death in her Caring Center.

4

Gullible's Travels

A headless body found in the Ocala National Forest was identified Friday as a twenty-three-year-old Apopka Beauty School student, Amy Amber Braccio. 'We think more than one person was involved,' Marion County sheriff Brad Smith said, 'and they were acquaintances of hers, possibly close friends.' Her head and the lower parts of her arms were found three months ago by a fisherman in Trout Lake.

OCALA STAR-BANNER

Spuds, Saturday 1st – Decide to avoid Ocala. On a whim. Call it chance. Or fate. Or the *Ocala Star-Banner*.

Waylaid instead by a town called Spuds. This is potato country, and I expect Marlboro man to ride out of the sun eating fries. At a diner I order a Black Bottom egg-'n'-burger. I've missed the town's Cabbage and Taters Festival. The Palatka Catfish Festival – with its prize catfish-skinning contest – also passed me by.

Spuds offers few local distractions, apart from standing at the crossroads and watching passing trucks.

'Excuse me, sir. What's that one carrying?'

'Potatoes, son.'

Call Katrin from a pay phone outside Spuds Campus.

Before the number connects an unreal electronic voice bids me, 'Thank you.' Yet Virginia Blue doesn't walk the streets at night without a pistol.

'When I was out this morning the puppy chewed the hall carpet,' says Katrin.

'Oh, God.'

'I gave her such a scolding I thought she was traumatised. So I fed her some Sad Cow.'

'Sad Cow drops? For the puppy?'

Sad Cow is Bach Rescue Remedy. Four drops on the tongue help to comfort and reassure.

'Jutta gives it to her geraniums.'

Highway 207, Sunday 2nd – Travelling without a schedule is liberating. It engenders openness, enables me to recognise things of value in the arbitrary, spares me the expense of buying a guidebook. I rely on my intuition. And intuition is a sophisticated form of planning.

Americans celebrate their freedom. Their faith in the ability to choose for themselves and to direct the course of their lives may be optimistic, it may even be a myth, but it lies at the heart of the American dream. Yet Cassadaga's clairvoyants consider journeys to be predestined. Virginia believes that events are ordained by God. Their confident assertions make me wonder at the assumption of free will. I pull onto the hard shoulder to try to put it into context.

Who visits Florida, and why? It seems a reasonable question to ask, as I'm here and don't yet know why.

The Spanish came first, dreaming of finding a promised land. And swiping its riches. Ponce de León, who had been a crew member on Columbus's second voyage, grabbed the limp penis peninsula in Easter 1513. He named it after the Catholic Feast of Flowers, *Pascua Florida*, even though he found only swamps, alligators and enormous black clouds of voracious mosquitoes. Its riches eluded him, unlike a native Calusa poison arrow.

Florida may not have had Mexico's gold or Brazil's cocoa beans, but at the time the land was of value because of its strategic position. The Gulf Stream swept up its east coast, speeding ships home on their return passage to Europe. Its location also attracted the attention of the French and British, who held it for twenty-odd years, yet for almost three centuries it remained under Spain's control.

White Americans turned up at the start of the nineteenth century. Andrew Jackson, who later became President of the United States, came to bash the Spaniards and hunt down Indians. His attacks helped to drive the colonialists out of North America and – with the assistance of European diseases – led to the virtual annihilation of the native Seminole. Next, Africans were shipped in to work the cotton, citrus and cattle farms. Those who stayed on after the Civil War and the abolition of slavery had to contend with a poll tax designed to keep the poor away from the ballot box. Their former owners ensured that discriminatory laws forbade 'Negro government' in this Utopia. The Ku Klux Klan had a formidable following in the Sunshine State.

Florida soon became a fashionable winter escape for wealthy northerners, as well as invalids from America's wars. The warm climate and allegedly curative mineral springs enticed sufferers of asthma and rheumatism. Henry Flagler, once the partner of John D. Rockefeller, created the East Coast Railroad, pushing south faster than the pace of settlement, building extravagant hotels, encouraging rapid population growth.

Flagler's ambition was to create an 'American Riviera', and down his rails came property developers and Bible bashers, gangsters and bootleggers, geriatrics and exiles. Babe Ruth, the legendary baseball player, retired to Florida for a time.

As did Lefty Turner, star of the one-time Negro Baseball League. He can still be seen riding his bicycle around Palatka.

Florida became accessible to all. Like California, it was touted as the place to live out the American dream, and still get in a swim before breakfast. Sun, fun and reduced hair loss. Its is a history not of seeing and believing, but of belief restoring sight.

Last night in Spuds I picked through a handful of free newspapers. In among the discount motel vouchers I found the story of the Goatman.

Every autumn for over thirty years up until the late 1960s, Charles McCartney left New York for Miami in a covered wagon pulled by a team of a dozen goats. He travelled south, living off cabbage and nanny milk, selling postcards of his retinue, sleeping rough, using his animals as blankets. 'The colder it gets,' *Florida On the Go* quoted him as saying, 'the more goats you wrap around yerself.'

Goatman McCartney hated the cold. To keep warm he made himself a goat-hide hat, leggings and jerkin. He grew a beard. His parents, who had been circus trapeze artists, had given up the travelling life and settled in the north. McCartney wanted to stay with them, but he couldn't stand the winters. The need to feel the hot sun on his face pulled him and his goats to Florida. Along the way injured animals rode with him in the wagon. At steep hills he and the kids put their heads against the tailgate and pushed. Every few nights he'd set up camp in a drive-in theatre, charging the public three dollars to meet him and his animals. He'd tell stories, do a little preaching and sell a few more postcards.

His whimsical, fancy-bred trek caught the public's imagination. The Highway Patrol was often called in to direct traffic during his annual visits. Local dignitaries went out of their way to meet him, despite the smell. McCartney even managed to marry three times. His last wife drove behind him in a new Cadillac all the way from New York. In my newspaper there was a photograph of her keeping up her hircine Quixote, dreaming like him of the warm sunshine.

They divorced not long after reaching Miami.

I turn around to reach across the Cavalier's back seat. Under Virginia's forgotten copy of *Try it Yourself Hair* is my discarded road map. I spread it across the dashboard. Highway 207 runs north-east through Saint Johns County towards the arbitrary pencil tear. The gash points at Saint Augustine, my obvious next destination.

The city is by the sea, protected by a barrier of sandy islands, rich in history. Ponce de León, Florida's original tourist, first landed here. Europeans lived on the site for more than fifty years before the Pilgrim Fathers arrived at Plymouth Rock. It was recommended to me by flabby Fran at Alamo Rent-a-Car.

Saint Augustine, Monday 3rd – I expect the past to anchor me, but as soon as I arrive in Saint Augustine Lady Luck casts off. She checks out of my motel and leaves me thrashing in the deep end of life's swimming pool. I lay myself open, engage strangers in conversation and get punched in the eye.

The old town seems charming enough. Spanish villas are encircled by oleander and hibiscus hedges, pink Mustangs park beneath massive oaks, flowering bougainvillaea tumbles down grey coquina garden walls. I wander under overhanging balconies, around sour orange groves, past a Huguenot cemetery caught between a dusty bus lot and Highway A1A. At the site of the Fountain of Youth Archaeological Park Ponce de León came ashore. Unlike me, he didn't have to pay $4.75 to drink from the spring. I cough up the cash. Sip the legendary sulphur water. Detect no obvious improvement to my mortal span or hairline.

To wash away the taste I order iced tea at the Orange Street Cyber Café. Internet access is provided 'in the authentic Old Drug Store complex'. Other visitors buy boogie boards and beads at Grist Mill Gifts. A waitress in mirror shades tries to undo the sulphur water's effect and speed me to ruin with a serving of Sudden Death Chocolate Blizzard Bomb.

'You've been to alotta places I ain't seen in my own hemisphere,' she says. She has never been to Cassadaga or Palatka. 'Saint Augustine is a small town, but if you want history you can't do better than Ripley's.'

On my way there I am distracted by the Tragedy in US History Museum. A peeling red, white and blue billboard declares, 'See President Kennedy's car! See each shot as they hit him in the Dallas Parade! See Spanish skeletons too!' But the old white building is in need of more than a lick of paint. Its sagging stars and stripes is moth-eaten. The owner died and his museum was closed. I've just missed the liquidation sale. As well as the Kennedy memorabilia, the items auctioned included Bonnie and Clyde's getaway car and a Civil War neckbreaker. The tragic past doesn't seem to be a money-spinner in feelgood Florida.

It's a different history next door at Ripley's Believe It Or Not!. The museum celebrates American normality by gawking at (for the most part) foreign aberrance. Robert Ripley was a chubby Californian cartoonist-cum-showman with bad teeth and a toupee. Early in the twentieth century he travelled the world searching for the odd and the unusual. His discoveries illustrated a cartoon strip which, at its peak, reached eighty million readers. In it he depicted Kuda Bux the Indian firewalker, dogs which ate razor blades and Beauregard, the six-legged cow. He noted weird sporting achievements ('A. Forrester of Toronto ran 100 yards backwards in 14 seconds') and the man whose nose measured seven and a half inches long. His critics called him an outrageous liar. To confound them Ripley brought home Tibetan skull bowls, Medieval chastity belts and Amazonian shrunken heads. These strange, exotic and often implausible artefacts were gathered together in an 'Odditorium' at the 1933 Chicago World's Fair. The exhibition and travelling shows which followed proved so popular that over the years twenty-seven Believe It Or Not! museums were established in cities as far apart as Niagara Falls, Pattaya and Blackpool.

I see the world's smallest domino set and its largest Meccano model. Gag at the toothbrush used for fifty years. Keep clear of the Iron Maiden of Nuremberg, an execution device pierced with fourteen spikes. There are Fijian cannibal forks, a jellybean portrait of Van Gogh and an eight-foot-high wax model of Robert Wadlow, 'the tallest man of all time'. A leprechaun's hologram glimmers beside a giant gallstone (weighing four pounds and donated by a relieved Liz Huff of Myrtle Beach, S.C.). Along one wall are photographs of El Fusilado, who was shot eight times by a firing squad and survived, and Laurello, born with a revolving head.

In front of the wax bust of Weng, the Human Unicorn, my disbelief rears its head. The Manchurian farmer had a thirteen-inch horn.

I laugh.

'It is impolite to mock other people's misfortune,' says the young woman beside me in emphatic English.

'I beg your pardon?'

'Do not upset our child, please,' instructs her beefy, cerise partner.

They are German tourists: blond, bored and burnt. Not having a good day either. He wishes to be on the golf course. She fancies her poolside lounger. Their son wants to get back to his game of beach Jokari. The shady, freakish museum is their unhappy compromise.

'I just don't believe it,' I explain.

I had read about an earlier sceptic, Wayne Harbour, who spent twenty-six years trying to expose Ripley's charade. He wrote over 22,000 letters trying to fault the Believe It Or Not! cartoons.

'Do *you* believe it?' I ask the man, poking at Weng's wax horn.

'*Lass das,*' he warns me. Hands off. 'It is not your property.'

I point at a seventeen-inch dwarf named Alypius. 'Or that?'

'*Ist es nicht echt, Mutti?*' asks the kid, now disappointed as well as dulled. Is it a fake?

'*Natürlich nicht, Wolfy,*' says the woman. Of course not.

'Tell the child that it is real,' demands the man.

'I can't do that,' I say.

'Just tell him.'

'No.'

Then he hits me. Hard enough to send my glasses flying. They land on the nose of a stuffed moose.

'Excuse me . . .'

My assailant yanks his family away. I scrabble for my glasses. Twist them back into shape. By the time I can see again the Germans have vanished.

I leave behind The Last Supper sculpted in pecans. In the sweltering parking lot a clown in a chicken suit waves a 'Free Wings' sign in front of my aching eye. I stumble past him and gaze down San Marco Avenue towards the Castillo. Run across the road to the 3-D World ('A Voyage Beyond Reality'). Look back towards the Tragedy Museum. The unhappy family are nowhere to be seen. I almost stop a bicycling policemen in shorts, then spot them ducking through a low white doorway. I chase down a narrow street and into Casa Avero, the Saint Photios National Greek Orthodox Shrine.

In 1768 the first permanent settlement of Greeks in the New World was established near Saint Augustine. At the time Florida was under British rule and London was reluctant to further drain its own manpower in settling the colonies. So a plan was hatched to recruit loyal foreigners to populate the new lands. Four hundred Greek immigrants jumped at the chance to escape their Turkish oppressors. But after ten ill-fated years, often surviving only on mullet and gopher turtle, the settlement collapsed.

I sigh. Inside the shrine there is no sign of the Germans. To try to will a little good into my wasted day, and to remember the settlers, I light a candle. Then the manager snuffs it out, along with all the others.

'I'm closing up now,' he says. 'I'll relight your candle tomorrow.'

I have a bad night, too. The long, lonely whistles of northbound CPX freights do little to help me sleep. One after another the six-locomotive, five-hundred-box-car trains rumble through the next room. Or at least the motel lobby. Half a dozen Landstar Ranger truck cabs sit in the parking lot, their drivers drinking away the darkness before hauling another load of potatoes north.

Saint Augustine (still), Tuesday 4th – I've escaped. A ceiling fan ruffles the pages on the desk before me. Outside are eager buskers and loud-mouthed touts. Venezuelan tourists ride calèches through crumbling gateways. Germans punch Canadians beneath pastel-coloured parapets. But inside no one speaks in a voice louder than a whisper.

I woke this morning and couldn't see. Couldn't find the car keys. Couldn't read the road map. My eye was swollen like a shiny Aryan egg. I tried soothing it with a sock full of ice cubes then walked into the bathroom door.

'Hold a book in your hand,' goes the old Hebrew saying, 'and you're a pilgrim at the gates of a new city.'

So this cyclopean pilgrim sought sanctuary in the Saint Augustine Research Library. It is housed in a mock-Moorish building behind a pseudo-Colonial Woolworth's. Here are ten thousand books on the state's history, bound volumes of Spanish Land Grant deeds and the records of the Bureau of Refugees, Freedmen and Abandoned Lands. And I can't read any of them.

Charles A. Tingley strokes his goatee with short, plump fingers.

'The business of Saint Augustine is history,' he tells me. 'We're one of the oldest towns which based its economy on cultural tourism.'

The genial, rotund head librarian and I sit in his shady side-office. Cool air tumbles out of his air conditioner. He's trying to ignore my shiner.

'Starting with before the Civil War, Saint Augustine was the most tropical place you could get to in the United States. Invalids or people with tuberculosis, one of the great killers of the nineteenth century, came here to get out of the cold of New England. Many of them died here. Ralph Waldo Emerson, for instance . . .'

'Emerson died in Saint Augustine?'

'He came here and recovered himself.'

He must not have met any German tourists.

'People came by steamboat, then on Flagler's railroad.' As they came to – then bypassed – Palatka.

'And what do you need with a railroad?' asked Tingley. 'You need hotels. So we have the Alcazar, the Cordova and the Pots.'

'The Pots?'

'The Ponce de León; it's a time capsule from the gilded age.' Tingley gushes with pride for the town's history. 'Next came A1A, the Coastal Highway, and the automobile tourist. Right up to the fifties Saint Augustine was *the* major tourist destination. Not Fort Lauderdale. Not Palm Beach. We have the Castillo de San Marcos here. We have the Spanish Quarter Living History Museum. Our alligator farm was founded in 1887. It has representatives of every crocodilian on the planet.'

Tingley brings to mind a confident schoolboy in shorts bragging about his late grandfather's achievements. He enthuses about the Bridge of Lions and the old British slave market. He calls the Pot's dining room – now the Flagler College canteen – 'one of the most spectacular Victorian interiors in the world'. He raves about the Spanish Castello with its soft yellow coquina walls, cemented together by burnt oyster-shells mixed with sand and water. As he speaks he leans forward in his chair. 'And we have Marineland. Marineland was the first major marine zoological park in the world. It started here in the thirties.' Then he sucks back his enthusiasm. 'Though now it's on its last legs . . .'

'But tourism seems to be booming,' I say. Forty-five million foreigners visit Florida every year. Nearly one and a half million from the UK. Four hundred and fifty thousand from Germany. And the domestic holidaymakers are too numerous to be counted.

'. . . because of the advent of Disney.'

'Disney?'

'Disney has changed Florida tourism so dramatically. People used to drive down the scenic route, down A1A, from points north, and stop here. Now they stay on the Interstate and head straight to Orlando. Disney has become the black hole of tourist dollars.'

In the library Tingley digs out books and journals, reads me extracts, describes in vivid detail photographs of Edwardian chignons and imprisoned Apaches. There are sixteenth-century Cathedral Parish Records and microfilmed papers from the Bureau of Indian Affairs ('Enrolment Cards of Seminoles 1898–1914'). He points out the stereographs and glass-plate negatives, plays oral histories of Saint Johns County residents and gives me a photocopy of Morris Phillips's 1891 volume *Abroad and at Home: Practical Hints for Tourists* ('At the majority of hotels you eat ordinary oranges. At the Cordova only selected "Indian River" oranges are used and instead of coming from the store-room they come from a refrigerator'). I try to focus on back-issues of the *Journal of Southern History* until my good eye starts to ache. I begin to taste the exotic past of frontier Florida, before it was transformed into a pleasant backdrop to the Disney experience.

'Are you from an old Saint Augustine family?' I ask Tingley. Why else would he make his life's work the preservation of the town's past?

'I feel like a bit of an impostor,' he confesses, shuffling his schoolboy's feet. 'My ancestors helped to supply the British during the siege of 1740.'

I laugh, relieved, disturbing a reader at another desk. 'So you're trying to make amends?'

Tingley shakes his head. 'I grew up in south Florida, in Clearwater, so I'm aware of what happened down there. Pinellas County got so overdeveloped in the fifties and sixties.' He strokes his trim beard faster now. 'Saint Augustine is the closest thing to the tel – the midden – of Jericho in the United States. You can go and dig a hole in the ground and see the layer of ash from when Governor Moore burned the town in 1702. That's why I'm here.'

It seems that for Tingley only the past can keep Mickey and Ripley at bay.

He returns to the shelves again. Volume after volume land on the desk until I too begin to feel like compacted ash, layered under the weight of history. He is generous with his knowledge. The history absorbs me. But the facts feel irrelevant in modern Florida, like so much old baggage in the trunk of a scarlet Corvette. I grow restless.

Tingley starts to read from the pamphlet *Fact vs. Fiction for the New Historical Saint Augustine*: ' "The program at Saint Augustine must be absolutely sound historically without any flimflams or phoney stories." In the thirties there was a movement to resist this becoming a catchpenny town,' he explains. 'Men like Verne Chatelain and Charles B. Reynolds tried to debunk the tourist myths.'

'Maybe the myths have always been preferred to the true history?'

'In town you can still find the *Oldest* Wooden School, the *Oldest* Drugstore, the *Oldest* House in America. We have the Fountain. Reynolds said that tourists who came here were taken on Gullible's Travels.'

'But isn't that why they came?' And continue to come to Florida.

More books follow: the *Standard Guide* of 1901, Henry James's *The American Scene*, and *Cheap Thrills Florida – The Bottom Half*. I want to recognise the valuable in the arbitrary, but nothing catches my imagination. I don't see my next destination.

Then Gloria Jahoda's *The Other Florida* topples off the stack, falling open at Chapter 4. Page 68. It is titled 'The Garden of Eden'.

' "It was right here in Bristol, Florida," Elvy E. Callaway told me one afternoon as we sat on his porch,' wrote Jahoda in 1967. ' "God created the Adamic man one mile east of Bristol. The original Garden of Eden was here on the banks of the Apalachicola." '

I stare until it hurts. Eden. In the real, phoney Florida. The notion is preposterous.

'Do you know a place called Bristol?' I ask Tingley.

'In England?'

I shake my head. 'On the Apalachicola River.'

'The Apalachicola is way over in the Panhandle.'

'This book says that the Garden of Eden was there.' So much for earthly paradise being in Mesopotamia. 'It quotes from the Bible: "out of the ground God caused to grow every tree pleasant to the sight – including the gopher wood trees."'

'I don't remember gopherwood being mentioned in the Bible,' says Tingley.

'According to this there's only one place in the world where it grows, and that's in Bristol.'

'Florida has always been famous for its somewhat carnival-ish roadside attractions,' Tingley explains with a dismissive shrug.

'It's fancy over fact again,' I say, straining to read. 'This Elvy Callaway claims to have spent seventy-five years studying the matter. Seventy-five *years*,' I repeat, excited and sceptical. 'He was a Baptist minister. Ran for governor, too – in 1936.'

'I never heard of him.'

'He believed that he was chosen "to uncover the evidence in absolute proof of the Bible account of purposeful creation". '

In my head the bells are ringing. Tingley pulls an atlas from the stack of books to show me the Apalachicola. Bristol lies on its eastern bank, close to the Georgia State Line. It looks like a small town. I run my finger down the distance chart. About 350 miles. I can make Tallahassee by dusk and be in Eden tomorrow morning. The route takes me right across the top of Florida, almost as far as Alabama. It's Inter-state most of the way, so I can drive with my bad eye shut. I don't even need my Alamo road map.

I turn to Tingley. He holds in his hands a rare copy of R.K. Sewall's 1848 *Sketches of St. Augustine (with a View of its History and Advantages as a Resort for Invalids)*.

'I've got to go,' I tell him.

5

Garden of Eden, FL 32321

In an attempt to show his congregation that sin was like Russian roulette, Melvyn Nurse, thirty-five, a Jacksonville minister, fatally injured himself when he pointed a pistol loaded with blanks at his head and fired. A blank casing shot through his temple.

TALLAHASSEE DEMOCRAT

Bristol, Wednesday 5th – The road to the Garden of Eden is lined by mobile homes and mailboxes, curb marts and gun stores. Along it run white prison vans and piggish logging trucks grunting under the weight of stacked pine.

Yesterday afternoon I crossed Florida from east to west, leaving behind Saint Augustine, skirting its World Golf Village, driving one-eyed along I-10 all the way to Tallahassee. I found the state's tree-lined capital surrounded by rich farmland, beaten from the wilderness by slaves in the nineteenth century. It's the only Confederate city east of the Mississippi which didn't fall to Union troops. I squinted into its suburbs as an apricot sun dipped behind the overpasses. Found a motel on an asphalt island between a tangle of highways. Went for a swim at dusk under an ultramarine canopy, serenaded by the roar of passing tractor-trailers. Then locked myself in my room with supermarket takeaway BBQ chicken.

Over a drumstick I considered Elvy Callaway's dubious proof for the existence of a swampy Elysium.

First, he quoted from Genesis that 'a river went out of Eden to water the Garden and parted and became four heads.' Callaway maintained that the Apalachicola was the only four-headed river system in the world, and cited a US Army Engineers' survey as evidence. On his map the Chattahoochee River was the Biblical Pison. The Flink was the Gihon. Spring Creek passed for the Euphrates and Fish Pond as the Hiddekel. He claimed that the rivers' names, like those of Syria and Ethiopia, had been transplanted *from* America *to* Asia and Africa after the Great Flood. I dug out a Gideon's Bible from the bedside table and read that the Gihon 'compasseth the land of Ethiopia'. Ethiopia, Callaway pointed out triumphantly, was the original name of a small community in modern-day Georgia.

I took another bite of chicken. My mouth was coated in piquant slime, as if I'd been gargling with curried Castrol GTx. I should have bought a fresh salad.

Next, Callaway drew attention to the Garden's rich supplies of onyx, gold and bdellium, or pitch. 'The best gold in the world is found in north Georgia,' he declared, 'where the Chattahoochee has its source before it flows into the Apalachicola.'

Next, there was the gopherwood tree itself. The *Torreya taxifolia*, one of the rarest trees in existence. It grew only to the north of Bristol – that is, in the Garden.

I wrapped up the left-over chicken in its foil bag. The flavour-enhanced fat coagulated on my fingers. I found it hard to believe that the dismembered, spiced carcass had once been alive. Almost as hard as it was to imagine how Callaway had come to believe that Adam and Eve hailed from Liberty County.

A sleek Sheriff's car slices past me, a dark figure slumped in its back seat. It cuts into the turning between the pines marked 'Liberty Correctional Institution'. Bulrushes raise their sausage seed-heads. A grackle picks at a black pancake of carrion. A leaden haze blocks out the sun.

For the first few miles the highest point on the horizon is the road itself, elevated above the bayou, until I come upon a line of pylons beating over the low-lying, featureless earth. But beyond Farr-away Farm the road tucks into rumpled countryside. It begins to roll over the land, curving, no longer running arrow-straight. Paltry clapboard houses sit back from the highway, gathered into tight clearings. I see signs to towns called Panacea, Sneads, Sopchoppy. There are no tourists, tennis courts or lawn sprinkler systems here. Only mile after mile of farmed pine and wild sweet gum.

The Panhandle is the poor corner of the state: hot, Southern and not overlaid with humanity. I'm curious to see if there is here some spirit of innocence and tranquillity, an up-country notion of perfection which might be exaggerated into a bogus Eden. I also hope that Callaway may still inhabit his earthly paradise.

The cloud lifts as I drive into Bristol, 'Our Friendly City' midway between Hosford and Niceville. It's a dusty town of dirt roads, shabby bungalows and yawning caravans. No building is higher than a single storey, apart from the red-brick jail. Behind it, in a caged recreation yard two prisoners hose down a patrol car. The deputy sheriff leans against the razor wire, under a basketball hoop, chewing gum.

I aim for the Court House, parking next to a black Ford pick-up with 'Kill'n . . . Time' painted on its tailgate. As with Cassadaga, Palatka and Saint Augustine, public buildings have become my chosen port of call, natural staging posts from which to reach into a new community. I walk into the ornate front hall. Ask for the mayor. Directed out a small side door.

Across the street is the utilitarian City Hall. With attached fire station. The single face of the town clock glares at a vacant lot. I cut across the coarse grass to the bare entrance. A forgotten note – 'Gone to sawmill. Back shortly. Art' – clings to the wall on a curl of Scotch tape.

I try the door.

It opens.

'I'm afraid you caught me where my hair's short, Miss Louise.'

Behind the glass partition a Confederate patriarch is on the telephone: ash-white skin, shadow thin, sitting bolt upright in the straight hard chair. His delicate-featured face is creased by age lines. He wears a crisp, tieless Sunday shirt buttoned to the collar.

'I don't know and I should know,' he admits in a high, inflectionless voice. 'I'll look into it for you and get back to you, Ma'am. Yes, Ma'am. Goodbye, Ma'am.' He hangs up and addresses the empty office, no change in his tone. 'She did tell me about it and I plain forgot. My memory's got as short as my little finger.'

His metal desk is bare, save for a tidy stack of counterfoils stamped and stapled together. As he composes a careful note to himself, I imagine him running rabbits or dark intruders through the pages of a Faulkner novel. He has to be older than seventy, despite his full head of silvery hair.

'Now, I can't say that I recognise you, son,' he says to me without looking up. He is at once amicable, courteous and guarded. 'You payin' the water bill for a relative?'

'I'm looking for the mayor,' I say.

'Mayor's gone up to Sink to catch bullheads. Won't be back till Friday.'

'Then I wonder if you know a Mr E.E. Callaway?' I ask.

'Sure do,' he replies, easing himself up from his chair, his movement stiff. 'But he won't be much use to you. Elvy's been dead near on twenty years.'

'Can you . . . ?' I start to say, then hesitate. Bristol is as much Eden as Dunblane is Gomorrah. I don't want his laughter to chase me back onto the hot, weary street. But I want even less to go back to Tallahassee. 'Is there anyone who I can talk to about the Garden of Eden?'

'The Garden of Eden?' repeats the old man.

I wait for the guffaw, or at least a chuckle. Instead he joins his hands together as if in prayer.

'They say it was here,' he says, lowering his guard. 'But it's only the whisper of a claim.'

'Here in town?' I ask. 'In Bristol?'

'Just up the road a few miles. Turn left off Highway 270. It's real near to the spot where the Ark was built.'

'*Noah's* Ark?'

'None other.'

I wasn't prepared for the Ark. I'm on a roll.

'I'm no oceanographer,' says the patriarch, 'but they say if you check the tides and currents of the oceans that was probable at that time, you'll find that they'd carry a vessel without a rudder straight from Bristol to Mount Ararat.'

He smiles. With my good eye I try to size him up.

'Why don't you come inside and sit down?' he suggests in his honeyed drawl. 'I hate talking through this glass thing.'

Willy Prophet is the Town Clerk. It's Wednesday, and he is collecting water rates. I take a seat in Biblical Bristol. Adam, Eve and Noah may once have paid their utility bills at the counter.

'The Great Flood has come and gone and a lot has changed since that time, so I don't know who you could talk to about the Garden. But it was here, sure enough. Excuse me for one moment.'

An untidy woman saunters up to the window, her chaotic hair in disarray, proffering a twenty-dollar bill.

'Good mornin' to you, young lady,' says Willy, taking her money. Is she Mary Magdalene? Jairus's daughter? 'If memory serves me correctly, you're Jimmy Revel's grandchild.'

'I'm his *child*,' she cackles, enjoying the flirtation, tucking a feral tendril behind her ear. Then adds, 'The good-looking one.'

'Never a truer word was spoken,' he says, stamping a receipt. He winks. 'Now, where's my tip?'

'You don't git one.'

A large black man in a singlet waits behind her. Zerah the Ethiopian perhaps? He sticks his payment through the window and holds his hand there for half a minute, in silence, while Willy counts out his change.

'Like I was sayin',' Willy says, returning to the desk, 'I don't know who you could talk to about the Garden. The best people in town aren't no good to you now. They've either passed on or they're like my old friend P.H. Hayden. Hayden would have helped you. He'd help anybody. Back in the Great Depression when folks didn't have the money for groceries, he paid for them. And afterwards he didn't get all flutterly like people do today.'

Willy has lived all his life in Bristol. He belongs to its streets as much as the jacaranda and flowering oleander. As much as the spittoons and prison vans too.

'But Hayden's in a nursing home now, and his mental facilities are narrowing down. He thinks he's coming back home but every time he walks a few steps he falls down. I know that the good Lord never makes any mistakes, but I sure wish He'd just let Hayden not wake up one mornin'.'

The telephone rings again. The beauty salon on Solomon Street is closing down and wants its water supply turned off. The caller asks if the order can be backdated by a week to avoid paying this month's bill.

'Yup, Hayden and I were fast friends,' remembers Willy. 'He was a good man.'

'Is there a tourist office that could help me?' I ask, drawing his attention back to my search for the Garden.

'Not this side of Tallahassee.'

'Then a guide to take me there?'

'We could look in the phone book.'

We check for 'Eden, Garden of', but there isn't a listing. 'Maybe it's entered under the owner's name,' suggests Willy.

'God?' I ask.

'The Apalachicola Bluffs and Ravines Preserve. Eden's run by the Nature Conservancy.'

The Conservancy is listed in the book, unlike the Almighty. Willy dials the number. As it rings he pulls a detailed map of Liberty County out of the drawer.

'Did you see the turn for 12 North when you came into town?' he asks.

I had.

'You head up there about five miles, then turn onto 270 and go about two more miles. There's a graded red clay road on the left. If you reach a community, you've gone too far.'

I scan the map for the Tree of the Knowledge of Good and Evil. 'I can't find the Garden,' I say. No prudent legend advises, 'Beware of Beguiling Serpent'.

'Here,' says Willy, pointing without hesitation at an isolated stretch of land on the east bank of the river: Garden of Eden, Bristol, FL 32321.

I see no direct road.

'There's always more than one way to go to a place, as you know.' Willy runs his finger along the various footpaths, then drops the receiver back in its cradle and rolls up the map. 'I wish I could be some help to you,' he says. 'What time is it, anyhow?' He glances up at the wall clock. Noon. 'The Garden's been around for a fair few years now,' he reassures me. 'Could you hold off seeing it until after lunch?'

Willy coasts along the unpaved roads with casual familiarity, avoiding potholes and acknowledging neighbours with equal ease.

'Bristol is a peaceful, quiet community,' he tells me, waving at the Sheriff. Red hibiscus blooms in front of the Court House, tended by prisoners in striped trousers. 'I can't remember when we last had a serious crime.' A resident sells 'collectable' jailhouse birdbaths across from Liberty High School. 'I'd sleep with the doors unlocked if it weren't for my wife. She's a nervous sort, you know. Watches too much TV.'

Home is a single-storey, white-shuttered bungalow. Willy drives across the front lawn and stops by the verandah. The screen door opens onto a neat living room of needlepoint cushions and keen memories. A beehived daughter beams in a monochrome graduation photograph. A crewcut son with dark eyes poses beside an Alaskan wellhead. On the wall are framed medals, an air force citation and a dangling lucky rabbit's foot.

Rose Prophet warms the little kitchen with Southern cooking and hospitality. She has fried their evening's chicken and baked short-dough biscuits, prepared collard greens and salad, opened a can of Green Giant sweetcorn and made Lipton's iced tea – all in the fifteen minutes since Willy's telephone call. Only the loaves and fishes are missing from the table.

'We thank you God for this food,' Willy prays, the three of us holding hands across the Formica, 'and for the visit of our new friend on his way to find the Garden. May you watch over him and guide him on his journey.'

Amen.

Over lunch I learn that Elvy Edison Callaway was a minister who never attended church in the last thirty-one years of his life. Also an early ecologist who did not believe in Darwinian theory. 'We have at last proved beyond any intelligent doubt that the birthplace of man is right here in Big Bend

Country,' he declared in a 1970 interview with the *Tallahassee Democrat*.

'Elvy's suspicions were aroused first by the anomaly of the gopherwood tree . . .' explains Willy. He unearths a copy of Callaway's treatise *In the Beginning* as Rose dishes out the chicken.

'I am personally convinced that man was created,' I read in its introduction. 'Until the Evolutionists can present more convincing facts that man evolved, I shall rest the conclusions herein stated to the judgement of those who seek only the truth.'

'. . . and second by the research of A.R. Jones,' continues Willy. 'You've heard of Dr Jones?'

I shake my head while accepting a generous serving of grits.

Willy produces a pristine copy of Jones's *Man Before the Flood*.

'The east bank of the Apalachicola River between Bristol and Chattahoochee, Florida is an area that has every Biblical description of the Original Garden of Eden,' I read over my plate. 'The Tree of Life mentioned in Genesis is here; the river of four heads; the gold and the purity of gold; bdellium and onyx stone near the head of the first or Pison river, as mentioned in the second Chapter of Genesis, cannot be denied.'

'They made a television documentary about Elvy,' Rose recalls, passing me another biscuit. 'He was a colourful character.'

'Do you think that the Garden of Eden was here?' I ask in disbelief.

'It is a very special place,' she confides, sharing out the greens.

'Let me give you a little background on how I personally feel,' says Willy.

I lay down my knife and fork.

'I'm a Christian. I'm doing pretty good here. I've got a few aches and pains, but I'm doing all right. When I leave here I'm going to heaven. So I got no problems at all. I mean, I'm a great believer in this.'

Willy smiles and I wait for him to say more. But he bites into a chicken leg instead.

We eat.

Callaway's theory relied on 'teleology', the compilation of information and a study of the Bible like the preparation of circumstantial evidence in a legal brief. He wanted his work to banish forever doubt as to the truth of the Biblical account of 'purposeful Creation'. As we sip our glasses of clamato juice, I wonder if teleology is taught at Liberty High School. I wonder too if Darwin's name is ever whispered in its corridors.

'Could you find the space for a slice of pie?' asks Rose, clearing away the dishes.

'I always says I married Rose 'cause her Mamma could cook,' Willy volunteers, sitting back in his chair. 'She likes to have guests. But we've been alone for such a long time she doesn't much get the chance any more.' Then he adds, 'I'm sorry that I can't think of anyone who you might be able to talk to about Eden.'

'Why don't you run him out there?' Rose asks him, cutting me a thick quarter-wedge of lemon meringue.

'I've upset your day enough,' I say. Not wanting to take advantage of their kindness. Wanting him to be my guide. 'You probably have to get back to City Hall.'

Willy looks at Rose. Looks back at me.

'I'm elected to that job,' he says, joining his hands together again. 'And I'm seventy-two years old. So don't tell anybody, but I do as I please.'

On the drive out to the Garden I see no cherubim with flaming swords guarding the way to the Tree of Life. More surprisingly, there are no roadside restaurants called Adam's Ribs, or grocery stores selling Eden apples. Willy remembers that there was once a kiosk at the end of Garden of Eden Road, but the building is now derelict and for sale.

'Is this it?' I ask him as he turns onto a dirt track.

We park at the edge of the sandhill forest and follow a drifting trail through the sparse, longleaf pines. It is hot in the sun, and Willy hurries ahead, anxious to reach the cool cover of beech and evergreen. 'Not good for anything much except to hold the world together,' he says, pointing at the odd clumps of wire grass, tufted like a punk's hair. 'Near extinct, too.'

His pace slows when we enter the pale shade of the slope forest. The green canopy darkens the path as it angles down to the edge of the steephead ravine. Over the lip, a hundred feet below, are the leafy tops of magnolias, sweetbay and oaks. Cicadas buzz in the trees beneath us. Black-winged dragonflies dart into the valley.

'Is that it?'

We plunge into the deep, narrow ravine, grasping for handholds on the sheer sidewalls, disturbing spiders' silk strung across the path. The treetops rise up to meet us, and we slide down beside their thick trunks. We twist through the snarled barrier of dense evergreen shrub, tangled with laurel and holly. The temperature drops again. I hear running water, smell sweet rotting leaves and fall into the humid embrace of the valley floor.

I don't ask again if we've arrived.

Over millennia a crystal-clear stream undercut the slope to create the hidden canyon. At the place where it springs from the toe of the valley wall I crouch down to lap mouthfuls of fresh water. There are newts and dusky salamanders in its sandy shallows. Water beetles push against its current, remaining forever still. Underfoot are soft mosses and minute, delicate ferns.

Man may not have been formed of the dust of this ground, the breath of life puffed into his nostrils. There may not be hereabouts every beast of the field and fowl of the air. But the valley does fill me with a sense of awe. I feel welcomed, at once tranquil and emotional. My scepticism deserts me. I thank Willy for bringing me here.

'I trust that my countrymen have been open with you?' he asks after a moment.

'Pardon?' I say, reluctant to break the spell. He's a Confederate in Eden. Then, 'Yes, most open.' I have never before heard one American refer to others as his countrymen. 'A German tourist did this,' I add, pointing at my black eye.

'When I was young, if you came to someone's house near sundown you were urged to stay,' says Willy, stepping across another finger of the spring. A chestnut-brown wren flies off from its feeding. Multi-coloured spiders the size of side plates hang on enormous webs laced between the trees. 'And anywhere near a meal time, you were urged to stay and eat. This was common courtesy.'

We walk through the fragile valley watching for diamondbacks and indigo snakes, maybe even for a serpent. I want to talk to him about Eden in Florida, about the value of the Garden's meaning, if not its existence. Willy seems more concerned with other matters.

'I don't think anybody locked their doors at that time,' he remembers. 'Literally.'

The divine ravine is shaped like a natural amphitheatre, the tiers of lush vegetation rising above us on all sides. Around us are trees unknown to me. I feel obliged to follow his lead.

'I can't reconcile that tradition of American generosity in the home with the suspicion, even danger, of life on the street,' I tell him. 'You invite me, a stranger, into your house,

yet my car-rental brochure tells me to keep my doors locked
and windows up. It's inconsistent.'

'It's because of today's overabundance of communication,'
he replies.

I thought the discrepancy might be explained by some
simplistic vestige of frontier society – the settler at odds with
the wilderness. But Willy has his own theory.

'Used to be we only heard of a crime occasionally,' he
recalls. 'At the time that I can first remember, if something
happened in Jacksonville you never knew about it in Bristol.
Odds were we didn't know even if something happened in
Tallahassee. Today somebody starts a . . . what do you call
him – a murderer who commits several similar . . . ?'

'Serial?'

'Serial killer. He starts off and the TV goes blabbing about
it and either he kills another one or somebody copies him
and, human nature being what it is, people start locking their
doors. People start looking at everybody they pass on the
street. Even if that first murder happened way over in Denver
or up in New Jersey. One crime in one town gets magnified,
and people become frightened, and then the copy cats get in
on the act.' The intensity of his address brings him to a stop.
He pauses by a clump of conifers, making a seat out of an
old stump. 'So, instead of the one killing, or perhaps two,
we have twenty before it runs its course.'

I have my doubts that television alone provides prototypes
for budding murderers. Man has slaughtered his fellow man
since leaving the Garden, since Cain croaked Abel. But the
cathode-ray tube does bring the persistent barbarism into
every living room, heightening the mayhem in True-to-Life
colour.

'You're saying that television makes people suspicious of
the outside world?'

'They go home and they slam that door tight,' he insists,
miming the action. 'Like I told you, Bristol's a safe town.

Nobody bothers nobody down here. Back a few years, most of the criminal stuff that went on, the Sheriff would look at what was done, think a minute or two and know who did it. He knew his people. Now he don't anymore. This is the problem that I see. People have lost track of the odds. But that's just one old man's opinion.'

Willy catches his breath and we carry on towards the Apalachicola, climbing up between the hickory and the oaks. The track rises out of the basin of sweet air and back into the sultry afternoon. We try to stay in the shade, ducking beneath the delicate brown flowerheads of the Spanish moss, but soon my back is running with sweat. After ten minutes my ears sing like the tree frogs in the serpentine limbs above us. I begin to melt. Willy, on the other hand, maintains his well-groomed lustre.

The Garden – or Apalachicola Bluffs and Ravines Preserve – supports a remarkable range of plant life. Conservationists classify it as a 'paleorefugia', a refuge of ancient flora and fauna stranded during the retreat of glaciers and unchanged for millions of years. There are subtropical pines on its sandy uplands, mountain laurel on the steepheads and northern hydrangea in the depths of the primeval ravines. Its river system sustains the greatest variety of amphibians and reptiles in North America. As far back as the 1830s, botanists puzzled over the valley's strange mix of native, northern and alien plant species, many of which were extinct elsewhere. As Rose Prophet said, it is a very special place.

Under the sun it occurs to me that what's special is not whether Eden was here, but that locals believe it was. Or want to believe in it. At first I thought that chance brought me to Florida. Then I saw that I've come looking for something different. It's the same instinct that brought Ponce de León, George Colby, Flagler, the invalids, even the endless ranks of retirees dreaming of extending their mortal days. It's the fear of the darkness beyond. The attempt to create here an ideal society as a bastion against nothingness. In an ersatz Garden of Eden, I realise that I'm hunting for the pure in a muddled world.

I wonder again why the site hasn't been developed into a tourist destination. The sanctity of the ravines could have been defiled by a Genesis Walk and a kids' Serpent Slide. The last few gopherwood trees could have been uprooted to make a replica Ark ('Meet Mr & Mrs Noah! Count the animals, two by two!'). The park shop would do a steady trade in 'Like Naked' Fig Leaf swimwear. The Reserve could be transformed into a homely family attraction that would be simplistic and idiotic. It might still happen, of course.

On the pine-needle path terracotta anthills mound on the beige sand, the red earth scooped up from the depths by the colony. There are gopher tortoises here, though we only see their burrows, and above us swallow-tailed kites. Willy leads me the last few steps through the upland forest and out onto the crest of the bluff. One hundred feet below the broad, khaki Apalachicola meanders from the southern Appalachians to the Gulf of Mexico. In the fiery sunlight my eye begins to throb again.

'So where are the apples?' I ask.

I walked through the Garden of Eden, and still checked into a motel in time to catch *Friends*. Callaway's 'birthplace of our first parents' is a beautiful spot, and the absence of Eve's fruit tree doesn't spoil it for me. But I want to know how Noah's Ark fits into his offbeat theory.

I leaf through Willy's copy of *In the Beginning*.

First there were the fossils. The existence of 'the fossilised bones or parts of bones of every animal known to have lived on this earth' proved to Callaway the 'building and loading of the ark in Big Bend Country'. Alum Bluff, on which I stood with Willy, is one of the South-East's most significant palaeontological sites. Its striations delineate the rise and fall of ancient seas over millions of years.

Next Callaway wrote, 'The Ark was built of gopher wood, selected by the Lord, because it is the lightest and toughest wood known. It grows only in one place on earth and that is just north of Bristol, Florida.' On our walk Willy pointed out a single surviving *Torreya taxifolia*. The demand for fenceposts, and fungal blight, have made it the world's most endangered conifer.

I look in the bedside table and again find a Bible.

'And God said to Noah, "I have determined to make an end to all flesh; for the earth is filled with violence through them; behold, I will destroy them with the earth. Make yourself an ark of gopher wood."'

I turn off the TV.

Finally, Callaway maintained that the Ark had been carried by 'the atmospheric drift' from Florida to Mount Ararat. Noah and his family did not know that they had landed in Asia, because they had no knowledge of the existence of the continents. They understood only that their first home had been left behind.

'Abraham and his people in Ur of Chaldea knew the description of the Garden of Eden, for it had been handed down to them by word of mouth from generation to generation, but they did not know its location. The Israelites in Egypt knew the description of the Garden, but not its location. In fact, every nation and every people on earth heard about the beautiful birthplace of man.'

As I read last night in Tallahassee, the names that Noah and his family had known at home in America, such as Euphrates, Ethiopia, Havilah and Assyria, were transplanted by them after the flood to Asia and Africa. The true, original Garden was lost for millennia, Callaway concluded, 'until under God's direction, I uncovered the absolute facts concerning the location.'

Turn the TV back on. *Buffy the Vampire Slayer* is on Channel 17.

'Some guy punched me in the eye,' I shout into the pay phone a few hours later. There is no telephone in my room and I've walked out to a gas station to call Katrin. 'And I think I've got sunstroke.'

'Where are you?' she asks.

'The Garden of Eden.'

Bristol, Thursday 6th – At the Snowbird Motel ('Finest in Liberty County') the Patel children play football across Highway 20. Traffic thunders over their pitch. Their ball misses a school bus and bounces off a Wal-Mart tractor-trailer.

Tell owner Vinod Patel that I'm staying in Bristol for a few days.

'Thank you very much,' he replies as his daughter retrieves the ball from behind a petrol pump. Vinod came to the United States from Bombay fifteen years ago, moving from a city of nine million to a town of twelve hundred.

Did he choose Bristol in his search for vestigial self?

'I came here because I couldn't afford Orlando.'

I plan to spend the morning exploring the town but am back in my room after an hour. Bristol consists of less than a dozen streets. Across from Noah's Ark Child Care an elderly couple in Hawaiian shorts sit on their porch counting the passing cars. Garden gnomes in convicts' ticking seem to be popular on Jeremiah Street. There is a bank, two gas stations and a 'Tallahassee 43 miles' road sign.

I've never seen a bayou, so I stroll down to the Calhoun bridge, scrambling up a rough embankment to catch a glimpse of the marshy wetland which borders most Gulf Coast rivers. The swamp appears as a tangle of black gum and dying oaks beneath the gleaming new span.

As a boy Willy shot squirrels and turkeys among the cottonwoods, spending nights out hunting with his brother. A generation before, Confederate troops had occupied the county. Their heavy artillery was intended to protect the interior of the South. But the Union troops didn't invade, and the waiting soldiers contracted yellow fever. Earlier still, De Soto's Spaniards crossed the Apalachicola on their trek into the interior. The river's strategic importance, like its history, had been washed downstream. If mankind had been created in the lush ravines, he couldn't wait to get out of the town.

'The Lord God sent him forth from the Garden of Eden.'

Bristol is the kind of place that most people leave behind.

Except for Willy.

After supper we sit on his verandah watching the light drain out of the day. A cloak of cobalt blue wraps the heavens. The night stirs with the sound of crickets and bare feet hurrying bedward. Game-show jingles and freetailed bats ride on the air. It seems that the further north I travel in Florida, the more south I find myself. At any moment I expect the mule wagon carrying Addie Bundren's coffin to pass by the door.

'Once I just let it happen,' Willy says, a lazy roll in his voice. We are talking about travel. 'Rose and I went up to the Smoky Mountains. First I'd choose a road, left or right. Then at the next place Rose would choose the road. If we saw an inviting log, we'd just stop and sit on it and watch the world go by. I'd gone to a lot of places in the air force, but you know, that was my most pleasurable trip ever.'

Willy saw America from the cockpit of a DC-4. He returned to Bristol after his tour.

'Rose liked Colorado best,' he says, looking out over pancake-flat Bristol. 'But I was guided back home.' He laughs, a soft croaking like a squirrel tree-frog. 'I believe we all are directed in many things, but not to the exclusion of chance or random activity. Not to the exclusion.'

Inside the house Rose watches *Seinfeld*. Neighbours also graze up and down the channels, remotes in hand, flicking between dumb sitcoms and self-important talk shows. The ubiquitous blue light of a hundred televisions casts a shadow across the street.

'I don't mean this slack in the way that God's got nothing better to do than to guide us step-by-step. I believe that a big part of life is simply left alone to us. But there *are* times when we are guided to do this or guided not to do that, and if we fail to accept it, then we are leaving ourselves open to catastrophe.'

'Isn't it simply a matter of recognising chance for what it is?' I ask.

'I call it divine guidance,' replies Willy. 'Of course, some folks have the idea that you're lucky either in everything or in nothing at all. Looking back over my life, looking at the bits and pieces, I can't believe that to be the true situation.'

'I heard somewhere that luck is a matter of enjoying the arbitrary as if it's meant to be, rather than allowing it to disrupt one's plans.'

Willy stares out into the fading light. Leans back in his rocking chair. Sips on his iced tea. 'I think sometimes we just aren't aware when the Lord directs us.'

On another porch a match flares, lighting a neighbour's face. I follow the trail of its flame in the darkness.

Bristol, Friday 7th – Stop at the Lucky Dip yard sale. Find a 1963 *Guide to Shooting Game* ('Chapter 9: Daily Bag Limits for Dove, Snipe and Crow') and an eight-track cartridge of AC/DC's *Highway to Hell*.

'Where you from, boy?' drawls the paunchy proprietor in a stiff Stetson. He shakes dewy rain-sheets off his cluttered display. I am his first customer of the day.

'England.'

'You know slavery started in Boston,' he tells me.

'Not New England. Old England.'

'It was you smart Yankees who came down here and sold it to us poor cotton farmers. Then you went all goody-goody and had the gall to tell us that it weren't right. What was a man supposed to do who'd just paid $2,000 for a big, strong, black slave?'

Around him a dozen tables are covered with rusty bread-boxes, patched paddling pools and mildewed medical books.

'You enjoying your stay in Liberty?' he asks.

I tell him that I had been.

'This here's a good county. We got a good understanding.'

'What's that?' I ask.

'You don't touch my stuff, I don't touch your stuff,' he explains.

I decide not to examine the broken bronze eagle statuette.

'I guess it's more than an understanding,' he elaborates. 'If you touch my stuff, I'll kill you.'

Don't much feel like browsing any longer.

'If somebody's trying to rob you or rape you, he's not going to hang on while you call 911. By the time the police turn up he'll be long gone. You got to take it into your own hands.' He shakes off another plastic sheet. 'Have a look round, boy, and holler if you need any help.'

Spend the rest of the day at the motel in bed with a cold compress on my head. Too much sun, again.

Willy stops by with a pitcher of Jean's iced tea. I'm drowning in iced tea. He tells me that he's an elder at Lake Mystic Baptist Church, and teetotal.

'You moving on tomorrow?' he asks, silhouetted in the open doorway.

Nod.

'Figured so. Everyone does, unless they're locked in jail. Any idea which way you're heading?'

'South,' I say. North is Georgia. West is Alabama. East is backwards.

'Stick to the small towns,' he advises. A hot, dusty breeze swirls around his feet. The cool air spills out of my room and away over the highway. 'One of the things America lost after World War Two was the home places in the heart of the big cities. Back in the thirties you could recognise people from the Bronx, Brooklyn, Hoboken, wherever, as soon as they opened their mouths. Now we've all been mixed and stirred and kicked back out. The big cities lost their roots somewhere in there. They'll never get them back.'

Outside the Patel children play chicken with the late-afternoon Greyhound.

'So if you want the real, down-to-earth – what's the word here? – friendly, faithful people, you need to go to the small towns.'

'I'll remember that,' I tell him, remembering too the yard-sale bigot.

'I give a good civics lesson from time to time.'

'And thank you for taking me to the Garden.'

'I'm only sorry I couldn't find you anyone to talk to about it,' he says, again.

Bristol, Saturday 8th – As I load the car a cool ember of memory flares to mind. I realise it's not the first time I've heard of Liberty County.

It was near Bristol that a British couple were shot as they slept in their rented Cavalier at a highway rest area in 1993. The gunmen blocked the car in its parking bay and opened fire at point-blank range when the couple tried to escape. Gary Colley died at the scene. He was the ninth holidaymaker murdered in Florida that year. His girlfriend Margaret Jagger survived bullet wounds to the upper chest and right arm. The killers fled.

In this sleepy town the memory of the cold-blooded murder makes me shiver. For all I knew Colley and Jagger might have stayed at the Snowbird, bought gas at Moses's Tire, gone swimming in Fish Pond.

On the outskirts of Bristol two prisoners plant geraniums at the foot of the 'Tallahassee 43 miles' sign. Along the highway police cars ferry inmates between court and prison. I drive at the speed limit. I check my mirror, slow down and signal well before the turning.

Out of the woods rise four watchtowers, half a dozen dormitory blocks and an immense American flag. The trees are cut back from the twenty-five-foot-high fence. Behind the razor wire, guards ride between the low buildings on golf carts. I park beside a row of white Bluebird buses and walk up to the main gate of Liberty Correctional Institution.

The United States has the second-highest rate of imprisonment per capita in the world. There are 1.8 million inmates behind bars. One in every 150 Americans.

Ask to see the Warden. Push my passport through the double metal hatch. It locks shut. The glass in the gatehouse window is an inch thick. Against the fence is a red trashcan filled with sand: Discharge Weapons Here.

J.D. Turnage, the duty officer, comes out of the gate to meet me. She is thirty-five and blonde. Pale, bone-china eyes. A swimmer's taut figure.

I don't know what I expect to gain from her. An explanation of the nature of evil? Clarification of the media's role in making murder a spectator sport? Enlightenment about the tension of living between real and imaginary worlds? The whereabouts of Gary Colley's killers? In the end I simply ask her about the prisoners I saw in Bristol.

'They're on work detail,' she tells me.

I ask if Liberty is a high-security prison.

'Low-security,' she replies.

I ask if I could meet a prisoner.

'No,' she says.

Make a mental note to delete investigative journalism from my list of career choices.

J.D. Turnage gives me the telephone number of the Department of Correction in Tallahassee. All arrangements for interviews are to be made through its information office. 'Speak to Brett,' she says. 'He's a honey.'

I turn to go.

'I really like your accent,' she says, not wishing to disappoint a visitor. The tradition of common courtesy. On her day off she probably broils on the beach and lends her snorkel to strangers. 'Have you been up to where Noah's Ark was built?'

I tell her I have.

'It's right here where the four rivers meet,' she boasts, standing beneath the watchtowers and razor wire. 'We love Liberty County. It's the real Florida. Anything south of Ocala you can forget. Up here we have trees. We have seasons. We have grass. It's paradise.'

On the long, empty road local signs offer small-town choices: Alligator Point, Chattahoochee and Wewahitchka. 'Buckle Up: it's the law', instructs a billboard. I do. Warden Turnage may be watching.

America is crazy about imprisonment. School systems

deteriorate while tax dollars build new penitentiaries. Militarised police forces serve drug warrants from armoured personnel carriers. According to the *New York Times*, in some states African-American males are now five times as likely to go to jail as to university. Prison is as much a part of Florida as Mickey Mouse and F-117A Nighthawk stealth fighters.

I pull up to a gun-metal-grey diner for a plate of comfort food.

'How y'doin'?'

The gravel-rough voice behind me sounds right out of *Planet Groove.* I turn around and come face to face with a slender Vietnamese teenager: burnished stone skin, thick ebony hair, blue baseball cap jammed on backwards.

'What'll y'have?' he asks.

I order pancakes. It's too early for catfish. The television above the counter is tuned to the Black Entertainment Channel.

'Say sir, will cranberries do ya?' asks the cook through the hatch, his inflection warm as bedtime milk. He has no blueberries. He is black.

'Been spending most our lives, living in a gangsta's paradise,' chants Coolio on *Rap City.*

There's a photograph of a trawler behind the till. While breakfast fries the teenager and I talk about fish: snapper, mackerel, red drum. His restaurant is forty miles from the coast, hemmed in by pine groves and bulrushes, yet he knows all about the sea.

'My old man was a shrimper,' he explains.

'Was?'

'He got killed.'

In the last few years Gulf shrimpers, frustrated by floods of imports and a net of new regulations, began attacking South-East Asian incomers. With boathooks and guns. His father, who had been plucked from the roof of the American Embassy in Saigon in 1975, was beaten to death in Louisiana.

'I'm sorry.'

'It's history,' he says without shrugging. 'Coffee?'

Billy Vu lays the cutlery on the counter, aligning each utensil with care. He turns the handle of the maple-syrup dispenser towards me. There is fragility in his precision. If he asks me to wash my hands, I'll do it.

After the murder Billy took his share of the insurance settlement and came to Florida, buying the diner with his friend the cook, keeping away from the sea. His mother moved to California to live with her sister.

'The joke is, his pa's killer ended up here, in Liberty pen,' says the cook, lowering the plate in front of me. Six thick pancakes, three eggs 'easy over', churns of butter and ice cream on the side. Glad I didn't order the deluxe. 'He should have gone down to a real prison. Liberty's soft. They clip hedges and go on therapy courses. Nobody kicks ass in there.'

The cook is as broad as Billy Vu is tall, his skin as coarse as Billy's is polished smooth. They are an unlikely pair, wearing LA Gear sneakers, running an isolated restaurant in the middle of a farmed forest.

'I thought America was tough on sentencing,' I say. Life-means-life. Three-strikes-and-you're-out. Old Sparky.

'Get caught with an ounce of cocaine and ya do four-to-nine,' snaps the cook with a flash of anger. 'Waste some fisherman and y're into macramé classes. We got some bad attitudes.' He gestures at my breakfast. 'Enjoy.'

On the counter is a copy of the *Democrat*.

'Now the highest-quality marijuana in the world is grown in the United States,' reports FDLE Special Agent David Broadway. 'We're dealing with a super-narcotic.'

Since America declared war on drugs in the mid-eighties, the article claims, the number of people jailed on drug-related offences has tripled. With no reduction in street drug-use or trade. Over the same period local growers quadrupled the home-grown strain's potency. Down the road in Lafayette, the Florida Department of Law Enforcement just seized 15,833 marijuana plants – almost two for each of the county's eight thousand residents.

I finish my pancakes.

It's Saturday and families are visiting inmates. A woman stops to buy a chocolate cake. She leaves the kids outside in the car. The cook recognises her and chooses his best from the display cabinet. 'With mini marshmallow fillin', right?' he remembers. 'See ya next week.'

Billy Vu ties its box with a neat bow of yellow ribbon.

A Dodge Ram prison van pulls in off the road. A white guard asks for four Danishes to go. The cook watches the prisoners waiting in the heat.

'Delicious,' I tell him, after he has bagged the guard's order. I didn't touch the ice cream. 'Thank you.'

'Glad y'appreciated it,' he says, clearing away the plates. The guard leaves without payment or thanks. 'Stayin' round here for long?'

'I've been in Bristol for a few days. A man named Prophet has been helping me out.'

'Willy Prophet? How in sweet hell ya hook up with him?'

I explain about Eden.

The cook roars. 'Man, that ain't real!'

'There's a rumour that last century some minister made the story up to sell land to folks in Philadelphia,' says Billy.

'It doesn't seem to have worked too well,' I observe. Liberty is Florida's least populated county.

'Where'd y'say y're from?'

I tell them.

'Is that where ya at?' says the cook, surprised. 'Where Princess Diana was?'

I nod.

'Some people are making a lot of money on that, aren't they? I tell ya, let the lady rest. Just let her rest.'

'How does it look over there?' asks Billy. 'Y'got problems like us?'

I assure him that we do, though we tend to have a lesser propensity to kill.

'We saw the funeral on TV and all,' recalls the cook. 'That Princess Diana, why'd they give her all them flowers? She's dead. Might as well give her steak and baked potato. Steak, baked potato and iced tea with lemon. What can she do with any of it now? Y've gotta look after people when they alive, not get all sentimental about them when they dead.'

'He can't stand all that thing,' explains Billy as I settle the bill.

'They lie on ya when y're living, and lie for ya when y're dead,' says the cook.

The cash register rings.

'Have a good one.'

Sawdust, Sunday 9th – Couldn't bear to go back to Bristol. Or to stay anywhere near the prison. Instead drove ten miles to Sawdust. Spent the afternoon in a motel trying to collect my thoughts and some words for them. For supper I ate two battered Pogo hotdogs on a stick and an Oscar Mayer Pizza Dunk Fun Pack. At home I eat organic vegetables and avoid white sugar. Here my diet revolves around Mexitos corn chips, cholesterol-packed pancakes and GTx chicken. Convenience food may be fast and easy but I'm missing my fibre. Tomorrow I'll buy a bag of carrots.

In the morning I climb back behind the wheel. I decide against making for the Redneck Riviera, the destination for beach-bound tourists from Alabama and Georgia. There clean-cut, clean-living Christians worship sun, sand and the Lord at pious retreats and in a gospel music hall shaped like the Ark. It's also *the* college spring-break destination, the one which I read about – and the puppy peed on – in England.

But I might run into Warden J.D. Turnage.

I also choose not to make a pilgrimage to Apalachicola, the city at the mouth of the river. It was there in 1851 that Dr John Gorrie, while struggling to control malaria, invented a machine to cool patients' rooms. He is the father of refrigeration.

Instead I jack up the car's air conditioning in homage to his invention and drive south beyond Ocala. Willy Prophet may be right about the 'home places' of 'friendly, faithful people'. Or he may not want to admit that a sleepy veneer can mask viciousness and violence. But whichever it is, I don't fancy another small town.

I know where I'm going.

Miami.

6

Gay Abandon

Hot Bi Cuban 32 seeks bi/straight male for
discreet encounters. I'm 5'8" 180, versatile.
You be W/H, 25–40, HIV-, safe & fun.
Bottoms preferred but not necessary. Love
hot showers, oral & more. Married OK.
Box 2434

MIAMI NEW TIMES

Miami Beach, Monday 10th – I didn't want to go clubbing.
After the five-hundred-mile drive from the Panhandle I
planned a quiet night: a pepperoni pizza, a swim in a motel
pool, a movie on HBO. But it didn't work out that way.

'Niles, right?'

'I'm sorry?' I say.

I am trying to buy gas on Collins Avenue when the freckled
redhead in a strapless number bounces up wearing a brand
new pair of scarlet fuck-me pumps.

'You're Niles from *Frasier*,' she says.

'I'm Rory from Yetminster.'

'I *love* South Beach,' she cries, swinging across the fore-
court. She isn't a day older than twenty. Confident, candid,
bedazzled. 'You meet all the stars here.'

I couldn't look less like a star: clip-on dark glasses, rumpled
clothes, piña colada yoghurt spilt down my t-shirt.

'We saw Gloria Estefan yesterday,' she tells me. 'And we've
heard that Stallone's in town. Hey, Mitch, it's Niles.'

'No shit,' says her boyfriend. He has mastered the black art of Miami petrol pumps. I am yet to learn that they are switched on only after you surrender a credit card. He reaches out to shake my hand. 'Man, we love your show. But you look thinner on TV.'

'You just hanging out?' the girl asks.

'I've just arrived.'

'You caught up with Sylvester yet?'

I pulled off the Dolphin Expressway and suddenly everyone was chilling out, catching rays or speaking Spanish. Latino matrons walk under parasols. Blade Runner cops ride in-line skates. Buff boys burnish themselves to a perfect sheen. Young blacks sport baggies low on their hips, exposing Calvin Klein boxers and a line of pubic hair. Here are bronzed skin, firm butts and melanoma. Hunchbacked old ladies drive gull-winged Thunderbirds. Yellow-haired bohunks squeeze into elastic cycle shorts. Miami Beach is an Art Deco feast of pink and ochre, of turquoise balconies and folly towers, of beachfront hotels called Winterhaven and The Tides. It is the coolest place to be seen on the planet, according to Tanya and Mitch.

'It's a head-fry,' says Tanya.

They are in from Chicago, courtesy of an inheritance. Mitch's uncle died. His parents wanted the money invested in a mutual fund, which would have pleased the late, Orthodox, insurance-selling uncle, but Mitch decided instead to blow it on a three-month rave in Miami. He and Tanya packed in their jobs, bought a lime-green '67 Mustang and buzzed south. They found an overpriced apartment on the edge of the Deco District, installed a futon and splashed out on a silver-plated cocktail shaker. The three months became a year and SoBe their idea of Heaven.

'So why Miami?' I ask from their back seat. I'd parked the Cavalier in a lot, changed my shirt and hid the clip-ons in the Pringles tube.

'Sun and salsa jazz,' raves Tanya, twisting around to meet my eye. We are driving down Euclid. 'Calle Ocho, *merengue*, all-night *bailables* . . .'

'. . . Versace, Desi Arnaz, Crockett and Tubbs . . .' adds Mitch from behind the wheel.

'. . . and screwing on the beach,' Tanya laughs, throwing back her head to expose a cinnamon-brown neck.

I'd convinced them that I wasn't an actor, which disappointed Tanya. She collects autographs. 'Mementoes, too. Last month Elton John gave me a feather.'

To soften the blow I invited them for a drink. Chance may favour the prepared mind, but I know no one in Miami, have no hotel room and, anyway, I like them. Their uncomplicated, dumb puppy enthusiasm attracts me. I've been thrown into their company and I'm not eager to be tossed back out.

Buy two rounds of tequila slammers and make friends for life, or at least until dawn. Tanya proposes dinner.

'The heat makes me *so* hungry,' she bubbles, delighted by her appetite. 'Like, I know it's crazy, but I'm starving.'

Mitch says that afterwards maybe we'll go on to a club.

Drive to their apartment together. The Bentley Hotel casts jagged shadows over Lummus Park. Sunbaked youths skateboard along the Promenade before the day's last swim. Tanya changes in minutes. Drops her scant clothes behind the closet door and slips on a white cotton pocket-handkerchief dress. There is almost nothing to her. She sits with me on the futon and we finish a tin of stuffed olives. Mitch spends an hour in the shower.

'Just visualise it,' he enthuses later over a terracotta tub of guacamole. 'At the dock, by the pool, with the margarita, with a Latino beauty queen, under the nice sky, with the neon. It's a peak-facet American dream, don't you think?'

'Tanya doesn't look Hispanic to me,' I say, and they laugh with such abandon that I imagine it was funny.

'I mean, in terms of the material lifestyle, there are few

easier places to have it than here. For far less money you can have far more fun.'

'That's not a bad reason to live here.'

'It's not the only one either.'

'It's pretty, too,' says Tanya, finishing her fish Creole. She has already eaten an overstuffed burrito.

'There's nothing wrong with pretty,' affirms Mitch. 'And Miami's fun. People may own a lot here, but they have a great time.'

A long-haired peddler – with 'Tet' tattooed on his shoulder – tries to sell us roses and shark's teeth necklaces. A tipsy Brazilian couple sway down Pennsylvania Avenue, falling against a palm tree to kiss. Gay men skate by our table leading dogs and partners onto the Lincoln Road Mall.

Mitch leans across the table, his mouth full of refried beans.

'This year's gay dog is the English bulldog. Last year it was the Shar Pei. "What happened to your Shar Pei?" you hear guys ask. "Oh, it ran away. Don't you just love my bulldog though? He's so cute."'

He beams with mischief.

'The lesbian dog is the pug,' whispers Tanya, as if not wanting to be overheard, then shouts out loud, 'I hate pugs!' Someone at the next table takes out a camera. It flashes and Tanya makes a theatrical show of covering her face. 'Please, no cameras! No cameras!' I look at her. She whispers again. 'So they'll think I'm somebody.'

First we go to Bash and then to Twist. We dance under the stars at Cuba Club Jimmy'z: me, Tanya, Mitch and about 350 other ravers. We stroll arm in arm along the sand between venues. Mitch tries to throw Tanya into the sea. She splashes him so thoroughly that we stop and hang his chinos on the lifeguard station to dry.

By midnight Tanya is hungry again so we ride the Electrowave to the Hamburg and buy her a quarter-pound turkey burger. Even while she eats she can't sit still, jumping up

from her seat every few minutes for ketchup, relish or flirtation. Mitch and I make do with root-beer floats.

I'm no lean, mean party machine. I need my sleep. I get
heavy-eyed around eleven. I've been known to doze off on
friends' floors at New Year's Eve parties, before twelve
o'clock. I spent one night in the early eighties at New York's
Xenon club staring at wannabe mime artists dressed as
Indians smoking peace pipes inside glass cubicles. My girlfriend at the time wanted to make love in the VIP lounge,
or at least to dance naked together on a scaffolding catwalk.
I hadn't fancied unbuttoning my shirt. So when I find myself
eating Tanya's greasy fries and not tasting them, I know it's
way past my bedtime.

'Let's check out Groove Jet,' she says brightly. I look at
my watch. 'It's *the* after-hours spot.'

'I'm on for it,' says Mitch, with equal enthusiasm. 'You're
only young once,' he reminds me.

My memories of youth grow dim.

'Come on!' the Good Time Kids chant in unison.

Groove Jet is a block from the sea. Its music is so loud
that if Katrin is walking the puppy along Chesil Beach she'll
catch a few bars of 'Hot in the City'. On the street a queue
of punters wait to lose their hearing. A mean, lanky thug in
a black Armani singlet guards the entrance. Tanya takes my
arm and leads me to the front of the line.

'Hey, look, it's Niles Crane,' cries Mitch.

In the resulting confusion we steal inside.

It is like walking into a tempest. A roaring tropical storm
has been unleashed in a warehouse. It throbs like a raging
wind, stopping me in my tracks, seizing my chest in a high-
fidelity grip. Iridescent lights lash out at the darkness, catching flashes of movement: bending buffed torsos, wailing
red-lipped queens, designer dykes in evening dress. In the
ear-splitting din bodies cavort, squirm and leap. Loved-up
über-babes swing to jungle music. Girls spin on tiptoes, lunge

at their partners, flourish young limbs around eager flesh. Hips meet, lips touch, hands grope. Slapheads savage one another in the shrill frenzy.

There is nothing to do but dance. Certainly any conversation on the relationship between pleasure and purity has been blasted out the window, assuming that there is a window. Tanya and Mitch pull me out onto the floor. One hand each. Gio and Paloma ripen with sweat. Lightning flashes. Slam-dancers shriek. Climie Fisher sings about 'Rising to the Occasion'. I think fondly of slipping under a duckdown duvet.

After Climie comes Kylie. 'I Should be so Lucky' morphs into 'Lost Ones'. I dance with Tanya. I dance with Mitch. We get down, strut, boogie. We join hands with strangers and cry out the nonsensical lines of nonsense songs. I move like a hyper hippo in Reeboks. Mitch unwinds like a windmill gone ballistic. Tanya dips and turns and thrusts her rump around and about. It is wild, exhilarating and exhausting. I am deafened and numbed.

Harry Pussy, the Miami noise band, plays 'Sex Problem'. Bomb the Bass follows with 'Beat Dis'. When Will Smith brags 'Gettin' Jiggy wit it', I retreat to the bar with the Good Time Kids in tow. I need a whisky to boost my flagging energy. Tanya orders Southern Comfort. Mitch tries to warn her off it.

'Nobody's ever going to intimidate me from having a drink,' she yells, kisses me on the cheek, swallows her bourbon and hauls him back into the crowd.

A chunky, hairless bodybuilder with skin the colour of marinated walnuts offers to refill my glass. I shake my head. It is refilled anyway. He asks if I'd like to go for a swim. It is 2 a.m.

'I'm waiting for my friends,' I shout.

'Don't have to be long,' he replies.

Ask a tall, icy blonde at the bar in a 'Look Better Naked' t-shirt to dance. She nods, then brings along her friend. The three of us swing to the Fugees, squeezed in between a bouncing Van Halen clone and a chap in a PVC corset.

'Do you come here often?' I wail at the blonde.

'*Dra åt skogen*,' she replies.

As we take a turn past Tanya and Mitch, he flashes me a thumbs-up. Tanya shouts in my ear, 'Two is *greedy*.' Squeezes my arm. Winks. 'Your lucky night.' I look up at the Swedes. They dance away.

'We can be heroes, just for one day-ay.'

After Bowie I need another break. Tanya and Mitch have hip-hopped off into the throng. I tack towards a dark corner with a cluster of sofas. Fall into an armchair. Feel something hard. Pull a pair of handcuffs out from underneath me.

'It's the sheer pressure of people looking at me and saying, "Jew",' yells a young man to his friend. Intense, impatient, oval wire-frame glasses. 'Just last night I was sitting here and some guys came in and said, "Ezra? That's a Jewish name. You're Jewish." Out of nowhere.'

'Knowing me, knowing you . . .'

A Puerto Rican goddess in a thong bikini top asks me to dance. We spin across the floor. She smells like honeysuckle dipped in chocolate. But I haven't even the stamina for Abba. My legs no longer support my weight. Slink back to the corner. Sink deeper into the armchair. Order another Scotch.

Along Miami Beach there are gay danceterias and straight nightclubs. The Warsaw Ballroom hosts a Boys Only amateur strip contest. It's Freaky Friends Ladies' Night at Zen. Fat Black Pussycat is the Monday-night theme at Liquid. But the majority of the Beach's clubs are mixed like Groove Jet: gay, lesbian and straight. In the next alcove a uniformed cop mounts a lad in fishnet stockings.

'Virtually all of the synagogues on South Beach have been co-opted for hedonistic use.' Ezra is still shouting. 'The Shadow Lounge, which was the Jacob Cohen Synagogue, is now a disco.'

It is 3 a.m. Swallow my drink. See Tanya at the bar with another man. Mitch jives with the Puerto Rican goddess. Smile at Ezra. Fall asleep.

'YMCA! It's fun to stay at the YMCA!'

I wake to feel a hand on my thigh. Think of icy Swedes and pocket-handkerchief dresses. Open my eyes. Mitch takes away his hand. 'Great club, huh?' he raves.

'Pity Gloria Estefan hasn't come by tonight,' I joke.

'She and Emilio go to Centro Vasco.' He has brought me another whisky. 'You want to get some air?' he asks.

'Where's Tanya?' I shout.

'She's a big girl. She can look after herself.' His hand is back on my leg. 'Come on.'

'No, Mitch,' I say. 'I don't think so. Thanks.'

'Too bad,' he smiles, and vanishes back into the melee.

'Even as a crack fiend, mama; you always was a black queen, mama.'

Ezra has stopped shouting at his pal. 'Friend of yours?' he asks me, nodding after Mitch.

'Sort of. He comes from Chicago.'

'People come to Miami,' he yells, 'because things are locked in up north.'

'How do you mean?'

'Here there's potential. There's openness. If you can visualise it, you can make it happen here.'

He makes it sound like a frontier town. The Wild West on the Gulf Stream. 'You been here long?' I ask.

'Since about two.'

'I mean in Miami.'

'Forever.'

Five o'clock. The crowd has thinned out. I can now see the mirrors on the walls. And the clubbers gazing at themselves. Avoid looking at my own reflection. Look like death.

Ezra has left. Bianca Jagger didn't show. A naked couple

didn't ride in on a white horse, as they once did at Studio 54. John Travolta hasn't danced to the Bee Gees and no one took off all their clothes, yet.

Tanya sits down beside me, glowing. She spreads herself across the sofa, ready to be plucked. She hasn't stopped moving all night and now, at the edge of dawn, she tucks herself up beside me.

'Do you mind?' she asks.

'No.'

She lifts herself up onto her knees, turns to face me and kisses my cheek. 'I guess for me a kiss has always been an intimate thing,' she says, moving closer still. 'You can fuck me over a barrel, but kisses are sacred.' Then she leans forward and puckers up. She thinks Kiss. I can see down her cleavage as far as her toes. I thought this only happened in the movies.

'I don't think Mitch . . .'

'Mitch is gay,' she tells me. 'I'm not.' I must look surprised. 'We kinda cover for each other so one of us will get lucky every time.' She giggles, dropping her head back, exposing again the cinnamon-brown neck. 'And tonight it's my turn.'

'Our puppy ate the hall carpet,' I say.

'Huh?' she says, unpuckering.

'Because I took its teething ring.' I pull the ring out of my pocket. 'It's chocolate flavoured.'

'Hey, I don't mind if you're involved.'

'Married.'

'Whatever,' she shrugs. 'It adds . . . spice.'

'Not for me.'

'Then just oral,' she offers, unabashed, a Good Time Samaritan running her hand up my thigh. 'Right here,' she says, excited by the prospect of a public display. 'It may be inappropriate behaviour, but even the President doesn't call it sexual relations. And your wife'll forgive you.'

But I'm not lying on the road to Damascus.

'Sorry,' I say, meaning it. Remove her hand. And the cleavage view is withdrawn.

I wake up alone under a Winnie the Pooh duvet on somebody's sofa in a North Beach apartment. My mouth tastes like three-day-old cabbage soup. My head hurts. My ears hum. Until I realise it's the air conditioner. It stirs the leaves of the tropical houseplants and induces nausea. The watercolour seascapes begin to roll across the curved, pastel-green walls. Deco vases of violet gladioli sway above the low glass tables. White drapes flap over the metal-framed window. I feel sick. Then a wild, sharp-clawed bulldog thunders across the parquet floor and licks me on the lips.

Miami Beach, Wednesday 12th – Yesterday didn't exist. It was rubbed off the blackboard of life. My single achievement was to stumble down to the beach and fall into the sea. Stumble. Lurch. Splash. Watched the waves wash away my footprints. Tried not to drown as a plodding geriatric with a metal detector combed the sand for doubloons under my beach towel. I thought he might make off with my Factor 15.

Miami Beach, Thursday 13th – 'What is the most beautiful part of a city?' asks Avi Mizrachi.

'Its waterfront?' I reply. 'Or its parks?'

'Its cemetery.'

I chanced upon the Holocaust Memorial. This morning I went back to Groove Jet to try to find the teething ring. It had fallen out of my pocket during the last dance. Across City Park and beside the pink Miami Beach Chamber of Commerce Visitor Information Center, I saw the remarkable bone-white monument.

'The cemetery is the one part that everyone wants to be beautiful,' says Mizrachi, its Israeli-born director. 'You don't want it full of trash to desecrate the memory of the ancestors.' He has a handsome face, a vanity of inky tint hiding the silvery hairs at his temple. 'That's why this place is the most beautiful part of Miami.'

The Memorial dazzles in the clear morning sun. Its bleached stones seem to be luminous. Even the bougainvillaea flowers and waterlilies are pure white.

'Everything is white,' he says, 'because white is the colour of remembrance and mourning. At Jewish funerals the Rabbi wears white and the dead are wrapped in a white sheet.'

The monument was conceived by local Jews, five of whom were Holocaust survivors. The stone was imported from Israel. The land donated by the city. A local architect entrusted with the design. Mizrachi, who had been raised on a kibbutz near Jerusalem, was appointed its director. On its completion in 1990 it was given to Miami as a gift, in the memory of six million victims.

'It has a serenity,' I tell him, lost for better words.

'It is a beautiful memorial,' he says in a clear, certain voice, 'to a beautiful way of life.' A way of life that existed before the war, before the Nazis eliminated two-thirds of European Jewry in the pursuit of their ideal society.

The broad circular plaza is backed by a bowed, black granite wall. At its centre rises a forty-two-foot-high bronze arm, tattooed with a number from Auschwitz. Cast naked figures struggle up the patinated skin. Brother reaches out for brother. A skeletal child is passed between relatives. An old, emaciated couple grasp each other in a final embrace. On the chiselled stone ground lie the dead. It is a hideous

Hieronymus Bosch nightmare under the bright Florida sun.

'When people come on holiday, like from your Cambridge University, are they going to go to a Miami library and read a book?' asks Mizrachi.

He has a fighter's physique, stocky and muscular, and a sculptor's broad, shaping hands.

'No,' I say.

'So this is the one text we want every visitor to read on vacation. But instead of in a library, we've put our book outdoors on the walls.'

He leads me along a polished colonnade. The history of the genocide is carved into the stone. I see my reflection in its mirrored surface.

January 1933: Adolf Hitler becomes Chancellor . . . *November 1938: Kristallnacht*, the Night of Broken Glass, almost every synagogue in Germany destroyed . . . *January 1942:* Wannsee Conference approves deportation of Jews to camps to be killed *en masse*.

Mizrachi gestures back across the reflecting pool to the entrance.

'We've tried to create an impression of family life during the Holocaust.'

The Memorial's first sculpture is of a woman, apprehensive, fearful, clutching her two children.

'Here, at the beginning, the family are alive.'

He points beyond the towering arm to the journey's conclusion.

'There, at the end, they are dead.'

The dark interior of the Dome of Contemplation is pierced by a single shaft of yellow light, burning through a Star of David window. I am led down a claustrophobic tunnel. Children sing songs from the Holocaust through hidden speakers. The names of the camps are cut into the narrowing walls.

The cry of a single child grows louder as we emerge into the bronzed nightmare.

'We want visitors to look into the faces of the sculptures, to hug them, to interpret the individual stories . . .'

Around us a hundred tormented, terrorised, lifesize figures weep, despair, die.

'. . . and then to appreciate the main objective,' Mizrachi explains, pointing at the inner circle of granite walls. 'The place for the lost ones.'

Thirty thousand names are etched into the black marble: Tama Szafir, Sara Gutfrend, Max Biegeleisen, Rachel Tila Katz, Family Freiheiter.

So many.

'This is not an archive. Every name has been sent to us by survivors.' The Memorial's founders decided not to search old *Wehrmacht* files for the names of the dead. 'Anyone can submit a name and it will be chiselled into the wall. That way there will be a place where the names exist.' The dead are given a resting place. 'It's a personal memorial. And a legacy for the grandchildren.'

It is also a sanctuary. As in Saint Augustine, the past is used to anchor the amnesiac present.

'How can you remember six million dead?' asks Mizrachi. 'It's impossible. The mind cannot conceive of such a number. But you can remember one.'

He holds up a single finger.

'You can mourn one.'

We walk behind the Memorial to a small park beside Collins Canal. Air-conditioned limos cruise up Dade Boulevard. Across the road are gyms and strip clubs. The Euroexim Laboratory offers Volume-Bust treatment to 'increase Volume and Reaffirm your Breast'. In parasol cafés Chablis drinkers dip their crabcake canapés into mustard mayonnaise.

A school group assembles under a billboard – 'Unleash the Wild Side! Fetishes, Fantasies . . . Whatever You're Into!'.

Thirty-five healthy, tanned teenagers sit on the trimmed grass by the canal, hearing about life in the Warsaw ghetto from an Auschwitz survivor.

'Hunger was the worst,' Nathan Glass tells them. 'The worst punishment a human being could have, worse than being beaten.'

These young men and women have never wanted for anything other than new rollerblades or a better Walkman. How can they conceive of starvation?

'We lived on starches alone,' Nathan recalls, running his hand over his full head of oiled hair. 'Our bodies puffed up and filled with water.'

It is mandatory for schools to teach Holocaust studies in Florida. The state is home to half a million Jews, 20,000 of whom lived through the Shoah. It has the largest concentration of survivors in the world after Israel and New York City.

'We watched our father, our mother waste away.' Nathan bends forward as he speaks; emphatic, dignified, his emotion held in check. 'You should know this.'

'We get 150,000 visitors every year,' Mizrachi says to me. 'Every month two thousand schoolkids. It's these people who bring the spirit here. They make the Memorial alive.'

I sit with Nathan Glass in the tiny white information booth, baked by the sun and cooled by a noisy air-conditioner. We are in America, five blocks from the ocean, free to speak, to travel, even to bear arms, yet in the enclosed cubicle I can't stop thinking about sealed European railway carriages and concrete gas chambers.

'Why do you relive it?' I ask. Nathan comes to the Memorial every day, meeting school groups, giving them his time for free. Even when his heart is bad. 'Why aren't you relaxing on the beach?'

'I think that it's two things,' he answers, his accent strong even after fifty years in the United States. 'One, I owe those people who perished.' He unfolds the word with care, as if opening a precious fruit. 'We are left over here to remember their names and to tell the story. So the future generation should know what happened.'

Mizrachi made us coffee. Nathan swallows his cup in a gulp. His Tupperware sandwich box is untouched.

'Number two, if we can explain, maybe we can prevent what should never happen again. This is Miami. When a kid from a Cuban family comes here he says, "What's special about the Jews? I've lost relatives." So we tell him. The Memorial's not just for one history. It's to teach us all about tolerance and hatred. To show what's happening if we don't get on.'

Nathan is stout, with ashen hair and crooked, nicotine-stained fingers. A web of broken blood-vessels spiders across his face. The burden of witness weighs heavy on him. Unlike his frugal lunch. Two pieces of white bread, a single Kraft cheddar-cheese slice, pickle. Nothing more. I know that he had no breakfast.

'Please don't let me interrupt your meal . . .'

He waves away my concern.

'Every day I see kids arrive here rowdy, running around, joking,' he tells me, sensing perhaps that I am thinking of the likes of Tanya, Mitch and the careless skateboarders on the boardwalk. 'Ninety minutes later they leave quiet, some-times so deep in tears that I take them on my side and say, "Now calm down, don't worry. It happened to me, maybe it won't happen here. You can prevent it."'

He holds a brown envelope full of handwritten essays col-lected by another class.

'I go to schools, lots of schools. I was yesterday in a school. Here, every student writes me five hundred words. About how I changed their outlook about the Holocaust. They say at first they know about it. They say they read a book. They saw a film. But completely different when they can meet a survivor who *really* saw and talks to them person-to-person.'

Nathan grew up in Pabianice, a medieval town near Lodz in central Poland. Before the war it was a prosperous textile centre on the old trade route between Krakow and Gdansk. Its population was 60,000, including 12,000 Jews. By 1945 all the Jews had been killed.

'Over here I know I'm an American and a Jew, so happens. But over there I was just a Jew.'

As he speaks he uses his hands. He points over *there* towards Pabianice, then jabs a yellowed finger down *here* at the floor.

'Over here we're living in the best country in the world, because we have a vote. We can see to it and not stay on the side like during the war when some of the Allies, sorry to say, stood by and didn't do a damn thing when they could have done a lot.'

He teeters at the edge of the black void. Thrusts his hands at me, grabs the air in front of my face and makes a fist.

'The world *knew*.'

The word is drawn out, accusatory.

'When I was in Auschwitz they were bombing the factories. They *knew* that they can save hundreds of thousands of people by bombing the railway tracks, by bombing the crematoriums. And if some civilians would have died, they died anyway. Better to a bomb than to a gas chamber. So the free world knew.'

He rolls up his sleeve and shows me the stark line of black numbers etched on his skin, his identity reduced to this for four terrible years.

'Yoo-hoo. Hallooo . . .'

A suburban couple appear at the booth's window. Sun visors and double-knit golfwear.

'Go in,' says Nathan, waving them into the Memorial. 'No charge.' But they only want to use the parking lot.

'Ten minutes,' says the man, spreading his fingers up against the glass. 'Just to go to the Gleason Theater.'

'We gotta get tickets for *Show Boat*,' explains the woman.

Nathan always needed to share his experience. He recorded his testimony for both the Washington Holocaust Museum and Steven Spielberg's Survivors of the Shoah Visual History Foundation. His memories, family photographs and the names of the lost ones were catalogued and cross-referenced. He has a video copy of his testimony at home.

'It wasn't easy at the beginning to talk about,' admits Nathan, quieter now. 'For instance, when I go to a school, I ask for a glass of water. I talk about my mother and my father and I just, like, swallow my glass of water. We are human. I break down. But without them realising. Because I cannot do that to the kids. They cry anyway in the middle of my talk. They wipe the tears. But then they see and believe. They always believe.'

In the cramped office the sandwich still lies between us. Instead of eating it, Nathan lights a cigarette. He draws on it, twice. The booth fills with its acrid smoke. The old air-conditioner strains. If it breaks down, we will bake.

'I know survivors who still cannot talk about it. After more than fifty years. Took me quite a lot of time, and energy. It still hurts,' he says, fingering the brown envelope filled with essays. 'There's no question, the biggest reward is the letters. Not that I need the letters, but at least it proves that they learnt something.'

'That you reached them.'

'Not only me, but other relics like myself.'

He drags on the cigarette.

'This place here, with the 30,000 names, it is a cemetery. I have my parents' names here, and my two sisters'. I don't know where they're buried. Some students asked me last week, "Mr Glass, can you tell us on which panel are your parents?" I show them. "Would you mind if we say a prayer for them?" They cross themselves and they say a prayer. Sometimes they light a candle and leave flowers. For this person who died for no reason at all, only because he or she was Jewish.'

Mizrachi comes into the booth to collect his wallet. He notices the lunchbox on the desk. 'There's another group at two, Nat,' he reminds him. Concerned. 'You taking a break for lunch?'

'Soon,' he answers, snapping his hand flat on the table.

Mizrachi looks at me. I look at the sandwich.

'I had my wife pass away a few years ago,' says Nathan.

Mizrachi slips out of the cubicle.

'She's buried over here in Florida. I go to see her grave. My daughter sometimes calls and I take her, you know, to meditate and pray. But this is the cemetery for my parents and my sisters. It's a very holy place.'

'A lot of German tourists visit Miami,' I say.

'Quite a bit.'

'Do they come . . . ?' I hesitate. 'Do they try . . . ?' Again, I can't find the words. 'I want to ask you about forgiveness.'

'It's not forgiveness. You forgive but you don't forget. We say in Hebrew "*zechor*" – remember, remember as long as you live.'

He stubs out the cigarette, the yellow smoke curling around his fingertips.

'A few years ago somebody put an advertisement in the university paper that the Holocaust never happened. It started a big *tumult* at the time. So I was invited to speak to a college. The professor gave me a warning. "Nat," she said, "the class is very educated. They want to know. But there are in the front row students who are revisionists, who believe it's all a Zionist plot, and who want to get to you." So, to cut the story short, I started in my speech, "Before we go any further, if somebody has something to say about things never happened the Holocaust, please prove to me. Because I was there. I was in the concentration camps. I was in the ghettos. I was liberated by the American liberators, by the English liberators, who saw all these things, who saw the bodies, the graves. So please speak out now." And no one spoke. So I gave them a very powerful talk on my life. Then after the people from the front came up and asked, "Can we please shake your hand?" And then, "Will you honour . . ."'

Nathan savours the word.

'". . . *honour* us and come Sunday to our church and be keynote speaker because you changed our whole outlook about the Holocaust." They sent me letters too. I still got them at home.'

Nathan holds up his hands, as if manacled, as if begging to be released.

'So we survivors have to do our utmost best to speak and remember and to leave behind a lot of tapes and books.'

He pauses then, looking at his lunchbox. I want him to eat. I will him to eat. But the sandwich remains untouched.

'A week before the liberation my father was in good shape,' he says. 'Then a Nazi soldier gave him a cup of tea, a luxury. The next morning he didn't wake up. It was poisoned, because he had gold teeth. So they pulled out his gold teeth and then they . . . nobody knows where he's buried. My brother was with him together. He couldn't even go to bury him. He was told that he was going to be buried alive with him.'

Nathan's anger mounts again as he relates the story.

'So *this* was the way we lived over there. We became very hard people.'

In the sealed cubicle he is suddenly shouting.

'It wasn't just survival. It wasn't just between life and death. It was to do with suffering. We had to have tremendous *will power* to live.'

He shakes his head, more in disbelief than regret.

'And a little bit of luck.'

He falls quiet, his hands at last still in his lap.

'Everything was timing, circumstances. Because every survivor could tell you how he and she survived. There won't be two alike. Not two alike. God gave me these years, so why did He not give them to my father? My mother? They were just as nice.'

'Over here', 'over there' isn't simply America and Poland. It is also 'here' in life and 'there' among the dead. Nathan Glass's heart remains in Pabianice, so many years after the end of the war, back there in the old world which had been destroyed forever. I leave him alone in the booth. Walk away under a cerulean sky knotted with clouds. Hear no birdsong in the trees. Then I realise that I've forgotten the puppy's teething ring. Turn back.

Through the cubicle window I see Nathan wolfing down his meagre lunch. Biting into the Wonderbread. Shoving the cheese slice down his throat. Gorging himself in a haunted frenzy.

Decide to leave the ring behind.

Miami Beach, Friday 14th – 'I have a friend – Albert Stern – who is researching the Yiddish word for vagina. Apparently there is none.'

'There isn't?'

'At least, it's really hard to find.'

I am sitting with Ezra Richler at Joffrey's coffee bar. Behind us cappuccino machines hiss and would-be supermodels poise on the brink of discovery. Miami's beautiful people rouse themselves with mid-morning fixes of Cuban zoom juice.

I called Ezra earlier in the day.

'Who?' he asked down the phone.

'We met two nights ago,' I reminded him. 'At Groove Jet.'

'Are you the guy who fell asleep on my foot?'

I hoped that Ezra could put the Memorial, Miami's Jewish community and SoBe's hedonism into context. What place does genocide have in the world capital of cute, kitsch and *chutzpah*? He said he could spare me thirty-five minutes. We agreed to meet for an espresso. He began by discussing Yiddish body parts.

'Albert spoke first to his father, and he didn't know one,' he delights, as excited as he was at the club. 'There are about thirteen or fourteen different words that I can think of right off the cuff for penis. But none for the female genitalia.'

'In Hebrew too?' I ask.

'In Hebrew there are plenty. It's a modern language, even if a contrived one. But Yiddish is Old Middle German, and they call it "that place", or "there". I hung out with Albert right after he did his research on this.'

Ezra calls himself a law professor and condo developer. A sentimental heart and a progressive mind. He is young, not yet forty, a lean, energetic man who pays tribute to life by always being in a hurry.

'He went round old South Beach talking to all the *alte kakers*, the old guys, and so many of them had serial numbers on their wrists from Auschwitz or Dachau.'

'Did they mind him quizzing them about their language?'

'These guys were considered. They'd say, "You know, I don't know." They were sitting there playing poker for pennies. It was a pleasure.'

'But none of them knew?'

'None of them knew.'

'So there isn't a word?'

'Albert wrote to Saul Bellow and to Philip Roth, and neither of them knew. Although Saul Bellow thought he knew.'

'*Thought* he knew? Was he going to share it?'

'He wasn't sure. He wanted to know if he was right. Then there was an Israeli at Tel Aviv University who claimed that there were twenty-three different words, and he would sell them all, but each had a certain price. They started at $20 apiece.'

'Did Albert pay?'

'He refused, absolutely refused. He wasn't going to look in a dictionary, either.'

'I'm sorry? He hadn't looked in a dictionary?'

'No. He wrote an article on it. It's somewhere out there. He figured he'd go to Nobels and the Pulitzers.'

Ezra has the spontaneous, boyish smile that comes to a confident man used to laughing. Good teeth, too. He is at home in Miami Beach, as much as Willy Prophet was a part of Bristol. We laugh until there are tears in our eyes.

'The point is what they *did* know about,' says Ezra, catching his breath, 'was Auschwitz and Dachau. The stories were . . . heart-rending.' He pauses and considers his coffee. 'I've checked out the Memorial, and it's difficult for me to go there.'

I take a sip of my 'Iced Tea of the Day'. At the next table airheads with pierced tongues flip through sheets of transparencies. Tourists wander in from Lincoln Road, between galleries and bookstores, to leaf through hip fashion guidebooks and foodie magazines. Few of them will take in the Memorial.

'But isn't the Memorial out of place in Miami?' I ask as a pair of garish rollerbladers skate in for *café con leche* to go. 'I mean, Florida seems all but devoid of reflection. Why build it here?'

'Miami may be Mecca for homosexuals. It may be a magnet for drug dealers and actress wannabes. But this is very much a place where a community of Jews settled two generations ago. People who are of my grandfather's age retired here. That community remembers Auschwitz in living memory. So it's like saying, "This is true. This is where we came from. We may be in this Tower of Babel but we know our past."'

'It's always seemed to me to be such a remarkable achieve-ment,' I say. 'Ellis Island poverty to Miami riches in a few decades.' I picture Nathan framed in the cubicle window. 'But don't some of them want to leave the horror behind?'

'The idea of Judaism is not as a religion of faith, it's a religion of action. It's a religion of doing,' Ezra tells me by way of an answer. 'Our grandparents came to America and were excluded from many of the trades. These very educated, very cultured people were forced to work in the *shmatta* business, as tailors or cobblers. My grandfather was a butcher.' Even in liberal Miami Beach Jews were restricted to living south of 5th Street through the thirties. 'Their children were encouraged – you know, the second-generation émigré work ethic – to go into the professions; to go into law, to go into medicine, to go into the entertainment business.' He shrugs with evident pride. 'A lot of them became very successful.'

In a city enslaved by the ephemeral, it seems remarkable that a community can hold on to anything of lasting value.

'You see, there's a debt that's being acknowledged.'

'How do you mean?'

'Here is a small, discrete, indigent population which is different: unwilling to integrate, with distinctive rules about food, clothing, religion. And it's a bad rap in all the Christian communities. There's the legacy of institutionalised anti-Semitism: pogroms, inquisitions, holocausts. If so many for so long have done their worst, I'm damned if I'm going to abandon my heritage. That's the debt. That's why the Shoah is not left behind.'

'Are you a religious man?' I ask, acknowledging the dang-ers of fanatic idealism.

'Not in any orthodox sense. But I think that truth and doing-the-right-thing has a biological power.'

Two college girls distract Ezra. The strawberry blonde is one of his students; petite, coy, with a gaping three-inch gash across her neck.

'Steph's doing stage and film make-up,' she volunteers. 'She's into deep flesh-wounds.'

The girl comes to Ezra twice a week to swot up for her law exams.

'I love your slacks,' Ezra says, feeling the material at her thigh. Tommy Hilfiger? FUBU? Maybe you should come around more often,' he jokes, playing the playboy playing the playboy. 'But without the prosthesis.'

She clutches her books to her bloody chest and giggles, a cross between *Happy Days* and *Pulp Fiction*.

'The University of Miami excels in tax law,' he tells me after they go. 'But little else.'

Ezra turns down my offer of gazpacho and Caesar salad. He hasn't the time. He is giving a litigation tutorial in ten minutes. As he gathers his books together I ask him if the Memorial is Jewish Miami's only collective endeavour.

'Not at all,' he says, pulling his dark glasses from his pocket. 'The cultural heritage of Judaism is a commitment to education. My grandfather tells stories of how his mother worked like a dog to support his father so that his father could study twelve hours a day. That was not uncommon. We have the Alfred Swire Talmudic University here. Across from there is the *yeshiva*. They're trying to get together under one roof.'

'Will they succeed?'

'If they do it, it will be the largest centre for Jewish studies in America. Right here in Miami Beach. Which is cool.'

Ezra leads the way out onto the street, high-fiving a passing acquaintance.

'If you're committed to figuring out how things work and how they fit together, if you're willing to take the time and make the effort, you can do well. If that's your basic cultural ethic, you'll do well as a community.'

'All of which keeps you in Miami,' I say.

'As well as the girls. Don't forget the girls,' he laughs again. 'Look, I went to school in Chicago. I spent some time in

New York. I get depressed in winter. It's almost that simple.'

'I don't believe you stay here for a negative reason.'

'I have a community of people who are important to me. I connect to them and it gives me a lot of pleasure to be around people I like and know and esteem. I think this is a magical place in that regard. You can have a quality of life and also do things that are worth getting passionate about.'

'Like Yiddish etymology.'

Shake hands. 'No place better.'

When we part the temperature is in the eighties, forecast to top out in the high nineties. Across the mall in an Art Deco-esque McDonald's, glassy-eyed kids order Chicken McNuggets and envy each other's Nikes. Young dancers from the Miami City Ballet pirouette behind plate glass. Up at Surfside their parents pop Prozac in Majestic Towers, shop at Saks Fifth Avenue, then have their bodies dowsed by Dr Mondshine. After cocktails they gaze out of their penthouses at the tinsel Spanish palaces of the Harbour Islands, where Mexican gardeners 'mow-and-blow' emerald lawns. The residents of Star and Fisher Islands in turn wish for covered tennis courts and faster Cigarette boats. They envy the Mars family, creators of the Mars bar, said to be worth $4 billion. They are neighbours, as is Edmund Ansin, son of a Massachusetts shoe manufacturer who revamped tired WSVN-TV as a tabloid news station – crime, sex, flashy graphics – and made $600 million. A mirage of skyscrapers shimmers across the hazy water of Biscayne Bay.

Behind the glitz of parties, stars and the skin trade, Miami is a unique piece of property. It's little more than a century since the city was invented. The Great Freeze of 1895 and the arrival of the railway ended Palatka's heyday and transformed Dade County's mangrove swamps. The fly-infested bog was drained, the beach widened, and America's resort nirvana was born. South Florida was marketed as a healthy, good-life fantasy land. Coconut plantations and avocado groves were grubbed up to make way for a pseudo-Iberian Valhalla. George Merrick turned his father's failing citrus farm into Coral Gables, an opulent model suburb, and pocketed $150,000,000 in a year.

Miami boomed. It was the gateway to Batista's Cuba. It survived the Depression, absorbed hundreds of thousands of Cuban refugees, rose above the Liberty City race riots. In the Reagan years shrewd entrepreneurs recognised that drugs were America's new growth industry. Then the 1986 Tax Act allowed write-offs for the purchase and restoration of historic buildings. The advertising machine promoted the Beach as the place to have a pied-à-terre. *Miami Vice* made slick heroes of cocaine cowboys and attracted international attention. South Beach became the world's gay resort.

'Miami is the only city in the world,' wrote William Jennings Bryan, 'where you can tell a lie at breakfast that will come true by evening.'

It is a cocky capital on the edge, embracing extremes in business, politics and sexual affairs. Smooth-cheeked boys check their hair in rear-view mirrors. Sun-dried *Marielitos* read *El Nuevo Herald* at a Hurricane Evacuation Bus Pick-up Site. Range Rovers and E-Class Mercedes park outside the Publix supermarket.

I snap a photograph of a jet-ski ripping up the Collins Canal. Its windblown rider splashes to a stop.

'I hope that was taken for a positive reason and not for a negative one, sir.'

He is a policeman in swimsuit and lifejacket. Armed with 9mm Sig-Sauer pistol, collapsible baton, pepper-spray grenade and sunblock. Maybe he's worried that his hair will look too ruffled.

Image matters here. It is no surprise that the Miami Ad

School, established only a few years ago, has become the top advertising school in the country.

Find myself at Wolfie's on 21st at Collins. When the city was still known as God's waiting room, this was the restaurant where 'ageful' residents came to eat corned-beef sandwiches, bagels and cheesecake. Its turquoise and pink leatherette seats probably haven't changed in fifty years.

'You look like you need happying,' says the waitress. Think for a moment that she's proposing Tanya's oral cure-all. It may even be on the menu. She returns with a single bowl of steaming hot liquid.

'Chicken soup,' she says, 'is the Jewish penicillin.'

Miami, Saturday 15th – Drive away from the beach, over MacArthur Causeway and into downtown. Gleaming neon towers rise above the cruise-ship basin. But impoverished Liberty City, once called Overtown, for 'over the tracks', reminds me of a warning.

'That part of Miami between the airport and the beach is bad,' Mario told me in Cassadaga. 'Tourists drive through in their rental cars, get rammed and robbed, all within their first hour in Florida. I pack my .357 Magnum every time I go down there.'

I take a turn up Biscayne Boulevard to catch a glimpse of the city's most notorious 'feelgood' motel. Outside the hot-pink Stardust prostitutes solicit for business. Its owner admits that the rooms have been used for occasional drug deals. The police are not so delicate. They say that so much cocaine moves through the motel that it should be connected to a ski-lift. A few months ago an undercover officer bought crack here with the help of a prostitute, who then offered to exchange it for sex. 'One-stop shopping', according to the police.

Drive on.

7

Gator's Tale

A Sweetwater woman was bound and raped by three men in Fruit and Spice Park early Saturday morning. The men threatened to cut off the victim's head but no weapon was shown. 'After the attack they said they were sorry and they were ashamed of themselves and all kinds of crud like that,' said a Miami Police spokeswoman. 'We don't know what their problem is but it's unusual.'

MIAMI COMMUNITY NEWS

Miami, Monday 17th – In Bristol Willy Prophet talked of television spreading fear. At the Memorial Avi Mizrachi told me, 'What kids see on TV only increases violence and racial tension.' Americans watch the box for an average of four hours every day, spending a quarter of their waking time in a fabricated electronic world. So I decide to spend the evening with a TV news team.

WFOR-TV's glitzy glass office building towers above an industrial estate beyond the airport. In the lobby are copies of *Fashion Spectrum* and *Miami New Times*, a free listings-magazine swelling with breast-surgery ads. Two passing executives enthuse in Spanish about the Dodgers' seven-player deal and calcium-replacement toothpaste. No one seems overly concerned about fear, violence or even hard news.

Ezra put me in touch with producer Scott Stachowiak of rival WPLG Channel 10.

'I'm doing hospitals this week,' Stachowiak said. He didn't think hospitals would appeal to me. Not up to the drama of *ER*? 'Why don't you call my spouse Kevin?'

Scott's spouse Kevin Kraus assigns crews for the CBS affiliate WFOR. My call woke him. He yawned into his mobile and asked why I wanted to go out with a News4 team. I explained.

'There may be an insurance problem,' he said.

I wasn't surprised. In my imagination I pictured an evening watching Venezuelan drug barons bleed to death on Philippe Starck sofas and twenty-car pile-ups on the Palmetto Expressway. Bold, hard-hitting, dangerous news. I couldn't have been more wrong.

'Yo, Carlos!' hails Lee D. Zimmerman, the station's effusive, popular Director of Communications. He is leading me through the news studio, gladhanding every man-Jack. 'We don't care about being the first at the scene or getting the scoop,' he tells me. A technician brushes down the anchor's armchair while manatees and weather maps flash across the backing screen. 'Our niche is to make news that works for the audience. *Como va, amigo!*'

A dolled-up presenter stands like a Greek statue at the centre of the operations room, recording ten-second inserts between commercial breaks.

'Scrub fires threaten Jupiter, and the truth behind plastic-surgery resorts,' she announces. 'Would you risk the snip and tuck? Tonight at eleven.'

Microphone leads dangle from under her DKNY jacket. The floor manager kneels at her feet. A ring of devoted reporters surround them, paying homage to the monitors behind the assignment desk, filing stories on condo zoning law in Coconut Grove. Telephones ring. Library clips are assembled. Cameramen are despatched to cover school board meetings. Al Sunshine, the station's 'problem solver', edits an item on dishonest car-repair shops for his *Shame on You* slot.

Lee passes me into the hands of Troy Dinkel, a thirty-year-old Texan who has joined the station from Sarasota. I feel as manhandled as a new boy at the Zanzibar.

'If you can keep a good head of hair until you're thirty,' Troy tells me, 'you're not going to go bald, only grey.' In the reflection of a VDU screen he combs his thick auburn locks. Just washed and blow-dried. 'Guess I'm going grey.' He winks. 'I'll go get us a story.'

I have an *All the President's Men* view of journalism. Bernstein, Woodward and their peers uncover corruption, expose wrongdoing and curtail the abuse of power. They are the white knights of the cut-and-paste society. The public is served and truth reigns, between commercial breaks. In my mind's eye all newsmen look like Robert Redford, too.

'News4 South Florida,' declares the sign above the despatch desk, 'is the only newscast dedicated to making our community a better place to live by aggressively exposing the real problems here and fighting for solutions, thereby making viewers feel empowered and reassured.'

Troy wanders up to the wire-service printer and leafs through the pages. There may be stories on Iraq, ozone depletion and the proliferation of AIDS in Asia, but he returns with two domestic AP clips.

'How about something on school lunches?' he asks.

'No high-school shootings?'

Troy shakes his head.

'Or drug abuse?'

'Nope.'

'What about the Fruit and Spice Park rape?'

'We're after human interest stories,' he explains. 'News you can use. Would you prefer nuisance alligators?'

He hands me a copy of the story.

'As development encroaches into undeveloped land, alligators are being driven out of their natural habitat,' I read. Et cetera, et cetera.

'Mating season's begun, and gators are on the move. They're turning up in gardens and swimming pools, and there are only thirty-seven licensed trappers statewide to handle 13,000 nuisance complaints each year.'

'I guess it's public-service information.'

'It's news,' insists Troy. 'Synchronicity,' he says, 'makes the best television.' Then he saunters off to book an OB van. At least he has Redford's bouffed hair.

By dusk we're on the road. The setting sun wraps the ribbons of concrete in pink chiffon. Headlights dance across brown exit signs. The rush-hour traffic slows at a fender-bender, drivers craning their necks to watch two overheated men fighting by the side of the highway. Their argument seems more newsworthy than nuisance wildlife but we hurry on, racing to catch the light.

Troy made a few calls and found Kevin Garvey, a licensed trapper. He had just caught an alligator in Boca Raton.

'Where is it now?' Troy asked.

'In the pick-up.'

'What you doing with it?'

'Releasing it tomorrow.'

Kevin drives his daughter to school every morning so she and her friends can admire his latest catch.

'Could you do it tonight?' Troy asked. 'At about 8 o'clock?' In time for the 11 p.m. news block.

Cameraman Caesar is at the wheel of the van, driving with ballsy abandon. Like 150,000 other Cubans, he came to Miami from Havana in the late seventies, during the Mariel boatlift. He may not yet have risen to head Coca-Cola, as did the ambitious Robert Goizueta, another young engineer who fled from Castro, but judging from his driving it's only a matter of time. Troy sits beside Caesar, hanging on to the handstrap, drafting his script. I try to keep up in the Cavalier.

We find Kevin at Pompano Beach, by way of a Wendy's cheeseburger pit-stop. On his front lawn is an alligator-shaped mailbox. In the back of his truck is the living version. Six feet long and frenzied. Fore and hind legs tethered. Eyes covered. Snout wrapped in black electrical tape.

Troy and Kevin shake hands. The trapper's skin is the colour of ripe pomegranates.

'This little'un was in a backyard pond,' explains Kevin. He wears shorts, workboots and two gold earrings. 'I mean, a gator this size ain't gonna cause no harm to nobody. It's just the *idea* of the alligator being there.' He curls his vowels. Ali-gay-ders. 'I pulled him out just to get folks, you know, kind of at ease.'

'And you don't get paid for this?'

'There's no money in little guys.'

'We're losing the light,' worries Caesar.

Trappers receive no salary. Instead they are paid $20 per foot for large animals. The local processing facility sells two thousand pounds of alligator meat to restaurants and super-markets every week. The hides are shipped to the Far East, then reimported as Nieman Marcus golfbags. But the smaller specimens must be released, though not too close to town. Otherwise they'll turn up in someone else's backyard. Or even try to return home. One alligator swam twenty-five miles through canals and storm drains to get back to its territory.

We head west away from the sea, driving fast through suburbia. Kevin leads us past shopping malls and Sans Souci pizza outlets, beyond taquerias and liquor marts. At Middle High School the lights come on for evening baseball practice. Caesar accelerates. Kevin too. At the next corner he glances the kerb and the alligator almost bounces out of the pick-up. I spill ketchup down my shirt.

On Wiles Road we break the speed limit. I overtake commuters on the inside lane. The Cavalier's speedo tops eighty. We're making for the place where the last housing development presses up against the Everglades. It is among the few remaining areas where young animals can be relocated. I swallow my burger. I slip on my clip-on shades. I find myself singing Jackson Browne.

'Looking out at the road rushing under my wheels . . .'

On the outskirts of Coral Springs Kevin shoots a yellow.

'. . . I don't know how to tell you all just how crazy this life feels . . .'

Caesar follows him in the van. I push the accelerator hard and drive through the red light.

The police car is hiding behind the Ocean Cadillac Body Shop. In seconds it is on my tail, its blue-and-red strobes flashing, pulling me over. I reduce speed as Kevin and Caesar vanish into the fast-fading day. I'll never catch them.

'I'm sorry, officer,' I babble, 'but I'm following that TV van which is following an alligator to get to the Everglades before the light goes to make a piece for the evening news.'

'Step out of the car, son,' he says.

I do. He is a big man. He wears an open holster. He sees the oozing red stain on my chest.

'Wendy's,' I volunteer, by way of explanation.

'Who's Wendy?' he asks.

I try to explain. I produce my British driver's licence. He unfolds it as if it is an Iranian death warrant. It has no photograph. He asks for my proof of ownership. I can't find the rental papers. His partner radios in the Cavalier's registration number. He asks me to step into the patrol car.

'He's with us!' shouts Troy from over the road. Caesar and Kevin saw the flashing lights and turned around. They wheel across the oncoming traffic and stop beside us. The dizzy, enraged alligator thrashes in the back of the pick-up.

'Kev, you son of a bitch,' says the policeman, greeting an old friend. Trappers work alongside the police in south Florida. Both are public servants. 'This guy with you?'

'We're doing a thing for the Channel 4 news,' Kevin explains.

'Tonight?' asks the policeman, tucking in his belly.

'At eleven,' says Troy.

'If we can set up before dark,' adds Caesar.

'Follow me,' orders the policeman.

The extended convoy races through the darkening streets; four vehicles, six adults and one angry reptile. The patrol car is in the lead, its siren wailing, jumping red lights. Traffic pulls out of our path. Stop signs are ignored. The chase music swells. Caesar looks at the dull sky and groans.

After ten high-octane minutes the streetlamps peter out. A displaced racoon retreats from civilisation. A sign announces 'Dead End'. We drive off the asphalt and down to a weedy waterway.

Night settles around the cat-tails and Caesar sets up lights, complaining to himself in Spanish. As he mounts the camera on its tripod, Kevin snaps down the pick-up's tailgate. The alligator hisses and fights against its shackles.

'How do you catch them?' I ask, standing back from the animal.

'You make the grunt.'

'The grunt?'

Kevin makes a guttural swallowing noise. He sounds like a constipated goose. It mimics the cry of a baby alligator.

'That's good,' says Troy. 'We'll get that on tape.'

'If there's a male in the area, he will correspond to that call and come to eat the baby. If there's a female, now that it's mating season, she'll come to protect it. Unless she's real shy.' Kevin grunts again. 'I've had gators come right from the other side of the lake for my call.'

I look over my shoulder.

'Then what do you do?'

'If it's small, you hook it. I rescued eighteen hatchlings out of that storm drain last month. I didn't get paid, but I wanted to do something. This here's a new industrial park.'

'And if it's big?' I ask.

'I caught one fifteen-foot-six with this,' says Kevin, pulling an aluminium pole with a metal noose out of the cab. 'It took me two hours just to get close enough to get him.'

'You see the one that ate a kid in Daytona last week?' drawls the policeman, leaning against the van, swallowing the words.

'I have it on video,' says Troy. 'I'm gonna use it tonight.'

'Those guys went about it all wrong, gittin' that gator on that catch pole and lettin' it go. That was a deadly weapon right there. If that pole would have hit somebody, it would have killed them, too.'

'A twelve-footer can weigh over a thousand pounds,' Kevin points out.

I move behind the camera.

Caesar switches on the generator. Night retreats beyond the edge of the frame. Kevin begins to release the animal, cutting two of the ropes, making it more agile and angry. Under the lights I see that its skin appears to be fissured like baked earth. It has stubby, powerful legs and sharp, gnarled claws. A sierra of spines runs down its scaly armour. It looks as if it has grown out of the ground.

'To tie them,' Kevin yells over the noise of its thrashing, 'I mount their back so they can't roll, and grab their eye sockets.'

He sits astride the writhing reptile. Troy, his tie straightened and hair recombed, steps in front of the lens to begin the interview.

'If one of these babies takes up residence in your pool, it could take weeks to get rid of him,' he announces into the microphone. Behind him Kevin wrestles his captive onto the tailgate. 'State game officials are the only folks allowed by law to trap gators, and Kevin Garvey is one of only two in the whole of Broward County. Kevin, Broward had 566 complaint calls last year.'

'That's a lot,' shouts Kevin.

'How do you cope?'

'This can be a time of frustration for people who have small to midsize gators like this one on their property,' he continues, trying both to talk to camera and to control the beast. 'Just don't be in a big rush to have your little'un removed, because we may be elsewhere trying to catch an eleven-footer that could eat somebody.'

He jumps clear as the animal rolls onto the ground.

'Cut,' says Caesar, lowering the camera. 'Could we take that again?'

'I kinda got the gator down already,' says Kevin, catching his breath.

'I didn't know you were letting him fall,' Caesar explains. 'The light's no good there.'

As Caesar rigs up another lamp, Kevin and the policemen heave the alligator back onto the bed of the pick up. Its agitation takes on an air of wild rage.

I stay back.

'Rolling,' says Caesar.

'If one of these babies takes up residence in your pool, it could take weeks to get rid of him,' Troy says again into the microphone. 'Kevin Garvey, this can be a time of frustration for people who have small to midsize alligators on their property.'

'Don't be in a big rush to have them removed,' Kevin shouts, 'because we may be trying to catch an eleven-footer that could . . . shit!'

The alligator flips itself up over the truck's side, its white belly flashing under the lights. The camera stops again. Caesar looks at Troy.

'Sorry, Kevin, but we can't have any profanities.'

Again Kevin and the policemen lift the animal back into the pick-up.

'Take three,' says Troy to camera.

'Third time lucky,' says Caesar.

'If one of these babies takes up residence in your pool, it could take weeks to get rid of him,' smiles Troy, his clean hair shining. 'Now, normally this one's not a priority because he's so small. Right, Kevin?'

'Right. There's not a dire need for us to get out and take care of the problem right away.'

'So what's the story here?'

As Kevin advises on dealing with pesky critters, he uncovers the alligator's eyes and unwraps the electrical tape. It opens its mouth wide, describing a ninety-degree angle. Troy steps back and the policeman puts his hand on his holster. Even this four-year-old has 2,500 pounds of biting pressure per square inch.

'If a gator's actually walking in your backyard, Florida Game and Fish will issue an emergency permit and we'll go out right away. If it's just swimming around, like this'un was, then we'll get the paperwork in the mail and work it from there.'

'So what can people do while they're waiting?' Troy prompts from off-camera.

'You can try to spook it back into the water. But I'd advise not to get too close to the animal. As you can see, they're agile.'

Kevin cuts the last rope. The alligator whips its body left then right, too disorientated to sense its release. Kevin tries to guide it to the water with the metal prod. It snaps at him. Only Caesar risks moving closer, holding the running camera in front of him like a shield.

'People come down from up north. They buy a waterfront property,' Kevin yells. 'They don't realise that there's *bound* to be an alligator in the backyard. They call it in as an eight-footer. They claim it's attacking their dog and eating the cat. I get an emergency permit. I go out there. We find an eighteen-inch baby.'

'But you take it out?'

'Sure. And within a two-month period there's another one moving in. We're doing the best we can, but we're loaded down.'

Inch by inch, six humans drive one alligator towards the canal. It resists, lunges at us, then smells the water and dives into the murk. After a moment its head rises up through the waterlilies. Caesar zooms in for a close-up. Then it vanishes into a culvert.

'So what are the chances you'll be pulling this guy out again in a few years?' asks Troy, confident again, positioning himself in a neat two-shot beside Kevin on the bank.

'Real slim. This canal goes around the bend and under the expressway back into the Everglades. He'll stay in there – if he's a male – and develop his own territory.'

'That was great, Kevin,' says Troy, lowering his microphone. 'Thanks.'

'It's development that's killing us,' Kevin says as Caesar switches off the lights. 'It's getting real hard to relocate animals, because we're running out of areas. You drain the swamp, build a retirement complex, and folks find they're up to their ears in alligators. Then they wonder why.'

Troy steps up into the van, turns on the editing desk and begins running through the tape. Caesar extends the telescopic aerial, tweaking knobs and adjusting the frequency for the live link back to WFOR's glitzy glass studio.

'Just watch them red lights, boy,' the policeman advises me before driving off to nab the glue-sniffers of Coral Springs. I hear rustlings along the bank. It seems very dark without the TV lamps.

'That was a beautiful creature,' I say after a moment.

Kevin pushes his cap back on his head. 'The gators are gettin' real sick right now,' he tells me, looking out across the sawgrass, quieter now. Our eyes adjust to the dark – or at least to the yellow glow of the halogen lamps from the encroaching Paradise Pastures subdivision. 'We don't know if it's the mercury or the food source.'

I look around at the OB van. Troy records his voice-over insert. Caesar talks to the control room on the mobile. They have their story.

'Troy told me that South Florida alligators aren't so big,' I say.

'They've got smaller because of the contamination.' Kevin gestures beyond a warehouse. 'Over there in Loxahatchee, I pulled out two nine-footers. They were so badly . . . what do you call it? . . . emaciated that they were shrinking up. I mean, they just had no fighting ability at all.'

'I don't know Loxahatchee,' I say.

'It's a wildlife refuge.'

As we talk, Troy cuts together his report. He runs through the library footage of the Daytona alligator and drops it into his introduction. He edits out the profanities. He trims the shot in which he tripped out of frame. He selects the best grunt and mixes it onto the FX track.

After a few minutes Kevin asks if he is still needed. He wants to go home and watch the finished piece on the news with his daughter. I walk him to his truck.

'See, all these gators are property of the state,' he tells me. 'And humans keep pushing into their area. I'm just a garbage collector for Florida Game and Fish.'

Above the canal is a microwave tower. An aircraft passes overhead. We transmit the finished report back to the station just after ten. It goes out on the 11 o'clock news, sandwiched between Al Sunshine's exposé on dishonest car-repair shops and the truth behind reconstructive breast surgery. 'News you can use', with catchy jingles. An ochre full moon rises above the industrial park.

On the drive back to Miami I stop to call Katrin. There are no alligators in our back garden. But she is short of sleep. Yesterday she woke at midnight. The puppy had chewed the television remote control, swallowed the 'on' button and settled down to watch *Pet Rescue*. Now the TV's stuck on Channel 4. At full volume.

8

Wild and
Free . . . ish

A seventy-seven-year-old Palm Harbor man with a sleepwalking habit awoke yesterday to find himself up to his armpits in alligators. When James Currens wandered from home, he stumbled into a pond and awoke in several feet of water, his legs stuck in the mud. 'Several gators came to visit,' he said. 'I fended them off with my cane.'

NAPLES DAILY NEWS

Naples, Tuesday 18th – 'We've had a good year for loons.'

'Loons?'

'And pelicans. Did you see the one with the dental acrylic beak?'

I had.

'It was probably broken off by a fisherman. We remade it.'

'In acrylic?'

'An oral surgeon, a dentist and our vet all donated their time one Saturday morning.'

On the Wildlife Rehabilitation Center's blackboard the morning's new in-patients are listed: a royal tern which swallowed a fishing hook, a hit-and-run bobcat with fractured legs, two ospreys with broken wings, ten orphaned opossums and twelve gopher tortoises with their habitat destroyed.

'My aunt used to care for strays too,' I say. 'Though she never used acrylic.'

'Cats?' asks Joanna.

'Pigs, mostly.'

'I like pigs.'

'She had a soft spot for boa constrictors, too. She once gave one named Beelzebub to a zoo.' Then I ask, 'Do you have any alligators?' The reason I've come to Naples.

'There's one in the pool that was hit by a golf cart.'

'A big one?'

'About thirty horsepower.'

'I mean the gator.'

Joanna nods. 'He had some serious lacerations and needed stitches. How anyone could hit an alligator with a golf cart I do not know.'

This morning I left Miami, with its muscle shirts and *botanicas*, and drove west along Alligator Alley. The dead-straight highway runs from Atlantic to Gulf through the Everglades. There are no curves in the road, and a ten-foot-high chain-link fence keeps man and beast apart, sort of. Bugs drum against the windscreen and the only stop along its seventy-eight-mile length is signposted 'Recreation Access: No Security.'

Away to the south flows the river of grass, the largest remaining subtropical wilderness in America. Here are the last woodstorks and cougars, manatees and loggerhead turtles. Migratory birds such as bobolinks and peregrine falcons stop on their way south. It is the one part of Florida where man still seems to be just a visitor; albeit the one with the asphalt-laying machines.

The Everglades only became accessible by motor car in 1928, with the completion of the Tamiami Trail. Before that south Florida's unique, oozing, 'sheet-flow' ecosystem had remained unaltered for millennia. Then the US Army Corps of Engineers undertook a vast programme to tame the land and to encourage development. A massive network of locks, dams and canals channelled water away to the new, thirsty coastal cities. Sixty per cent of the wetlands vanished, drained for orange groves, sugar plantations and holiday homes. The programme proved to be the most destructive diversion of water in history.

After the evening with Kevin's 'small to midsize' four-year-old, I wanted to see adult alligators in their undisturbed natural habitat. I also needed a break from packaged, artificial glitz. The national park seemed to be the obvious destination. I headed to Everglades City, where driftwood motels rise on stilts above the sighing grasses, expecting to find scores of wild saurians.

But running down gators *au naturel* proved more difficult than armadillos, the creature most often seen mashed into the tarmac. I placed my future in the hands of the gods, and they rolled a pair of fixed dice. I was having less luck than a softshell turtle on the interstate.

'Alligators?' said the warden at the Everglades Visitor Center. 'You'd better go see Mike Owen at the Fakahatchee State Preserve.'

Mike turned out to be a botanist. So I went on to the Big Cypress National Preserve to look up Deb Jansen. It transpired that her work was with Florida panthers. She was trying to save the fifty remaining animals from extinction. I chased from ranger station to empty gator hole until I began to wonder if I should have settled for Disney World's Animal Kingdom. I could find any number of genuine beasts there. Zazu from the *Lion King* too.

Then, in the Park office lunchroom, a biologist took pity on me. Over spaghetti bolognese left-overs, she told me about the Naples Wildlife Rehabilitation Center.

'You should go see Joanna Fitzgerald,' she said.

'Does she have big alligators there?'

'Usually.'

'Like, *really* big ones?'

The botanist gave me a strange look. She could have directed me towards rare Everglades kites, one of the few remaining apple-snail colonies, or even a pink flamingo.

'You know,' she said, stabbing a slice of carrot, 'big alligators are very common in the park.'

'Here,' instructs Joanna Fitzgerald, foster parent to Florida's strays, handing me an opossum before taking me outside to the reptile pool. 'Hold this little guy first.'

The tiny, squirming curl of life wraps itself around my finger and urinates into my palm.

'A Doberman killed its mother last night. With ten babies in her pouch.' She puts her hand back into the crowded incubator, removing a two-inch-long rabbit from beside the nine orphans. 'This bunny's on the wrong side. You're supposed to be with your brother, you ding dong.' The tiny cottontail half-crawls, half-hops back around the divider to the warm furball of sleeping opossums. 'We've had so many orphans this year,' she sighs. 'So, so many.'

The Rehabilitation Center is in a leafy suburb of the affluent 'Golf Capital of America'. Its half-a-dozen wooden buildings are assembled around a garden of wild Allamanda and cabbage palms. At its door the foundlings arrive in cardboard boxes, brown paper bags and the backs of vans. Two thousand animals a year are cared for by staff, volunteers and six local vets.

'You never know what's going to be in the box,' marvels Joanna, then blushes.

She is a twenty-eight-year-old zoologist. Plain and pleasant. Her wavy hair is cut in a practical bob, and she has never owned a pair of contact lenses. Unlike most Floridians, she is awkward with strangers. Her cheeks flush when she is asked a question. Yet she crackles with New World enthusiasm, though not for the usual passions of fashion or wealth. Instead she is happiest in the company of animals, saying 'born' rather than 'hatched', 'babies' instead of 'chicks'. In a crumpled, moth-eaten t-shirt she comes as a breath of fresh air, standing among the cages, her feet planted on the ground. I imagine her rereading *Lassie Come Home* and *Walden* at the weekend. She'd cancel an evening out to drive across the state to put a splint on a sparrow's broken leg.

'How did you start at this?' I ask her.

'As a chick parent at the Crane Foundation in Baraboo,' she says.

'Is that in Florida?'

'Wisconsin. My parents divorced when I was three, and my sisters and I were raised by my mom. I worked at the Foundation every summer through high school and college. No matter how tired I was, once I started cleaning the chick runs I felt revived.'

Her teenage years were spent bent over bird cages, her glasses slipping down her nose, scrubbing away every last bacterium and germ. No crane dropping escaped her attention.

'Then I did an internship here, and got totally hooked on rehab.' She shrugs as if to acknowledge the inevitability of her fate. 'This is where I'm meant to be.'

A tiny Seminole bat, no bigger than a walnut, grasps the side of its incubator. Joanna checks its notes. 'Two of them arrived yesterday. One died today. When these guys first come in they are so scared.'

Beyond Intensive Care are wooden cages containing cottontails, squirrels and dozens of chattering, chirping songbird chicks, each of which needs to be hand fed every thirty minutes during daylight.

She holds a finger to her lips.

'A man out kayaking found this one,' she whispers, lifting a corner of cloth curtain. 'Isn't she beautiful?'

It is a glossy, streamlined loon, relative of the Great Northern Diver.

'She was probably hit by a ski boat. There's fluid in her lungs so she won't eat on her own yet.' Joanna speaks as if in a sickroom. 'See, she's just starting to get her breeding colours.'

The curtain lowers and the injured loon calls out, filling the clinic with the haunting cry of the Canadian lakes.

In the next cage is a cormorant, hunched over its long, hooked bill.

'This one swallowed a hook and had surgery. But he's eaten over fifty fish this morning, so as soon as he's got his medicine he'll be released.'

Sport fishing is a major cause of injury to native wildlife. One pelican was found tethered to a tree by a line, with five hooks in its wings and gut. Other dangers include hunters, automobiles, habitat loss, pollution and attack from domestic animals. A recent ornithological study estimates that 4.4 million birds are killed by cats in the United States *every day*.

Outside is like the doctor's waiting room for the natural world. In the flight cages are two barred owls. One was hit by a truck in Big Cypress, the other found crucified in a backyard. They are 'permanents', like a bald eagle scooped off I-75 with a broken wing, unable to fend for themselves, destined to live out their days at the Center. The other animals – the pelicans, egrets and herons by a shady pond, the ospreys and sandhill cranes in recovery pens – will be returned to the wild.

'And the gator?' I ask.

'In a minute.'

Joanna leads me into an open enclosure. Its sandy ground is filled with the burrows of tortoises.

'These are our great horned owls,' she thrills, explaining that the pair were resident for over five years without producing any offspring. 'All of a sudden one of the volunteers came in and said, "The owl's sitting on the ground on eggs." And it was like, wow! We tried moving the eggs into a basket up in the air, but the mother wouldn't follow them. So we had to leave her out on the ground and build up all this brush and stuff. We learnt our lesson, and had the basket in nice and early this spring.'

Her excitement is contagious. I notice the birds' sombre plumage and downy tufts near the ears. Lucky are the unlucky animals which pass through her caring hands. A flash of movement reflects in her glasses. A fifth owl, an orphan which fell from its nest near Goodland, swoops across the compound. It has been fostered with the mating pair.

'Now we need to make sure that they can hunt live prey,' Joanna says. 'We'll get a big trough out here with mice. So the babies and orphan can be set free.'

'My aunt used to breed mice to feed her boa,' I tell her. 'They escaped during a dinner party and one of them ran up a guest's trouser leg.'

'Then she gave the snake to a zoo?'

'That's right.'

'I couldn't work in a zoo,' she says, shaking her head, 'because the animals aren't released.'

'My aunt let her animals rule the roost. Would you like to see a photograph of her pig?'

She does. It is in my wallet, along with snapshots of my nephew picking heather, the puppy gnawing on a basket and Katrin's foot; arbitrary mementoes of a life's passing. In the photograph Winston the pig dozes by the hearth, next to the fire-dogs.

'He looks very contented,' says Joanna. 'What happened to him?

'That's another story.'

177

I remind her again about seeing the alligator.

'Follow me.'

Joanna walks on through the Center's gardens, planted with eight-legged spider lilies, wild coffee and scruffy Fakahatchee grass. Along the way we pass snapping turtles, confiscated from a pet shop, and an empty bear-enclosure.

'We've had kind of a lot of large mammals this spring too: bobcats, white-tailed deer and *two* bears.'

'Black bears?' I ask. I had glanced through a report at the Big Cypress ranger station.

'First we had a gorgeous three-hundred-pound male,' she says, nodding, 'hit by a car. He was so huge that there wasn't an X-ray machine big enough for him this side of Gainesville. His number thirteen vertebra was broken, so he ended up being euthanised, which was tough, because we were really rooting for him. Then a 270-pound female was brought in. She had six fractures in her jaw.'

'Had she been hit by a car too?'

'A truck. Her upper palate was crushed. Dr Noble saw her immediately and did four and a half hours' surgery. She was returned to the wild last Thursday,' says Joanna, smiling. 'We had lots of releases last week.'

'How did you feed her?'

'Real carefully.'

'But her jaw was broken.'

'At first she got pureed dog food with bananas, to give it a little flavour. Then, after about a month, lots of fruit. Bears don't eat meat, really.'

'You didn't ruin her tastebuds with hot dogs?'

'Some of our' – again she avoids referring to her charges as animals – 'guys get things that they wouldn't eat in the wild, like bananas for the possums. But the bear's diet worked. She weighed over three hundred pounds when she left. We didn't want her to get overweight, but we didn't want her to get bored either.'

Joanna stops beside a large, fenced pool. It's empty.

'Uh-oh,' she says. 'Looks like the alligator was released today too.' She frowns, not wanting to disappoint me. 'With a lot of these guys there's a certain time frame that you have to work with them. If you go too long, then they start to go back downhill. They lose their gumption. You've got to get them out when they're ready. Sorry.'

On the way back to the front gate I'm told about comforting an orphan sandhill crane by placing a life-size plastic heron in its enclosure.

'When he first came here he was always making a big peeping call, the contact call for his parents,' she recalls. 'Now he stands quietly right next to that statue the entire time, even though it's a Great Blue. He's totally pecked its nose off trying to get food from the parent.'

Every day a thousand people move to south Florida. Forty million tourists visit each year. Their sewage, gasoline and sun cream has poisoned much of the state's drinking water. Sixty years ago there were 300,000 nesting wading birds in the Everglades. Today fewer than 15,000 remain. I ask Joanna about the uninhabited places to which the recuperated animals can be returned.

'It's getting tough for them to stay out of areas settled by humans,' she admits, sighing again. The anxious foster mother. 'For example, the gopher tortoises are having a hard time. They make their burrows in sandy ridges, right where people want to build their homes. So the poor tortoises are displaced. Dozens of them get picked up on construction sites, you know, but there's bulldozers around, so obviously the tortoises can't be put back in their natural habitat. They get run over.'

I remember the squashed turtles on the road into Naples.

'The volunteer who made the pelican's beak does a lot of neat things for them too, like doming cracked shells with acrylic.'

'But what's the point?' I ask her, admiring her values yet appalled by the futility of her work. 'You may save one damaged stork or a couple of tortoises, but that'll never preserve the species. It's like sticking a plaster over a cancer.'

'It's just . . . I feel like I'm doing something good,' she tells me, speaking from the heart with plain, unaffected selflessness. 'The animals don't say thank you, but they can't talk back either. I guess I'm giving them another chance.'

On the way out of Naples a line of electricity pylons marches along the western edge of the park. A single, stoic heron – not plastic but flesh and feathers – flies beneath the power lines and into man's world. I pass the Teddy Bear Museum, 'a whimsical dream home for 3,000 teddy bears'.

I find my adult alligator in the end. On the Shark Valley Tram Tour fun ride.

9

Off the Deep End

Paul Shimkonis filed suit against a Clearwater topless bar, claiming he sustained
injuries to his neck and head when stripper
Tawny Peaks struck him with her size 69
HH breasts.

ST PETERSBURG TIMES

City of Mermaids, Wednesday 19th – I met my first mermaid more than a decade ago. She came to me in a dream,
taking my hand and leading me into the sea. We plunged
into the waves, surfaced to catch breath, soared through water
and air like flying fish. Then two dolphins appeared at our
side, swimming with us, becoming a part of us. Together we
dived down through the silver curtains of liquid sunlight,
grasping for something that lay in the deep. I reached out
and my fingers touched an old steamer-trunk. I undid the
lock, threw back the lid, and dozens of birds fluttered out,
filling the dark-blue ocean with a wonder of tropical colours,
of vermilion feathers and emerald wings. They flashed upwards
in an iridescent spray, sunbeams picking out every gesture and
sign. One bird circled above my head and perched on my shoulder, staying with me as both the mermaid and I turned to reach
for the surface, into the air, into the light.

Call me a modern romantic. Call me gullible. But in America, if you want to meet a *real* mermaid you can. On US 19. For $16.95. I read about it in the Sun Coast Dream Vacation fun pack.

I decide to investigate dreams at Weeki Wachee Spring.

The soulless Sun Coast lies north of Clearwater-Saint Petersburg, the condo county where 3,055 residents crowd into every square mile. Tire Kingdoms and CITGO gas stations line the broad, flat highway. Here are Momma's Cool Gazebo restaurants and 'gated golden age' communities guaranteed to bring on an early death. Riverridge Retirement Homes sells itself as the place 'where nature surrounds you'. But hedged in by Toys'R'Us and an EconoLodge, I don't see a single tree. It isn't simply that the natural world has been eliminated, rather that the earth itself is reduced to a platform on which to erect neon signs.

Palm Harbor blurs into Holiday which dims into New Port Richey, no town distinguishable from the next, each unworthy and unattractive, replicating itself for mile after mile like some rampant plastic fungus. The Sun Coast is soulless not only because it has no history, but because profit alone motivated its development. It exists to make money from the passing trade, both drive-bys and dyings.

Once this was the pretty county that Charles Tingley, the genial Saint Augustine librarian, saw despoiled. 'Don't east coast the west coast,' pleads a single, faded wooden hoarding. Much too late.

I keep my eyes on the road, motoring on through the agglomeration, past identical mix-'n'-match shopping malls, dismal strip clubs and a fifty-foot-high gas-station dinosaur. Sunlight dazzles off the rows of new cars at Gulfview Motors, which offers no view of the Gulf. Hot boiled peanuts are sold out of the backs of vans in Pizza Hut parking lots. 'Seeing Blurry?' yells another sign. 'Call Dr Sanchez Now at the American Eyecare Center.'

Beyond a Florida Cremation Services billboard ('$495.00 – Call for In-Home Appointments') rises a white, phallic column. Atop it stride two naked acrobats, cast in heroic socialist-realist pose, with fins splayed and nipples erect. A grey dove nestles on a board-flat concrete belly.

I join the queue at its foot, snaking towards the turnstile, eager to enter the City of Mermaids.

Weeki Wachee translates as 'Winding River', not, as an obese ogre in the line beside me suggested, 'We can watchee watchee.' He's a mouse-eyed weirdo with an air of unwashed socks and ill intent. Something sinister lurks behind his bland, pasty face. I suspect he divides his time between the mermaids and Port Richey's Pink Pussycat Club. He gives me an exaggerated nudge and I step away.

In 1947 Newton Perry, a retired US Navy frogman, stumbled across the Weeki Wachee, saw its potential and dreamt up the idea for a curious tourist attraction. He dropped a ship's hull into the waterhole as a makeshift viewing platform, then hired a shoal of attractive, long-legged swimmers. He taught them to breathe through hoses and to control their buoyancy with the air in their lungs, dressed them in clingy swimsuits and stood them at the side of the highway to flag down passing cars. The first Florida mermaids took tickets and flipped hamburgers until enough spectators had stopped to fill the ship. Then the girls dived into the surrounding pool, into which 174 million gallons of clear springwater rose every day at a constant 74.5 degrees, and performed strenuous acrobatics sixteen feet beneath the surface.

The shows were a success. Even Elvis Presley stopped by to gaze through the portholes. ABC bought Perry's spring, the hull was replaced by a purpose-built underwater theatre and the site developed into a two-hundred-acre family entertainment park.

Now kids ride Buccaneer waterslides and cuddle pygmy goats in the Animal Forest Petting Zoo. Gift stores sell *Splash* videos and *Flipper* toothpick holders. Visitors sail on the Wilderness River Cruise and enjoy the 'zany cockatoo entertainers' in the Exotic Birds Show. Yet for all its crafted artifice and state-of-the-art animatronics, the City of Mermaids remains a vision from the fifties.

'I'd like to meet a mermaid,' I say to the woman in the ticket booth.

'In your dreams,' jokes the fat man, his frantic winks bringing to mind a dying fly buzzing in a tub of lard.

Dennis Brungardt, the Operations Manager, comes out to meet me. He is a welcoming, busy man with the look of one who has suffered tragedy.

'There's nowhere else on earth I'd rather be,' he tells me, gesturing at the overweight children bobbing in the lagoon.

I believe him.

'I was a police officer, and my son was killed in a car accident in Texas,' he says, shaking his head as if to dislodge a nightmare. 'After that I started drifting; came past here and this guy asked if I'd like to help out, on a casual basis. I just loved it. Here were families and kids having fun. In five years I've worked myself up from part-time to Operations Manager. I live on-site with my girlfriend. I don't believe now that you should do anything in your life that you don't enjoy.'

'I'd enjoy meeting a mermaid,' I tell him.

'Why, sure,' he says, and picks up his walkie-talkie to call one.

Dennis's devotion to the feelgood is sincere. Beyond him holiday-makers float in multi-coloured rubber rings, tuck into ice-cream sandwiches and lie on the fine white sand working up their tans. Couples wander through the Mermaid

Museum. Parrots squawk in their cages. Cash registers make lucrative music. I wonder if we should wait by the water.

'Hi, I'm Wanda.'

I turn around to behold clear blue eyes, blonde hair and an all-American smile stretching from coast to coast. She could be my mermaid – were it not for the legs . . .

'This is Wanda Flip,' says Dennis.

. . . and her hands. They are warm to the touch.

'I don't want to cause offence,' I say . . .

She's not wreathed in red and brown seaweed. Or combing down her hair and humming an alluring tune.

'. . . but you're not a mermaid.'

'Not any more,' laughs Wanda. 'I'm now Mermaid Manager.'

It seems that promotion at Weeki Wachee effects metamorphosis. The Peter Principle meets urban myth: every employee rises to his or her level of fantasy.

'The younger girls are a bit shy,' explains Dennis, meaning that this is as close as you get. 'And Wanda is very protective of them.'

'I'd rather hoped that you'd have a tail.'

'It appears when we jump in the water,' she says, pointing at her feet. 'We like to keep the how kinda mystical.'

Wanda glows with good health, youthful energy and an unquestioning faith in the value of her work. She is on the fresh side of thirty and wears no make-up apart from a flick of mascara. For a moment I am at a loss for words. I can't square the difference between my dream mermaid and this twinkling, piscine bimbette. What does one say to a sea sprite in Tactel trousers?

'How did you become a mermaid?' I ask.

'I put in an application, kind of like a normal job.'

I picture the form. Distinguishing features: vestigial gills. Previous employment: rescuing drowning mariners. Interests: singing siren songs of love.

'I'll let you two talk,' says Dennis, and paddles off into the crowd.

'You must be a good swimmer.' It's like asking if birds enjoy flapping their wings.

'Actually our best girls are not very good on top of the water,' gushes Wanda, slowing only for superlatives. 'But they are *beautiful* under it. That's the secret. They can *move.*'

A Weeki Wachee mermaid doesn't spend her days sitting on a rock organising her collection of seashells or raising storms at will.

'We bring the new recruits in, have a water audition, do some surface work, then try a couple of beneath-the-surface moves, buoyancy – that's a big thing for us – being able to exhale out of your nose, especially while keeping your level, and doing some ballet movements when you're going upside down.'

She speaks as she must swim, without pausing for breath, as if being underwater has taught her to get by on less air. I wonder if she dives with dolphins.

'And you have to keep smiling,' I say.

'Right. Senior mermaids can hold their breath for two and one half minutes. Each senior takes a new girl under her fin and teaches her everything, like flotation, like how to catch the airhose, like the *moves*. Some kids take to it real quickly. Others need a little more time. It needs a good three months before you're ready to swim in a show.'

Wanda's walkie-talkie crackles with a marine ditty. 'I'm sorry,' she apologises, maybe for not communicating by sonar. She unhooks the radio from her belt. Her fingers aren't webbed. 'Eighteen. Go ahead.'

'Can you 2-5 with Sarah at Admissions?'

'I'm in the middle of something right now. Can she wait about fifteen minutes?'

'OK, Wanda.'

'10-4,' says Wanda, then turns back to me. She seems unlikely to lure mortals to death by drowning.

'Tell me about the shows,' I say.

'We do three or four every day. One's twenty-two minutes long and the other's thirty minutes.'

'The girls are underwater the whole time?'

'And they're really cold afterwards,' she shivers. 'Last month we did an experiment. Checked our body temperature before going in the water. Then after. It actually drops two degrees. The mermaids get a half-hour to warm up afterwards.'

'It can't be healthy.'

'We use lotions for the skin, but the hair . . .' She pulls at a long blonde tendril. 'Conditioners are a big thing for us.'

'I mean, we're not made to spend thirty minutes underwater.'

'Speak for yourself,' she flashes, laughing again. 'The first time on an airhose we all get that I'm-not-supposed-to-be-here feeling. But then being underwater becomes something that's just . . .'

Wanda's brisk delivery falters. She hesitates for the first time.

'. . . incredible. I don't know how to explain it. If you're out of the water for a while and you go back in, there are so many things that you accept as normal. You hear the bubbles. You sense every time someone takes a breath. You feed the little Brim fish. It's like you're really a part of that world, not this world.'

'Does it affect your dreams?'

'Yes, definitely. It affects your dreams.'

'Did you know that mermaids are supposed to be in possession of foreknowledge?' I ask her.

According to Homer, meeting a mermaid is fatal not because of dangerous seas or alluring, unattainable love, but because of the shock of foresight. In her song the siren sings of all that is to come. No mortal can survive the burden of such knowledge.

'I didn't know that,' grins Wanda.

I think again of my dream and the old steamer-trunk. I can't say if my mermaid was piffling or prophetic, if the spray of iridescent birds divined anything more than a love of free flight. I dip my toes into the waters of fate and determinism, fearful, perhaps, that neither exists at all.

Wanda invites me to watch the afternoon show. As we walk towards the theatre she says, 'Later this month we're bringing back all the mermaids and mermen for our *Tails of Yesteryear*.'

'There are mermen?' I ask.

'Sure,' she bubbles, pushing to open the glass door. 'Though the guys tend not to stay in this career. The show's kind of a tribute to our fiftieth anniversary. We'll bring back the deep dive, the Coke-drinking scene, the eating bananas underwater, all the popular things that we did in the past.'

Over the past half-century the thirty-five different shows have included *The Mermaid Follies*, *Perils of Pearls* and *Underwater Dream Girls*.

'What's on today?' I ask as Wanda leaves me in a plush seat, staring at a curtained wall.

'*The Little Mermaid*.'

The audience arrives in bunches: kids with parents, couples arm in arm, an evangelical church group, the fat ogre. He catches sight of me and spreads himself across the two adjacent seats. We are the only single men in the dim theatre.

'You find your mermaid?' rasps blubbergut, catching his breath. It smells of raw onions. He saw me talking with Wanda.

'Sort of,' I answer.

'She looked all right,' he concedes. 'But I like them younger and firmer, you know, with a pretty pink tail.'

'Do you?'

He probably trawls Internet porn sites.

'You British?' he asks, setting his Caterpillar cap onto his belly.

'I live there.'

'You know Germany?'

I nod.

'I flew Skymasters into Berlin during the airlift.'

His voice has a tightness which seems out of place. I take another look at him: flabby flesh, clammy brow, dumb Pilsbury doughboy grin. I can't imagine him fitting through an aircraft cargo door.

'I wasn't this heavy back then,' he adds.

In 1948, the year after Perry stumbled across the waterhole, Stalin cut Berlin off from the West in an attempt to starve the population. In response the British and Americans flew in food, medicine and coal to keep the city alive. Few times and places could have felt further away from Weeki Wachee Spring.

'We didn't have no schedule,' mumbles the ogre, filling his mouth with a chocolate bar. 'We just flew back and forth. When we couldn't fly no more we found a place to sleep.' He crumples the wrapper and looks at his watch. 'One minute to showtime.' He leans towards me and whispers, 'I really go for the little blonde in this one.'

'You've seen *The Little Mermaid* before?' I ask.

'Fourteen times.'

'Fourteen times?'

'And *Pocahontas* twelve times. All in the last month.'

The canned music swells before I can move to a vacant seat. The lights dim and the curtains rise. The aquamarine waters of the lagoon appear beyond nineteen four-inch-thick plate-glass windows. A single, blonde mermaid swims up from the depths, flicking her pink tail like a lycra whip. She performs a somersault, smiles and waves at the audience. Everyone including the ogre waves back.

'*The little mermaid,*' drones the mellow-toned narrator, '*lives in a place as old as time and as new as a dream. It is a lovely place to live . . .* '

'That's her,' he says, sucking in his breath.

She wears no mask, airhose or tank, and looks as fresh as a newly shelled shrimp.

'*She and her sisters have a happy, carefree life . . .* '

Two more mermaids glide across the dolomite cliffs that encircle the base of the spring. A fourth swimmer bursts from a submerged fairyland castle across the waterhole.

'*The sisters of the ocean, as happy as can be, tend their gardens and never grow old . . .* '

'She's my favourite,' breathes the ogre.

'She's very attractive,' I admit. She is Eve in a benign Eden, raking her tidy allotment in a wet idea of paradise. There is no Tree of the Knowledge of Good and Evil growing among her sea cucumbers.

'Get it off!' the ogre suddenly shouts at the glass, startling everyone in the theatre. His breathing is shallow. 'Strip it all off,' he hisses, a suet pudding out of control.

The couple sitting beside us move their children away. I too try to change places. In a moment an usher shines a torch on him.

'I'm sorry,' he apologises, bowing his head, his manifold chins multiplying. 'It's the last time, I promise.'

'This is your final warning,' snaps the usher, and flicks off the torch.

The performance is not interrupted, for the silly swimmers can only hear the sound of their own bubbles. They smile and wave, but the audience remains distracted by the fat man.

'*Happy, happy mermaids living under the sea . . .* '

A contented turtle floats by the windows.

It takes the calypso birthday-party scene to recapture our attention. The four swimmers dip behind rocks and emerge in wild Caribbean outfits. They jive and pirouette sixteen feet beneath the surface. A fish-shaped birthday cake sweeps across the lagoon, frightening a school of mullet. The little mermaid bubbles lip-sync to an asinine song.

'She reminds me of a girl back in Germany,' whispers the ogre to me.

I don't respond.

'Lots of girls used to hang round the perimeter fence. We weren't allowed to fraternise. But this one was real cute, you know what I mean?'

A woman behind us shushes him.

'One day she slips me her address. Says, "Come round." Like, "*Please* come round." So I did. Hers was the only building standing on her street. All the others was bombed out. I knock on the door and she opens it and she's standing there buff naked. Rubble all around, but not a stitch on her. "Come in," she says. "*Please* come in."'

The woman behind us goes to find the usher. The calypso party reaches its climax, and then a shimmering wall of air bubbles obscures our view of the waterhole. Curls of weed are caught in the current. Beyond them I catch sight of the swimmers pulling up their tails.

'I called her my little mermaid – "*meine Wassernixe*" in German –'cause she was all smooth and wriggly, just like that girl. I think maybe she wanted to come back with me to the States.'

'You didn't see her afterwards?' I hear myself ask. The Berlin airlift lasted fifteen months, and prevented Stalin from seizing Berlin.

'Got transferred to Pensacola.'

He gestures at the figures beyond the glass.

'I've been coming twice a day to watch that little one, to keep it all in my head, on account of my operation.'

'What operation?'

'Cataracts. In both eyes. Tomorrow.'

For a moment in the reflected half-light the ogre looks vulnerable, even frightened, and I imagine him aged twenty-one, a slender Skymaster pilot, flying coal into Templehof, the escape hatch open so the dust won't foul the control cables, dreaming of the vitality of a young woman.

The usher's torch flicks on. Without another word the ogre heaves himself up out of the seats. The only sound is the rush of bubbles up the plate glass.

The airjets cut and the show proceeds. A handsome prince falls off a passing ship and is rescued by the little mermaid. They fall in love and decide to marry. She gives up her fin, sprouts legs and transforms herself into a football cheerleader, complete with white pleated skirt. Hers is a seamless progress from one kind of Eden to another, towards a saccharine vision of goodness. Around me the audience applauds, identifying with the mermaid in themselves. To the tune of the grand finale the sisters, the prince and a reformed sea-witch wiggle their hips and swim away into the American Dream.

I stay on US 19 at the Valu-Lodge, formerly the Dream Inn, before that Howard Johnson's, next door to Crabby Bill's. 'Under Renovation' warns the notice in the lobby, which means cockroaches in every cupboard.

The room is like all the others I have rented in Florida. And probably not dissimilar to the 3,700,000 others on the continent. It measures about twenty feet by fourteen, boasts a shag carpet, curtains and matching bedspread. It has a doorless wardrobe, a telephone, cable television and a gasping air-conditioner. The familiarity lends it a homely comfort: the cigarette burns, the smell of Glade air-freshener, the paper-wrapped lavatory seat. Dial '9' for an Outside Line. Ice Machine Behind Reception. Outside are mile after mile of Burger Kings, Best Westerns and Li'l Champ Gas and Food stores.

Nowhere in the States is a traveller more than a few minutes away from a king-size bed, a rerun of *Baywatch* and the unvarying taste of Chicken McNuggets. It is the quick, reassuring, sugar-and-additive fix of everyday America. Accessible. Seductive. Anonymous. Sweet drinks, fast food, youth, sex, pork roast, revenge, murder. Here today and gone tomorrow.

'With the supermarket as our temple and the singing commercial as our litany,' wrote Adlai Stevenson, 'are we likely to fire the world with an irresistible vision of America's exalted purposes and inspiring way of life?'

Well . . . yes.

I decide to keep out of the motel pool, as the creatures who inhabit it are unlikely to be mermaids. Instead I fall into a deep, dreamless sleep.

10

Goodness Gracious

She was a mother in her thirties. Her four-teen-year-old daughter was severely dis-abled by cerebral palsy. In desperation to help the girl, the woman turned to a tele-vangelist, thinking he might intercede with God for a cure. The woman made a $1,000 'vow of faith' and went without pay.

The girl was not healed. She grew worse. When her mother called the evangelist's hotline to ask why the girl had not been helped, she was told she must have a secret sin in her life.

In a final desperate act of penance, the mother went into her back yard, doused herself in gasoline and struck a match.

CITRUS COUNTY CHRONICLE

Saint Leo, Sunday 23rd – Seventeen pages of churches are listed in the Sun Coast Yellow Pages: Baptist to Buddhist, Charismatic to Lutheran, Presbyterian Orthodox to Primitive Brethren. I read through the holy-roll in bed over a sixpack of spiced cranberry muffins. It's Sunday morning. This is America. I decide to go to church. But which one?

I brew a cup of tea while making up my mind. Turn on the TV.

'It is a *must* that you prove God and mail in your largest bill in Bible faith,' demands the Reverend James Eugene Ewing, misquoting Malachi 3:10. 'Is your largest bill a twenty-dollar bill? Or is it a fifty? Or a hundred? Whatever your largest bill is, do what God is saying. You may have had other plans,' acknowledges the quiffed head of Church-in-the-Home-by-Mail, 'but change them.'

I flip through the channels.

Kenneth Copeland's Liberty, Praise and Worship Institute has been on air since before dawn. As has Faith Partners on Channel 52.

'Come on down!' rants Pastor Zachary to his whooping congregation. Zachary marches to a different drummer, one who is partial to a rock-gospel beat. 'Can you feel it, brothers and sisters?' Choristers swing and vergers wail. 'Hallelujah!'

'What is Mother?' asks John Butler Book on *Christian Viewpoint*. 'It may be Dad who brings home the bacon, but it's Mother who stays up with you when your bones are aching.' Reverend Book wants to 'bring Mother out of mothballs', and declares, 'Women's lib is the devil's fib.' He also catalogues 'the ever increasing dangers which face our home and nation', among them homosexuality and working women.

I slop my mug of tea all over the bedclothes.

Two thousand five hundred televangelists work America's airwaves in a $3.5-billion-a-year business. Using Census Bureau demographic data they target elderly women, the poor and the desperate, as well as wealthy Christians anxious to justify their all-American acquisitiveness. The most poverty-stricken zip codes provide the richest pickings. In a leaked memorandum one of James Eugene Ewing's aides praised new computer software that isolated low-income neighbour-hoods and netted Church-in-the-Home $2,411,184 from 615,426 letters.

'The size of each special area is about two or four city blocks,' noted the memo. 'Thank God there are 10s of thousands of them across the nation.'

I'm put off my muffins.

Some teletheologians have had their come-uppance. Jim Bakker's PTL ('Praise the Lord') Network collapsed under allegations of fraud and conspiracy. The Reverend W.V. Grant, whose 'miraculous' ability to read minds relied on pre-broadcast interviews, served time in an Oklahoma federal prison for tax evasion. His wife Brenda claimed Grant's imprisonment was 'something that could happen to anyone who made a mistake on their tax information'. The flamboyant Texan Robert Tilton was implicated when thousands of unanswered pledge letters were found in trash cans behind his bank, their donations of cash, food stamps and even wedding rings removed. On air Tilton had promised to pray over each individual plea and to lobby God for wondrous improvements in his parishioners' health and finance. At its peak his $125 million-a-year *Success-N-Life* infomercial show appeared daily in all 235 US television markets. He drove a Jaguar and owned a fifty-foot Carver motor-launch. He lived in multi-million-dollar homes in Dallas and San Diego. He used donations to pay for plastic surgery, explaining that ink from the prayer requests had seeped into his blood and created bags under his eyes. An ABC TV investigation drove him off the air, temporarily. He moved from Texas to Florida to prey anew. Today he continues to call down silver-dollar miracles.

I dump the muffins, pack my bag and check out of the motel. A television is on in the lobby too.

'Call now and salvation is yours!' cries Dr Sherman Elijah, offering free tickets to the Promised Land. He holds aloft his flaming Good Time Bible. A toll-free number flashes on the screen for those wishing to make a snap donation. 'Please have your credit card details ready.'

As I pay my bill the front-desk clerk asks a six-year-old, 'Where'd you get your beautiful hair, darling?'

'From God,' she answers.

On the car radio Spirit FM pleads, 'Will you remember us with a financial gift?' In Shoney's Classic American restaurant Muzak blares out of a speaker above my head.

'People get ready,' sings Crystal Lewis, 'Jesus is coming! Soon we'll be going home!'

I am numbed by the ranting, raving racket. How can anyone think – let alone pray – with so much noise?

I turn inland, leaving behind the Holy Ghost Revival Center and a GMC 4x4 truck with the licence plate R BIBLE. I switch off 107.7 Magic FM's *Contemporary Christian Music Hour*. The gated communities and funeral homes fade into the distance. A line of chained prisoners walks up the highway on both shoulders and the central reservation, picking up trash. Behind them follows a police car and a white prison bus. Its bumper sticker reads, 'Never drive faster than your angels can fly.'

Away from the beaches, beyond the last Charisma for Christ ministry, Highway 52 winds up into the Pasco hills. A sea breeze stirs the elms and cedars. Thoroughbred horses feed in pristine paddocks. Yachts on trailers are moored under broad oaks. Houses fall back from the roadside, spread their wings, nestle among the trees.

I have no destination, just an instinct to flee the hustle of hard-sell. My compass needle swings east, then north, waiting to settle. I skirt Gower's Corner, home of Florida's largest nudist camp, and cross US 41. Ten miles ahead is I-75. Tampa is twenty miles to the south. Wildwood away to the left. I carry straight on, steering away from cities, staying on the back roads.

Outside San Antonio, farmers gossip over fences. Wives and daughters wait in pick-ups, anxious not to be late for church, checking their hair in the rear-view mirror. A grackle picks at a potato-chip packet.

At the edge of town a sign catches my attention. 'Saint Leo Abbey two miles.'

A monastery. In Florida.

The road climbs past the Stonehenge Apartments to a white Romanesque church surrounded by citrus groves. Saint Leo is perched on a hill overlooking Lake Jovita. If global warming melts the polar ice-caps, the abbey will tower above the flooded Sunshine State like Mont Saint-Michel.

I park in the shade of the bell-tower and walk into the orchard. The air is heady with the scent of orange and pine. Mockingbirds call in the trees. Leo the Great was the Pope who prevented the barbarians from sacking Rome in the fourth century. He devoted his pontificate to preserving the purity of the faith. I lie down on his dry, red earth and close my eyes.

'May I help you?'

I wake. Startled. Disorientated. A cartoon-cutout figure looms above me. I blink at the apparition. A few miles away blonde mermaids are cavorting in pools. Children meet Dumphrey the Dragon at Busch Gardens. Tourists cruise along the Elvis Presley Follow that Dream Parkway and the desperate dial in donations to the Ministry of God's Love Incorporated. But my feet are planted in the real world. I think. I blink again. It's true. I'm in an orange grove shaking hands with Friar Tuck.

'I just happened upon the abbey and fell asleep,' I say. 'I'm sorry.'

'You are most welcome here,' says Father Paul, a chubby monk in sandals. He has a face like a soft cushion. Or a pan of warm tapioca. Bright fish-eyes gleam out of the pap. 'A lot of people are guided to us.'

'It's a very peaceful spot. Have you been here long?'

'The Benedictine Order was founded in the sixth century.'

'I mean in Florida.'

'The house began in 1889,' he squeaks. If Paul were an orchestra, his body would be a tuba, his voice a piccolo. Its lightness doesn't suit his physical mass. 'A priest in San Antonio thought the climate and temperature recommended it as a good place to start a foundation.'

'The first monastery in the state?'

'And still the only one. I came in '46.'

'In 1946?'

Paul doesn't look much older than forty. Seeking God on earth must have spared him a few temporal worries.

'I was just a boy. The abbey ran a camp. I came back to the school in 1950. Then in 1959 I made my first vows. And that's a while ago,' he says in a pitch-pipe falsetto.

Paul was obedient to the monastic tradition during the hippie sixties and the Vietnam War. He didn't cast aside his black habit during the sexual revolution. He kept his vow of poverty through the materialistic eighties. He has never smoked dope, made love in a VW Beetle or owned shares in Microsoft. And in the dappled shade of the grove he appears happy, humble and filled with a gentle wish to listen.

'Would you like to stay for lunch with the community?' he asks me, holding up a jar of Dat'l Do-it Devil Drops hot sauce.

Before the meal there is medies. Father Paul sits me in a pew at the back of the empty abbey church. The broad building is white and clean, with plump arches and a high, pitched wooden roof. Abstract banners hang from the pillars. A vast rose marble crucifix dominates the altar wall. It is flanked by two faithful air-conditioning units.

The bells sound and the monks enter the nave in silent

single file. They pass through tinted beams of sunlight, the red of Saint Augustine's heart and the green of Saint Patrick's cloak, their sandals shuffling on the flagstone floor. Thirty brothers – one black, one Korean, five other Asians, the rest white – divide themselves to left and right, taking their seats in the choir.

'I praise your Name, my King and my God.'

The psalms are recited by alternate sides, back and forth, then repeated together.

'We praise your Name, our King and our God.'

With heads bowed and wristwatches left in their cells, the brotherhood attempt to live out Saint Benedict's Rule. They give up their own will and do battle for Christ so they may deserve to share His Kingdom. Their prayers measure their days, flowing forth like the rhythm of life. Their black habits stand out against the chalk-white walls. Beneath the high stained-glass windows, the community seems less a physical place than a spiritual world, a space for reflection distant from the lusting layman.

'That new incense really stinks,' grumbles Brother Amos.

'I don't mind it at all,' chirps Brother Malachi.

Father Paul guides me to a chair and introduces the two monks. Malachi is a slender man, balding, in his mid-fifties. Amos is a decade younger, his hair dishevelled, his temper bolshie. Eddie Izzard in a habit.

'Do you sort out your differences through confession?' I ask them, not used to the sight of quibbling holy men.

'I'll take your confession any time, brother,' teases Amos.

'Don't hang around waiting for it,' retorts Malachi.

There are a dozen round tables in the refectory. Monks queue at the self-service counter. Lunch is roast chicken and vegetables. Iced tea comes out of a machine. Coke is available too, its name now familiar to more people on God's earth than His own. A gay-and-lesbian Christian group on retreat sit together in a multi-coloured, badge-covered huddle. The wallpaper is patterned with entwined daisies. The blinds are pink. The cheery atmosphere is far removed from the austerity of European monastic orders.

'Saint Leo is different from the other monasteries...' explains Paul, shaking a dollop of his Dat'l Do-it hot sauce onto the chicken.

'Because of the quality of the brothers,' jokes Amos.

'... because of the climate. We are Southern. Southerners move slowly. We're not in a hurry to do nothing.' He swallows a mouthful of chilli oil. 'It's real different from the monasteries up north. There they roll up their sleeves and get the job done. We like to think about it for a while.'

'And then do it?'

'In God's good time.'

'It is a Southern trait to move slowly,' says Malachi.

'Now that's *smokin'*,' gasps Paul, his voice climbing an octave.

I'm finding it hard to correlate piety with jocularity, holiness with Happy Face tablewear. I try a dab of Devil Drops. Then gulp a pint of water. Hotter than hell's fires. When my eyes stop watering I ask, 'Are there really no other monasteries in the state?'

'There are mixed-sex friaries in Tampa and North Palm,' says Malachi.

'Mixed sex?'

'But we're the only real men,' mocks Amos. 'We don't read the instructions when we assemble things.'

'So what did you do before joining the order?' I ask him.

'You don't want to know,' interrupts Malachi, spiking the casual banter. 'It's too sinful.'

'Then how about you?'

'I was a photographer.'

'Brother Malachi was Head of Communications at the United Technologies Corporation in Hartford, Connecticut,' corrects Paul, dipping a potato into the sauce.

The little brother of seven sisters, Malachi trained as a barber, then a printer and finally as a photographer. He rose to the top of the career ladder, travelling the world documenting corporate enterprise.

'I first came to the monastery ten years ago, stayed a few months, left. I wasn't ready. Then last year I hit a wall.'

At the peak of his career he recognised that the time for change had come. He gave up job, travel, salary and home to take the vow of poverty.

'When I did that, when I arrived here, I felt like I'd died and gone to heaven.'

'Whereas it made me feel quite the opposite,' interjects Amos.

Malachi raises his fist in playful threat.

At the next table is Simon, an elderly monk with an anchor tattooed on his arm. Before hearing the call he led a 'colourful life' in the merchant marine: running guns to Nicaraguan Contras, whoring in Macau, scuttling pirates in the Malacca Straits. He maintains a vow of silence, apart from the nights when he wakes shouting out for his drowning shipmates.

A rosy-cheeked virgin from Fort Lauderdale sits beside him. 'I'm just a trainee,' he apologises, pulling at a shirt button. 'I've only been here for ten days.'

'Why did you come?'

'Because it felt right.'

'We're just a bunch of sinful men living together,' explains Malachi. 'Like everyone else, we fall down and get up. The only difference is that here we do it together.'

For the sweet course there is Divine Dessert, mixed fruit in whipped cream served with pink Marshmallow Bunnies. Father Paul tucks into a double portion. I have never seen a monk eat Marshmallow Bunnies.

'I just spent a couple of days around Weeki Wachee,' I tell them.

'Bless you,' says Amos.

'I've travelled all over Florida, and it's the first place I hit a traffic jam. Why is the Sun Coast so popular?'

Paul lays down his third, decapitated Bunny. He pauses to loosen the leather belt around his ample waist. 'The parks are very expensive,' he explains. 'People from up north drive south for the winter. They can't afford Disney's prices. So they go to the cheaper places. Places that only exist to separate the tourists from their money.'

'Don't you find that disheartening?' I ask.

'The poorer tourists don't really have any choice.'

'I mean, here at the monastery you are obedient to God's word. There, greed is god.'

'The almighty dollar,' says Amos without a smile.

'It's because of there that we're here,' answers Malachi. He, like the other monks, lived in the world and entered the Church by choice, not chance.

'Have you heard of Zephyrhills?' asks Paul.

I had seen its name on a road sign.

'Back in the twenties and thirties when nobody had any money it became the first tin-can tourist residence in the state of Florida.'

'Tin-can tourists?'

'They were northerners who built their own trailers out of aluminum, then drove south to spend the winter in Zephyrhills.'

'In home-made caravans.'

'The tin cans became more and more elaborate. They became mobile homes. Next they became recreational vehicles. Now there are one thousand tin-can parks in Zephyrhills. One *thousand*.'

'That's a lot of people.'

'So our role is essentially to be available to folks,' he says.

Tourists and residents, dreamers and realists.

Paul swallows the last Bunny. Amos gathers the plates. Malachi plans to e-mail an acquaintance in Atlanta about the nature of frailty. As the monks begin to slip away for afternoon study and prayer I surprise myself by asking, 'May I stay here for a few days?'

I need a break from schlock. A pit-stop for the soul. The affection of the brotherhood appeals to me, as does the sanctity of the location. The monks' devotion isn't extreme or ascetic. The rule lays down 'nothing harsh, nothing burdensome'. It aims to 'amend faults and safeguard love'. I feel comfortable here. This is a chance to gather my thoughts and strength. And to prepare for my trip's inevitable, final destination.

'You may stay, as long as you remember the OTIS elevator inspector in your prayers,' Amos responds.

'I'm sorry?'

'It's broken.' Amos may devote his life to finding a stairway to heaven, but he wants to ride the monastery lift up to his room. 'And I'm fed up with having to walk upstairs.'

I am taken in, fed, offered a haircut and the use of a washing machine. I spend the afternoon alone under the trees jotting down these conversations. After the inferno of the coast the gardens are a paradise. Songbirds stir the hibiscus around me. Jays move through the palms. Turtles paddle through Jovita's shallows. There are no fairy lights, crystal angels or satellite dishes. In spring when the orange blossoms are out the smell must be intoxicating.

The white church and monastery buildings – refectory, monks' cells, abbot's office and obligatory gift store – crown the hill. I am given a room in the Retreat Center. On the desk is a copy of Augustine's *Confessions*. Next door is the library. 'Blessed are those who return their books on time.'

Among the hymnals and psalters, the copies of Cicero and J.F. Woods, there is a board game called *Bible Trivia* ('The Game where Trivia is not Trivial'). I flick through its playing cards.

'How many years did Noah live after the Flood? 100, 250, 350 or 500 years?'

'Why must we consider the lilies of the field?'

'Who kept all these things and pondered them in her heart?'

The San Antonio Catholic Colony was established by Judge Edmund F. Dunne in 1881. Dunne created the territory as a Catholic bastion against the spreading Baptist Bible Belt. His vision was of an international city, San Antonio, surrounded by a ring of small towns peopled by different nationalities. Saint Joseph was to be a German settlement. Saint Thomas was to be Irish. There were to be English, Spanish and Italian communities. Saint Leo's monastery and a convent would be built at the centre to provide spiritual guidance. But the French settlers didn't like the area. Saint Thomas closed. The Spanish went off to Sarasota. Only German Saint Joseph survives today as a Catholic town.

At 5 o'clock the bells call the monks to vespers. The single condition of my stay is that I join in the abbey's services. I sit in the choir beside Brother Malachi. He lays the psalter before me, opens it, even turns the pages.

'Great is God's faithful love for us.'

The *Opus Dei* fills the void.

'Let us praise God with all our hearts.'

As we chant the church ceases to seem too large for the few monks. I realise that the building was not designed simply to be useful. It is itself a prayer, built to last, a bridge between the physical and spiritual worlds.

'The idols of the nations are sil–ver and gold,
the work of hu–man hands.
They have mouths but they–cannot speak;
eyes but they can–not see.'

The monks seek sanctity through their devotion. They strive to change and to better themselves. Their lives are not static, not an end, but a beginning.

'If my old workmates could see me now, folding bedlinen and peeling potatoes, they wouldn't believe it,' says Malachi as he trims my sideburns too short.

After evensong and a light supper he offered to cut my hair. He told me that mechanical actions give him time to think. He may be a fine monk, but from what I can see in the mirror, it is a blessing that he gave up being a barber.

'When you joined the order, what happened to your past life?'

'You mean money?' he asks.

I nod and almost lose an ear. 'And your home.'

'I didn't own a house. I was always an apartment-dweller. I never felt the need to settle.'

Malachi hadn't married, choosing to concentrate on his career alone. His photography too must have been more successful than his hair-cutting.

'As for my investments, I'm still a novice so I can keep them until I take my final vows in March. Then I'll either sign them over to my family for education or give them to the monastery.'

The scissors nip my scalp. I close my eyes and wish for him a steady hand.

'You'll stay here forever?' I ask, not looking.

'I will die here,' he says, cutting off an extra long length. 'There's a tranquil little cemetery out the back. This is where I'm meant to be.'

'I thought *I* was meant to be in Germany,' I say. I've begun to look as if I've quarrelled with a chainsaw. 'I spent months planning my visit there; then at the last minute it felt wrong, and I decided to come to Florida instead. Ever since then, things have fallen into place.' I look at the lumps of hair in my lap. 'Most things.'

Malachi lays down his scissors. Hallelujah. My prayers are answered.

'If you don't have faith, you're going to ascribe the encounters of your journey to chance,' he tells me. 'If you have faith, you will be looking for guidance from those coincidences.'

'I'd say it's a matter of being positive and open. Maybe even of creating luck.'

Malachi sits down in the second barber's chair. 'When God wants us to do something, He's going to see that we do it. Generally He shuts every door in our face. There's one door left open, and that's the one we go through.'

'If we choose to,' I say carefully. 'If we listen.'

'Listening,' hurries Malachi, suddenly excited, 'is the basic attitude of a mystic.'

'I'm no mystic,' I say, able to shake my head again without fear of mutilation. 'For years I pleaded for guidance, terrified that I might actually get it. At night I lay in the dark praying to my father, to my uncle, to God, wanting to be directed, ready to dive under the covers if I was shown a sign. Now on this trip I've tried to find the courage to listen. It frightens me, of course. But it also comforts me against the real nightmare.'

'Run while you have the light of life,' quotes Malachi, 'that the darkness of death may not overtake you.'

'I don't hear voices. I know it's not simply whimsy or chance. It's just a sense, for lack of a better word, that I now realise may have been with me all the time. I'm learning to trust the intuition which tells me whether to pull into one town or to drive like hell to the next. Sorry, Father.'

'Call me brother. You give me more praise than is due.'

'I get it wrong loads of times.'

'I think that everything that happens to a person in their life is a part of God's plan for them,' Malachi says. 'So who knows, from this experience with this monastery, God may be leading you to become a monk.'

He picks up the scissors again.

'Uh-oh,' I say.

A novice is allowed to put forward three possible names on entering the Benedictines. Malachi's second choice was Augustine, a late bloomer like himself. His third choice was Philip, a name favoured by his deceased parents. But he couldn't come up with a first choice. So he waited. He prayed. And after a time he went into the choir and picked up his Bible. It opened at the Book of Malachi. He knew that Malachi was a minor prophet who had travelled to Jerusalem, a stranger too in his own land. He had chosen to leave behind his own identity and become someone else. So Brother Malachi put forward the name as his first choice.

Saint Leo, Monday 24th – The bells ringing through the night do not disturb my sleep. Unlike the 3-D Last Supper alarm clock on the bedside table. Its tick is so loud that I hide it behind the stuffed Jesus doll. The bed is a single and the sheets smell of incense. There is a sea-painting by a departed brother ('his Hawaiian period') and a plastic frog with arms outstretched declaring 'I love you sunny Florida.'

The monks doze at morning prayers. They yawn, stirring themselves awake with psalms. I sit in my place, again in the left choirstall beside Brother Malachi. Once more he lays open my psalter. Under-pew fans cool our thoughts and feet. A lone woman in black prays at the back of the church. She mouths the words of the canticle, then collapses onto her arms in tears.

For breakfast there is Cap'n Crunch, Cheerios and Coco Krispies. English muffins and Danishes are on offer. Paul's bacon and eggs – though not his Dat'l Do-it Hellish Relish – grow cold. He lingered behind in the church to console the weeping woman.

Brother Amos was up at 4 a.m. searching for an elderly monk who had once been their abbot.

'He's apt to wander off in the middle of the night talking about his childhood with Jesus,' he explains to me.

'And how they played on the swings together,' adds Malachi.

Saint Leo, Tuesday 25th – 'Some people arrive filled with enthusiasm for a week's retreat,' mumbles Malachi, three clothes pegs protruding from his mouth. 'Then leave after twenty-four hours.'

I am helping him to fold bedsheets. The monks contribute work to the house each day.

'Because they're not used to being alone.'

The feel-good-fast-food-quick-fix does not engender reflection. It unlearns patience and heightens intolerance.

'My friends considered me crazy because I often ate alone

with a book. It gave me time to think. And made it easier to adapt to this life.'

The monastery offers retreats, seminars, workshops and pastoral conferences to groups and individuals. The monks participate in the sessions, leading reverent discussions or shaking beribboned tambourines. The Center is booked every weekend from next Friday until Christmas.

'Sometimes people ask me what they should do here. I tell them, "Just listen to the oranges grow."'

Saint Leo, Wednesday 26th – The OTIS elevator inspector arrives in answer to Amos's prayers. We have meatloaf for lunch.

Saint Leo, Thursday 27th – Father Paul was once a jazz pianist in a five-piece combo. He had a single night of rebellion, playing one concert at the Georgia Tech Interfraternity Council. Then he applied to become a monk. In his room are hundreds of 78 rpm records: Garner, Hines, Tatum, Peterson. At Mass today he leads the monks in an improvised rendition of 'Let us go to the house of God!'

Afterwards he asks me, 'Have you seen the grotto?'

I hadn't.

The abbey's stab at a tourist attraction lies across Highway 52. Paul sails ahead between the cars, his black habit billowing behind him.

'There were a lot of rocks around the grounds. Brother Aleutius decided to get rid of them and started piling them up, and all of a sudden it became a grotto,' Paul says, leading me into the garden. 'We put in a couple of statues and now it's a copy of Lourdes.'

Aleutius's grotto brings to mind a quarry with benches, not a place of pilgrimage.

'I got two hundred dollars in the mail a couple of months ago. A lawyer saw the Saint Leo sign on the Interstate and decided to visit the monastery. He just sat here for about an hour, then went on down to Tampa. He sent the two hundred dollars because he'd had a peaceful time wandering around.'

The site doesn't inspire me to part with any cash. Or even to wander. But I do admit to having been touched by the spirit that the monks give the abbey.

'We don't give it. We receive it. The abbey has been a very holy place since it was founded. Welcome to our own Massabielle grotto,' announces Paul.

The shrine is not reminiscent of Lourdes. Instead of an underground basilica there is a quaint cave, ringed by sea-shells collected on the Sanibel beaches. Inside is a small statue of the Virgin. The walls are not covered by discarded crutches and votive bandages.

The original Benedictine apostulate was pastoral work and education. But from 1965, after the Second Vatican Council, all Catholic houses started shedding priests. Saint Leo had to let go of its pastoral duties. It could no longer afford to send priests to university so gave up its educational role too. As a result the abbey found itself providing the ancient practice of hospitality alone. It encouraged contemplation, lost parishioners and fell into slow financial decline. Being faithful to the rule does not fill the collection plate.

'Maybe you should start a TV programme,' I suggest. *Saint Leo's Red Hot Peppers*? 'You could play a Jelly Roll Morton medley out here in the grotto.'

'Television evangelism is a way of making money,' says Father Paul, 'from folks who are hurting.'

It occurs to me that during my travels in Florida, the room in the Retreat Center is the first I've slept in without a TV.

'So many people today have this thing wrong or that thing wrong and they are looking for some solution. And these guys on television say, "I have a solution."'

'Are they doing any good at all?' I ask.

'They're making money. They convince people that they have the solution, and they profit from pain. *Pain*,' he repeats in falsetto. 'For instance, I was talking with a bank manager in Dade City yesterday. A very well educated man. He faithfully watches certain evangelical shows every week.'

'He phones up and makes a donation?'

'I don't know if he makes a donation. But his devotion to Robert Schuller and the Crystal Cathedral tells me that he's *hurting*, like so many other folks.'

The televangelists sell gold-plated salvation in the name of Feeling Good.

'Adolescents seem to be especially susceptible to pain,' Paul says, taking a turn around a solemn cairn of broken stones. 'Kids get filled with rage, steal a gun and go out to shoot a bunch of people.'

A young woman approaches, wanting Paul's blessing on a gift. The silver cross flashes in its gift store wrapping.

'Would you mind? It's for my niece who's joining the Marines. Thank you, Father. God always sends you at the right time.'

'I don't understand how anyone can pick up a gun and kill,' I say after she leaves. 'It's such a . . . failing.'

'I think maybe it's because there's no structure to life any more,' Paul says, swaying down onto one of the concrete benches. The smell of dry earth wafts up from the orange grove. 'There is so much money. People buy what they want to buy. If they don't have the money, then they buy it on time. Or steal it. There is no self-control.'

I try not to stumble over the two-foot-high replica Church of the Rosary.

'Children used to be heavily disciplined in school. Now

teachers don't dare touch them. So they grow up like weeds and think the world owes them a living. They get angry when they don't get what they want.' He sighs, wishing perhaps that he could provide me with a more uplifting outlook.

'We've been conditioned to believe that possessions bring happiness,' I say to a man who for fifty years has denied himself all earthly indulgences, apart from pepper sauce and the occasional Marshmallow Bunny.

'The abbey tries to do its bit. During the summer we bring disaffected kids up here to give them experience of living in the community. To convince them that there *is* another way to live.'

'Without commercial breaks.'

'I tell them a true story about the televangelist who went to work with a Christian care-worker,' he says with a piccolo laugh. 'A drug addict was brought in to them, so ill that he was covered in maggots. The Christian worker picked them off by hand. The televangelist said later, "I wouldn't do that for a million dollars."

'The care worker replied, "Neither would I."'

Call home.

'I'm just off to vespers,' I tell Katrin.

David, who wanted me to get laid in Florida, telephoned her yesterday to ask how I was getting on. She told him I was at a monastery. He laughed and laughed.

Saint Leo, Friday 28th – Brothers Malachi and Amos argue over the Fruit Loops. Paul jabbers with such excitement that he's forgotten about his Hot Licks spicy bagel. Together the three monks are planning my itinerary. I am Goldmund to their Narziss, leaving behind the patterned order of the cloisters, plunging into the wild world of blood and lust. Or at least unleaded gas and double cheeseburgers.

'There is *so* much to recommend,' squeaks Paul. 'Of all the parks my favourite is Homosassa Springs. Because you can feed the animals.'

'It's a lot of fun,' says Malachi.

'And there's Kumba at Busch Gardens.'

'The best rollercoaster in the South-East.'

'Have you been to Tarpon Springs?' Paul asks.

I shake my head.

'It's the centre of the sponge industry in the United States,' he raves. 'And a Greek settlement.'

'They dive for sponges, dry them and sell them,' explains Malachi. 'They have a magnificent Epiphany celebration on January 6th where the Patriarch of the Greek Orthodox Church throws the cross out in the bayou. Local teenagers jump in and try to bring it up, and the one who gets it is kind of king for a day.'

'I don't think so,' I say.

'Then how about the Seminole Indians' bingo?' suggests Amos, looking up from his Fruit Loops with dubious intent.

Paul and Malachi do not approve of the suggestion.

'They used to run buses up here to take people down there to gamble,' says Paul. I had seen the signs for the SunCruz Casino on US 19.

'Not a good destination,' Malachi advises me, with a firm shake of his head.

'At least he'd see why Americans are known as greedy people.'

'I recommend the Monastery of Saint Bernard in Miami,' says Malachi.

'I thought this was the only monastery.'

'Saint Bernard's is the Episcopal Diocese's head office.'

'It's the oldest building in America,' chips in Paul. 'Some of the Celtic columns date back to the seventh century.'

'William Randolph Hearst shipped it over from Spain.'

'Hearst bought a whole monastery?' I ask.

'The stones arrived in ten thousand numbered crates. But there was an outbreak of foot-and-mouth disease in Spain. So Customs opened the boxes and burnt the straw packing. Then they put the stones back into the wrong crates. The buildings could never be reassembled in the right way.'

'There's always Yeehaw Junction,' proposes Amos, again tempting me astray.

'That's not a suitable suggestion either,' states Paul. 'Yeehaw Junction was an infamous railroad brothel which . . .'

'. . . has lost its original attraction,' interrupts Malachi, dismissing any notion of me leaving men of the cloth for women on red satin sheets.

'It's closed.'

'He might still find it a fascinating . . .'

'No, brother.'

'But . . .'

'I'm warning you,' says Malachi, raising his fist in a mock threat.

I thank them all for their suggestions. I have made up my mind. After utopian fruitcakes and the Garden of Eden, emaciated alligators and drip-dry mermaids, there seems to be only one obvious choice left.

'It has to be Disney World,' I say.

'Oh,' sigh the monks. They look down at their plates. Paul takes a bite of his forgotten bagel. Malachi toys with his cereal. Goldmund is off to meet Goofy.

'At least you'll have TV there,' says Amos.

11

Thy Kingdom Come

'Get this ride started,' shouted Douglas Buchanan, 'I'm ready to go' were the last words of the four-time murderer executed today.

FLORIDA TIMES-UNION

Orlando, Saturday 29th – Next Exit Magic Kingdom.

If Brother Malachi saw the sign on I-4 he'd get down on his knees and pray. And be run over by a Greyhound bus.

I turn off the Interstate, leaving behind the morning rush of commuters, and onto a sleek multi-lane highway running through the woods. There are no billboards on the manicured embankments. No hoardings advertising all-you-can-eat lobster feasts. No heaps of trash along the roadside. A single notice directs me to tune my radio to 1030 AM. I spin the dial. Chipmunk laughter.

'Zip-a-dee doo dah, zip-a-dee ay . . .'

Mickey Mouse announces the parks' opening hours. Minnie lists the day's special events. Pluto plugs the re-release of *Fantasia*.

'My-oh-my what a wonderful day . . .'

The drivers beside me reduce their speed, smile, relax.

Their squabbling kids fall quiet. Winnie the Pooh and his friends speak to us from the Hundred Acre Wood.

'Piglet, I have decided to catch a Heffalump.'

We are still five miles from the Magic Kingdom parking lot, seven miles from Cinderella's Castle, yet already we are in America's promised land.

Walt Disney World is twice the size of Manhattan. Its parks – the Magic Kingdom, EPCOT Center, Disney-MGM Studios and Animal Kingdom – cover forty-three square miles. Every year thirty-two million people visit them, drink half a billion Cokes, eat five million hot dogs, snap 4 per cent of all America's amateur photographs. Every day the 45,000 Vacation Kingdom 'cast members' dispense goodwill and pixie dust, plant over five thousand bedding plants and take in an average of a hundred pairs of sunglasses at the Lost and Found. In a year they sell enough Mouse Ear hats to cover the head of every man, woman and child in Manchester. And sufficient character t-shirts to put Mickey's face on the chest of every Scot. I am no pioneer here. As my tyres purr on the smooth asphalt I lose any claim to being an intrepid traveller. Seven per cent of Britain's population has driven down Buena Vista Drive before me.

Thirty years ago this land was a swamp. Three-quarters of it was underwater during the summer. The site was bought in secret, designated the Reedy Creek Improvement District and declared an autonomous, self-governing community. It became for a time the world's biggest construction project. Fifty-five miles of canals were dug and landscaped to resemble natural springs. Two new lakes were dredged. Millions of cubic yards of fill were moved to raise the flat land by fourteen feet, making room for extensive subterranean 'utilidor' service tunnels under the Magic Kingdom. Florida's two highest peaks, Big Thunder and Space Mountain, soared above the scrub. In less than four years the central Florida bog was transformed into a place of pilgrimage. The most visited tourist destination on earth.

I park at Tigger 32. The original Disneyland in California would fit into this parking lot and still leave space for a thousand cars. A Chip'n'Dale caterpillar tram shuttles me and hundreds of others to the Ticket and Transportation Center. 'Meeters and greeters' in bellhop uniforms marshal us towards the air-conditioned monorail. Steamers whistle at the ferry-boat landing. Wheelchair visitors are whisked to the front of the crowd. I feel like a five-year-old at a vast children's birthday party, guided from sponge cake to blind man's bluff, cared for, carefree, controlled.

'*Donde está Peter Pan, Mama?*'

The queue snakes up to the loading platform and onto the streamlined five-coach trains. One after another the monorails glide out over the coiffured topiary, along the water's edge, above the paddle-wheelers and Water Sprites. So many watercraft ply the lakes, canals and lagoons that Disney is said to have the fifth largest navy in the world.

'*Regards! C'est Ariel!*'

'Anything can happen in the Magic Kingdom . . .' I catch through the polyglottal chatter. Every hour ten thousand passengers hear the same recording. 'Pinch yourself to know you're not in an enchanting dream.'

Here are black school-groups, Asian newlyweds, sunburnt English families and Brazilian holiday-makers. All are speaking at once. All are too excited to listen to the saccharine welcome in English and Spanish, apart from me. No one else seems to have come by themselves. No one is poor. No one is hungry. Most of us wear white socks.

We pass through the lobby of the Contemporary Resort Hotel towards the fantasy spire of Cinderella's Castle. The monorail doors swish open and the fun-loving herd stampedes to the turnstiles. Above us rises a red-brick Victorian train station. The puffing *Lilly Belle*, named after Walt's wife, is ready to depart. 'Aaaall aboard.'

'Do you want to ride the train, honey?' drawls a young mother. 'Or go to the next land?'

Adventureland, Frontierland, Fantasyland, Tomorrowland: all are places of the imagination. *Lilly Belle*'s theatrical steam swirls up above the grey shingled roof, wraps itself around the Old Glory flagpole and obscures the station clock. There are only five public clocks in all of the Magic Kingdom. The Disney experience is designed to exclude time.

'Good morning, sir,' smiles an amiable employee at the admissions booth. 'Single Day or Value ticket? The All-In-One Hopper Pass includes Pleasure Island.'

I step onto Main Street USA, the quintessence of mythical America. This is the old town that Palatka wishes it was: a nostalgic Hollywood vision built by Disney, and now copied by cities across the country.

'*So alles ist in Ordnung; erst, Splashberg; zweites, Big Thunder Eisenbahn.*'

It's just 9 a.m. and already the park is full of people. In Town Square they surge around the turn-of-the-century City Hall, with white portico and kitschy-cute cupola, and surround the Sun Bank, which provides cash advances on credit cards. An orderly queue of pram-pushing parents waits in its dependable shade to meet Donald Duck. Across the crowded square is Captain Hook. I gaze into the vast Emporium, selling fairy-princess wings and interactive 'Talk'n'Sing' Kovu lion cubs. The shop is packed with more grasping kids than would fill a dozen monasteries. Purchases may be picked up at the park exit or delivered to a World Resort hotel. There are popcorn vendors and pastel façades, stuffed Brer Rabbits and Pooh figurines. The smell of baking cinnamon buns is pumped out of the Main Street Bake Shop.

Families tuck into the day's first hot dogs at Casey's Refreshment Corner (hosted by Coca-Cola) before booking a Disney Character Dinner at the Liberty Tree Tavern (presented by Stouffer's). The chipper staff smile, joke and thank them for their custom. In the Penny Arcade are repro Kiss-O-Meters and digital interactive *101 Dalmatians* games. Cruella DeVil masks and glow-in-the-dark wands are sold from the House of Magic. The Dapper Dan quartet sings outside the Harmony Barber Shop. The Yough Cougars High School Band leads the Magical Moments Parade. Batons twirl. Tubas puff. Cinderella and the Lion King come to life in 'this land where Once Upon a Time is Now'. A child's handful of balloons escapes, as they must do every hour on the hour, and floats away over the cinema.

Main Street celebrates the ascendancy of commerce in a fairy-tale version of late-nineteenth-century America. It conjures up hazy memories of a cosy society uncluttered by immigrant slums or racism. Every 'guest' is funnelled along it, the only entrance to the Magic Kingdom. Its pavement is clean, its sidestreets are safe. It is a shopping mall that is open both one hour earlier and one hour later than the rest of the park. Each year every American child receives on average forty dollars' worth of Disney products. Here Walt reaches deep into his visitors' pockets.

I follow the hordes, allowing myself to be jostled forward, swept along by the park's assured operation. A plastic-shod Belgian drafthorse pulls the Main Street trolley, followed by a costumed streetsweeper with pan and brush. Inane tunes emanate from speakers hidden in every other fake gas lamp post.

Snow White blows me a kiss and I wave back. She's like a china doll with bon-bon sleeves and plucked eyebrows, wholly artificial except for the pale blonde hairs on her arms.

A stupid frou-frou bow in her black wig makes her look like a primped pedigree puppy. She waves again and I realise she's interested in the disabled kids riding ECVs behind me, off to twist and turn on the Barnstormer in Goofy's Wiseacres Farm.

Cinderella's fibreglass Castle draws us past the Hunny Pot shops and Fast Snack Sites towards the Plaza-Hub. Its six spokes lead off to the various dreamlands. I'm pushed left and, beyond the Liberty Square Potato Wagon, find myself in the queue for The Hall of Presidents.

'Sorry folks, this show's full for wheelchair access,' apologises a beaming cast member. 'The next one's in ten minutes.'

'The next one's *now*,' snaps an irritated guest, not enjoying wheeling his disabled father-in-law around the park.

'Yes, sir,' the cast member replies instantly, diffusing the anger, letting the group into the attraction. 'I'm sure we can accommodate you.'

In the darkness of the theatre, shadows of men and women recite the opening lines of the Preamble to the Constitution.

'We the people of the United States of America ...'

Patriotic music puffs and swells. Lumps grow in throats. The handwritten document is projected on the screen.

'These immortal words, when first they were written, proclaimed to the world an idea new among men,' intones the pedagogic narrator. The same actor may have recorded the *Mulan* voice-over. 'They expressed a shining wish for a better way of life.'

In five minutes the presentation encapsulates 'the most impressive moments of American history': the Wright brothers launch the *Kitty Hawk*, Edison invents the lightbulb, NASA reaches for the stars.

'*This* is the American dream.'

The multi-screens rise and AudioAnimatronic presidents appear on the stage in 'life-like realism'. Lincoln speaks of the immortality of man, Tyler confers with Jackson, George

Bush scratches his plastic cheek. Ronald Reagan's robot appears to be more animated than its flesh-and-blood original. Bill Clinton delivers a speech written and recorded especially for the show. Here is history as Disney wishes it to be portrayed, distilled and nostalgic, not simply reproduced but improved. There are no lost wars or dispossessed natives, women are not disenfranchised, the Space Shuttle *Challenger* does not explode in Technicolor above Cape Canaveral. A plastic president raises a pneumatic arm as 'The Battle Hymn of the Republic' booms out of the speakers. The perfect sunset turns into the American flag, the theatre doors swing open and a thousand patriots are released back into the Florida heat.

'When you wish upon a star . . .'

Among the audience I notice a group of young Japanese couples. The women cling to their husbands with the ardour of new love. The men glow with morning-after pride. For years young Asians have been flying to Hawaii and California to tie the knot. Now they appear to be travelling further afield.

I catch up with them outside the Haunted Mansion and ask if they've come to Florida for their honeymoons.

'No,' says one of the men. He wears a Jiminy Cricket tennis shirt and pressed Bermuda shorts. 'Come to marry.'

'In Wedding Pavilion,' giggles his wife, her jet-black eyes set off by a paste Tinkerbell tiara.

'There's a Disney Wedding Pavilion here?' I gasp.

'Over there,' the man gestures, pointing back towards the Seven Seas Lagoon. Then adds, 'Mickey Mouse was our best man.'

In disbelief I catch the monorail away from the Magic Kingdom, around the western shore of the lake to the Grand Floridian stop. The sprawling gingerbread hotel is like a transplanted multi-storey Tesco surrounded by broad verandahs and groomed white beaches. On the balcony of its

Grand Lobby a big band entertains guests sipping English tea. To the east is the Polynesian Resort and, beyond it, Wilderness Lodge, with a waterfall in the courtyard. If one spent a night in each Disney guest room, it would take more than sixty-one years to sleep through every hotel on the property.

Follow the white boardwalk along the water's edge, past more picture-perfect couples towards a private island. Stop in my tracks. Cannot believe my eyes.

Under the palms Disney's newest bridal pair climb into Cinderella's glass coach. A flock of white doves is released from behind the pavilion. A bewigged coachman, in cream-and-gold livery, gees on the team of dapple-grey ponies. The happy couple ride off to their Fairy Tale hotel and a life of everlasting happiness.

'It's *so* intimate,' marvels a blue-rinsed spectator beside me.

Outside the motorway-restaurant-cum-Baptist-chapel the day's nuptials are listed on a pink Wedding Ceremonies board: Yamada/Miyazu, Ono/Kawaja, Chan/Lai, Yu/Rabinovitch, Quinn/Letizia, Gomez/Castrillo, Waldo/Wishheart. One every hour.

My sense of astonishment grows like Pinocchio's nose. Dumbfounded, I slip through french doors stencilled with climbing-rose motifs.

Brides-to-be sit with their mothers on reproduction Provençal sofas. Disney Wedding Events Managers guide them on their choice of entertainment, balloon enhancements and fancy favours for attendants. Special options include laser-die-cut Cinderella's Castle invitations, mousse-filled white chocolate slippers and 'crystal collectibles that will make an ideal keepsake of your magical time together'. Gowns are bought or rented from Franck's Angel Threads, a salon recreated from the Touchstone movie *Father of the Bride*. Happily-Ever-After honeymoons can be booked aboard the Disney Cruise Line. The Fairy Tale Weddings brochure promises 'the sky is the limit for couples looking for a truly unique, memorable wedding – all in the privacy of your favourite theme park setting'.

'You've come at a very opportune time, because we're getting ready to celebrate our ten thousandth wedding this Sunday.'

'And Rebecca's been here for every one of them.'

The Fairy Tale Weddings Senior Sales Development Manager is Rebecca Grinnals. 'As in Grin-All-the-Time,' she tells me. 'It's an Irish name.'

Rebecca has the look of a happy woman: clear brown eyes, glowing golden skin, an oh-so-sincere Disney smile. Her earrings are chiming hearts and interlocking keys. She wears a tailored peach suit. I suspect that she is pregnant.

'We've got thirteen different countries represented here this month.'

'This *month*?' I say, staggered by the popularity of the service.

'We have a couple from Venezuela, another from Costa Rica, the United Kingdom, Holland, Germany, Italy, Japan, China – I mean, all over the place,' Rebecca gushes with sunny enthusiasm. 'Which is really neat for us, because we have the opportunity to make some special friendships along the way.'

Rebecca oversees the arrangements for the two thousand special friends who get hitched every year at Disney World.

'This weekend we're marrying a *very* wonderful couple who have had a lot of hardships. He was a hometown hockey hero in Michigan who was diagnosed with a rare form of cancer. He played throughout his chemotherapy and the hearts of his town opened up to him. They wrote in to the Lifetime Cable Network and told them his story. We were looking to do something special for our ten thousandth. So we all hooked up. It's going to be aired on *Weddings of a Lifetime* next week.'

Around us are vast white flower arrangements, floating pearl candles and a five-tiered Magic Kingdom wedding cake. Beneath a reproduction Monet a bride's father hands over his American Express card ('Use the Special Purchase Account feature of the Card to pay over time for your special day').

'We're giving them an all-expense-paid wedding: glass carriage, herald trumpeters, a gown designed in New York, bridesmaids' shoes, thousands and thousands of roses, I mean everything they could possibly want. We're flying in thirty family and friends. He's coming down Main Street on horseback. They're getting married in the Rose Garden. And what they don't know is, at the end of the show we're going to be surprising them. They still have about six or seven thousand dollars in medical bills. We have arranged to pay those off plus give them ten thousand dollars as our ten thousandth couple to start them in their life together.'

Even a wedding becomes a show in the hands of the Disney Corporation.

'We oftentimes have the chance to make dreams come true, but rarely can we give someone a wedding like this.'

I resist the temptation to ask how many of the marriages have ended in divorce. It would have flattened the pre-nuptial froth.

Rebecca tells me that her grandmother was a seamstress. As a child she loved to help her unfold the bolts of silk and crinoline, to trim the veils and trains. Soon after starting at Disney she was asked to join the wedding task-force.

'And it has just been the most incredible ride,' she gasps, her intensity almost sexual. 'I mean, I love it. It's the perfect job for me. I just got married here two months ago.'

'Congratulations,' I say. Wedding No. 9,656?

'After the ceremony we cruised around the world for an hour and a half, then docked at the Grand Floridian and went to one of the ballrooms for our dinner and dance. We had three hundred guests. It was the most incredible day of my life. And I was worried that it wouldn't be, because, you know, friends say, "What is a Disney wedding? Isn't it kind of hokey?" So we just kind of blew their minds away.'

Outside, a white stretch limousine waits to whisk the next couple away to their reception. Another dozen doves – or white pigeons – are released as the party walks across the humpback bridge. Rebecca takes me onto the island and I ask her about the morning's Asian couples.

'In volume Japan brings us more weddings than the United States,' she explains. 'During the week it's almost exclusively Asian. They come over for fourteen days. They rent their gown in Japan with the tiara and veil. I mean, they're decked to the nines. It's a status symbol over there to get married abroad.'

We step aside to let a cleaner hoover up the stray petals of confetti. For the third time this morning. The non-denominational pavilion is being transformed for a Jewish ceremony.

'Many of the Japanese choose to incorporate characters into their reception,' says Rebecca. 'Our American weddings tend not to have characters at all.'

'I was told that Mickey can be your best man,' I say.

'Not at the wedding. None of our characters take part in the wedding. We don't allow that. But at the reception they'll come in top hat and tails and cut the cake. They'll pose for photographs. They'll mix and mingle with the guests. The Japanese love that. Their faces light up. It's really been neat for us, because we've learnt a lot about the Japanese culture.'

Or about the pervasive reach of America.

Sunshine floods through the tinted panes, casting prisms of colour across the rostrum. The body of the pavilion is open and airy, lined with plastic-coated pews and hung with silken drapes. It looks sweet and rich, like iced vanilla cake with five scoops of ice cream. Beyond the podium the central window looks out across the lagoon towards the Castle.

'When we started doing business with the Japanese, one of the things they wanted was a Western minister who looked the part: elderly, white-haired, in a robe . . . and speaking Japanese. Talk about a needle in a haystack,' Rebecca continues, walking me up the aisle. 'Luckily we found a few retired service chaplains around here who had been stationed in Japan. Hi, sweetheart.'

'Hi, honey.'

As if acting out a well-rehearsed scene, the Reverend Jack Day, a photogenic Southern minister, appears on cue. His eyes sparkle as brightly as the clear waters behind him. He has a thick head of silver hair and a Hershey's chocolate syrup voice. Central Casting could not have found anyone better. On his lapel he wears an Orlando Police Department badge. On his tie is a Mickey Mouse pin.

'On one side of my life I'm chaplain for the police,' he explains after introductions. 'I help the officers, their wives and families through times of trouble or turmoil. I'm the man who knocks on someone's door at 2.30 in the morning and delivers the bad news.'

'And the upside?' prompts Rebecca.

'My other side is I come out here and perform the wedding ceremonies for people from all over the world.'

'We meet some amazing people.'

'I have such a happy time. I'm having more fun than any person should be having.'

'Jack does the weddings and then, a few years later, couples call and have him baptise their children.'

'You've got a Baptism Pavilion too?' I wouldn't be surprised to hear that they have an Eeyore Pension Fund, or a Twilight Zone Crematorium.

'We do it unofficially,' replies Rebecca, *sotto voce*. 'In their hotel room, or in a garden.'

'It's because they want to come back to the place where it all began,' stresses Jack, speaking with gooey gravity. 'They bring grandmothers and grandfathers, godmothers and god-fathers, eight or ten people in a hotel room somewhere. We have a little christening and dedication service. That makes me feel good.'

'Because you've touched their lives,' says Rebecca, *con brio*.

'And they've touched mine. I receive far more than I give.'

Fresh flower arrangements arrive from the in-park florist. Carnations are exchanged for stephanotis. New Order of Service sheets are laid out. The pavilion is transformed from virginal white to pretty pink. The staff videographer sets up his equipment. Rebecca glances at her watch. The transformation runs like clockwork.

'Bye, sweetheart. I'll see you,' she says to the Reverend.

Exit stage left.

Around the island are swaying palms and boat landings. Brides can arrive by outrigger canoe. Mississippi steamers might collect wedding parties from the pier. Arches, bowers and careful landscaping focus nuptial photo opportunities. Every aspect of the environment is controlled to 'ensure that your wedding ceremony fulfils every vision you anticipate and is perfectly preserved for years to come'.

No real marriage can sustain this candy-floss fable.

The Magic Moment Management reminds me of 'concept videos' which, rather than document weddings and anniversaries, dub and splice to spice up ordinary life. Professional 'memory makers' reshape 'life cycle events' using elaborate scripts, stock footage and sophisticated editing techniques. They create *Ghostbusters* birthday-party romps and wedding pop fantasies lip-synced to the B-52s' 'Love Shack'. A couple's mundane first date is transformed into a candy-cane-sweet encounter which in time replaces their recollection of the true circumstances. Karaoke meets memory, whimsy rules and reality is remade.

'I'm not sure I understand why people get married here,' I admit as Rebecca shows me around the solarium. 'A wedding is an intimate celebration. Isn't Disney's involvement invasive?'

'I think there are three fundamental reasons for our success,' says Rebecca. 'First, we have the people who grew up with Disney. It holds a very special place in their hearts. So, whether they had a rough childhood or just liked dreaming about fairy tales, it's natural for them to get married in a place they love so much.'

Across the bay launches run between the resorts. Red-and-white sailing boats dart away from the beaches.

'Then there are the couples with the Cinderella fantasy. Where else in the world can the bride arrive in a glass coach?'

A Dixie trio plays on the deck of a passing stern-wheeler.

'But the majority of our weddings are for couples who have *never* been here,' thrills Rebecca. Her excitement all but drowns out the tinkle of calm canned music. 'In America people are not necessarily marrying their high-school sweetheart any more. They're maybe getting married a little bit later. Or meeting someone from a different city. And all of a sudden they're faced with planning a wedding with guests who are coming from every corner of the country. They could pick a beautiful mansion somewhere to get married in, but then they'd have the hassle. Who's going to cater it? Who's going to do the music? Here we take care of everything. We offer a one-stop shopping service. We have a staff of thirty-seven people, so they don't have to worry that the flowers might not be nice. People know that we're going to put on a wonderful show.'

Rebecca steps under an elaborate blossoming portal. I resist the temptation to touch the bounty of champagne roses. They might be artificial.

'You know, no matter how crazy my day can be, I find that when I'm showing a bride and groom around here, it's so tranquil.' A soft breeze puffs off the lagoon to stir her loose curls. 'And when I sit down and talk to them about getting married, about how in love they are, I mean, it is an incredible experience.' She turns to face me, framed against the Castle's make-believe spires. 'As hokey as it sounds, we really are making dreams come true.'

'Nothing sells like sincerity.'

'It's a wonderful market for Disney. None of us would be here if there wasn't a reason to do it from a business standpoint.'

An Intimate Wedding in the pavilion, which includes sixteen 'amenities', from accommodation to 'officiant to perform ceremony', costs from $4,100. I wonder how many weeks Virginia Blue's Caring Center could operate on that amount of money.

We walk back across the bridge ahead of the next wedding party. A bow-legged cowboy carries a Plexiglas slipper to the island. Two cowpoke guitarists follow a clutch of bridesmaids. All that's missing is the Lone Ranger on Silver.

I read this morning in a newspaper about another wedding in Orlando. The bride's former boyfriend had burst into the ceremony, fired a gun at the groom and killed the best man. The rabbi, who had been a Green Beret, wrestled the offender to the floor. I ask Rebecca if she can explain the discrepancy between behaviour inside and outside the park's gates.

'You know, that's probably one of the reasons why I love working for Disney so much. People say to me, "Rebecca, you're not in reality." But it's like what we do. It sounds so kitschy, but if you can live and work in a wonderful place and touch people's lives, then why not? Why not?'

There are no shoot-outs in Fantasyland.

'So many people in the world are born into lives of crime,' she adds. 'No one has ever taken a moment to give them that helping hand, to give them a reassuring hug, to be there for them.'

'It's not just people from underprivileged backgrounds who commit crimes,' I say. 'It isn't so simple.'

We stop at the circular drive outside the office. A reproduction country-and-western stagecoach pulls up carrying a bride and her holster-wearing father.

'I think that once people experience good, they realise the power of it. They want to help others. They want to share.' Rebecca smiles as the bride passes us. Her father raises his Stetson but doesn't draw his six-shooter. She turns back to me. 'Not everyone has the luxury of meeting a good Samaritan in their life.'

There's a story told of a naked couple found *in flagrante delicto* by undercover officers beneath a bridge near Cinderella's Castle. Not only were the transgressors ejected from the park, they were banned from Disney property worldwide. Banished from Eden with no fig leaves provided. For defiling an icon.

On the way back to Main Street I see no newlyweds making love in the bushes. But the sight would have surprised me less than does the mass of humanity now flooding through the turnstiles. In the past hour the park's population has doubled. I step down from the monorail and hesitate before entering the crush. Never in my life have I seen so many stupid grins. Then, across the sea of heads, a stocky, frizz-haired retiree catches my eye.

The Magic Kingdom employee moves lightly as he works, dancing while stamping the hands of visitors leaving the park. Fred Astaire on Geritol.

'Give me that little hand, honey. Come on, it won't hurt.'

I cut across the flow to reach him.

Spurgeon Griffin doesn't at first appear to fit the 'Disney look'. He may not flout the dress code, or sport muttonchop whiskers and sequinned spectacles; he simply seems to have too much individuality to be anyone's 'cast member'.

'Let's see, I think I started here in '89,' he tells me, pausing in mid-jig, raising his voice above the noise of the Hoover Groovers Showband. 'I was a police officer in New York City.'

'From Gotham City to Loonytoons?' I shout.

'You know, if you've been used to being active all your life, it's hard to go home and sit around. Here, honey, give me your little hand,' he says, swinging around to brand a departing troop of Girl Scouts, enabling them to return later in the day. 'Let me have that other little hand over there.'

A dozen white children cluster around him, holding up their palms.

'I'm having a ball out here,' he tells me above their heads. 'I would love to meet Michael Eisner and hug him. I wouldn't kiss the dude, but I'd sure hug him for letting us old timers have a little gig out here. Come on, man,' he tells a shy boy in a Planet Hollywood t-shirt, 'this isn't going to hurt. It ain't no needle. Little kids get afraid of the stamp cause they don't know,' he explains as the queue bunches up behind him.

Spurgeon nods down the rank of turnstile attendants. 'We have one man working over here who's eighty years old. He's got all his faculties. His hearing is good. His eyesight is good. He's really sharp. He's Jewish, you know.'

'Does he dance too?' I ask.

'We all do,' he laughs. 'I tell you, right here is the only place in the United States you'll be treated decent.'

I laugh too.

'No, I'm serious about this,' he insists. 'I've been to the Playboy Club, to gambling casinos from New York back to California. This is the only place you'll be treated decent.'

'Why is that?' I ask.

'I don't know, but I'll tell you one thing for sure . . .'

A visitor interrupts us asking for directions to the Animal Kingdom. Spurgeon gestures past the Floral Mickey towards the nearby bus facility. Disney employees are not permitted to point. They are required to smile. Spurgeon beams as he jives through the throng. After a few moments of energetic stamping, the crowd has thinned out again.

'You were saying?'

'When I first came down to Florida about five years ago I was *shocked* to turn the TV on and see no crime. I used to tell my wife, "This place is wide open. *Wide* open." Cops didn't wear no bulletproof vests. Cops worked alone in radio cars. We didn't have that stuff going on in New York. We have two cops in a radio car up there, you know. Now more and more people are moving down here and bringing their little badass kids. And Florida's going to have to start dealing with them like we did up north. Hey, give me that little hand there, beautiful.'

The arriving *Roy O. Disney* locomotive rings its bell as a frustrated guest tries to jump the queue.

'Mister, come over here with me,' offers Spurgeon, stopping his shuffle to snap open another gate.

'We've had enough,' complains an unenchanted customer, pulling his hand away from the stamp. 'We're leaving.'

'Hey, I don't want to give you nothing you don't want. I tell you,' Spurgeon assures me, 'most people are decent. In police training we had a psychology class. They said you have three classifications of people in the world.'

'Only three?'

'That's right,' he nods, and lists them. 'Ladies, Gentlemen and what we call That Other Thing. Now, you're not going have no trouble out of Ladies. You won't have no trouble out of Gentlemen. But you're going to have trouble out of That Other Thing. The rule is out on the street to treat Ladies as Ladies, Gentlemen as Gentlemen, and That Other Thing like That Other Thing. And it's so unfortunate that I can't do that here in many instances.' He glances in the direction of the angry visitor. 'Give me that little hand, baby.'

'Thank you, sir,' says the child's mother.

'How do we get to EPCOT?' asks her husband.

As Spurgeon directs him, the surge of passengers from the train swells the queue.

'Some guests, they come in and act in any kind of way. I ain't never seen nothing like it. Come in and get away with so much lowdown stuff that they shouldn't be allowed in the park. I've seen them teaching their children to lie. To *lie*,' Spurgeon repeats, distracted for a moment from his stamping, working himself into a sudden fury. 'Man, if we didn't lie we wouldn't have all these problems that we're having in this country today.'

The queue bunches up behind him. A French tourist starts to complain. Spurgeon returns to the outstretched hands.

'It makes you wonder...'

I could go home now. I could turn around, make for the airport and wake up at Gatwick. But I haven't been on a single ride. I haven't sat in Pluto's lap. It's time to step into a world where timeless stories and favourite characters come to life. Or something like that. In the name of research, I walk back into the theme dream.

'Zip-a-dee doo dah, zip-a-dee ay.'

The Diamond Horseshoe Saloon Revue, archetypal setting of a thousand TV Westerns, is like a walk-through movie set. Beyond it is the Enchanted Tiki Room. Here *Aladdin*'s Iago and Zazu from *The Lion King* re-enact their big-screen antics.

'I *love* Iago the parrot,' a sparky nine-year-old in a queue confesses to me. 'Because he's always got a big mouth on him, and my mother says that sometimes I've got a big mouth too. I guess that's why I like him.'

Above us spread the 800,000 vinyl leaves of the vast Swiss Family Treehouse. The cement banyan tree was recreated from the Disney film *Swiss Family Robinson*. Next door Pirates of the Caribbean packs more animated characters into the celluloid culture.

'But really it's Sebastian in *The Little Mermaid* who I *adore*,' admits my self-appointed guide. 'He's funny. And a very good singer. "Under the sea, Under the sea, Take it from me . . ." And you *really* don't know him?' she asks me, breaking off her tuneless song.

I admit to the failing.

'Oh, God,' she despairs, rolling her eyes. 'Duh?'

I decide to skirt Fantasyland's eternal childhood, where youngsters meet Ariel in his grotto, and fast-forward myself to the concrete plazas of Tomorrowland. Here Buzz Lightyear defends the planet from evil. Star cadets buy battery-powered rayguns from the Merchant of Venus. I tuck into soft-serve ice cream with fifteen Dandy Lions Pre-Schoolers at Auntie Gravity's Galactic Goodies. Next door Cool Ship Fast Snack does a brisk trade selling refreshment to a thirsty galaxy. Eating and drinking are intermissions in the cinematic day.

I prepare myself to experience SpaceRanger Spin. Or Astro Orbiter? Or The Timekeeper? Or . . .

The 180-foot-high white steel cone of Space Mountain dominates the concrete square. I remember friends at school discussing the ride. So I jump to the absurd conclusion that it's educational. A summary of the Apollo missions and planned Mars flights, perhaps? The heat and noise must be getting to me.

'It's *really* bad,' says an eleven-year-old in front of me.

'There are two real big drops,' adds his friend.

Drops?

The queues, which from outside appeared to be short, snake through the dark under the mountain for forty-five minutes. Holographic comets and futuristic television news reports flash above us. Astronauts Scott Carpenter, Gordon Cooper and Jim Irwin took the inaugural ride. Maybe I'll learn how quasars are formed. Or understand the process of planetary accretion.

'Like, Thor puked on his first time.'

'He's a flake.'

The two lines merge and double back on themselves. Guests begin removing their glasses. Not so very far away, people are screaming. I realise too late that Space Mountain is a rollercoaster in the dark.

'I'm sitting in the front.'

'No way, it's my turn.'

'Sorry, guys, you're below minimum height,' says our space-suited executioner. 'You, sir,' he tells me, 'you can sit in the front.'

Our rocket ship is winched up beyond the spinning earth, above model astronauts walking on the moon, into a swirling galaxy. As we climb it grows darker. The cart's ratchets bite into the rail. The metal cogs click on the wheels. Disembodied shrieks waft up from far below us. Then we stop.

We teeter.

We drop.

Our rocket falls into the void, hurtling towards the ground, heading for death. As we are wrenched around right-angle corners, the boys behind me start laughing. I bury my head in my hands and worry about metal fatigue. When was this ride built? When I was growing up. When were all those Boeing 737s grounded? When I was growing up.

'Try standing,' cries the kid behind me.

'I'm going to barf,' says his friend.

We jerk back up, then drop again. I wonder what on earth I'm doing. I'm learning nothing about astronomy. Or even space exploration. I hang on to real life and feel my right shoulder rip. I close my eyes and wish for the end to this torture in a black hole.

The ride lasts three terrible minutes and twenty-two long seconds. I stumble out under the sign 'Prepare to re-enter Tomorrowland'. I'd feel safer in today.

'Let's go again,' say the kids.

The crowds press me forward, sweeping along in a feelgood daze, until I find myself in the queue for the ExtraTERROR-estrial Alien Encounter. This time I read the small print.

Warning! The ExtraTERRORestrial ride is an intense theatrical experience that may be too frightening for young children.

And me.

Portions of this attraction take place in total darkness at which time guests are confined in their seats by a restraint system that applies pressure to the neck and shoulder.

At least I won't spin out into a nebula.

Persons who develop anxiety in dark places or those with neck and shoulder conditions should not experience this attraction.

My shoulder hurts. My feet too. I need to sit down. I submit myself to the attraction and confront an animatronic *Alien*. A carnivorous space creature breaks out of a faulty teleporter. My seat shivers, hidden speakers whisper in my ears and jets of compressed air blow at my feet. It's exhausting. At least the screams in the dark don't bother me. Because I'm not being dropped from a great height.

'Please exit the Convention Center, those of you who haven't been eaten,' advises the solicitous controller. 'Don't forget your belongings and smaller carbon-based life forms.'

Not only have I lost any claim to being an intrepid traveller, I realise too that I'm no starship trooper.

I need to get back to Florida, so retreat with the under-tens to the safety of the Jungle Cruise. I hope that the excursion will recapture for me the excitement of the first Palatka subtropical river cruises. But there's no room for imagination aboard the *Orinoco Ida*. The ride is inspired by the Bogart/Hepburn classic *The African Queen*. We glide down the Nile, sail up the Congo, then flip across to the Irrawaddy to seek out the secret bathing pool of the Indian elephant. In eight and a half minutes we navigate eight great rivers, sailing scene-by-scene through a clockwork, unthreatening world. Parrots squawk, gorillas steal pith helmets and the friendly natives wear fezzes. President Jackson doesn't annihilate the Seminole people. There are no Islamic fundamentalists. No Hutu death squads. No *Tatmadaw* press-gangs. As with history, Disney offers us a playful, pseudo-exotic geography. Travel the globe, and still be home in time for *Jeopardy!*. Maybe I would be more bedazzled if I wasn't alone, if I'd come with children; but maybe I would be less critical too. I'm not even splashed by the mechanical hippo.

'No, we cannot do that ride again.'

'Don't you come cuddling me now.'

At end of the day, temperatures fall and tempers rise. Cranky children argue, tired teens strop, husbands curse the absence of alcohol in the Magic Kingdom. We're all funned out.

'Stop dawdling.'

I slump onto a bench, overshadowed by a larger-than-life statue of Walt and Mickey holding hands. Disney's right arm is raised, reaching out to cheer on his flagging guests. Aldous Huxley wrote, 'Experience is not what happens to a man; it is what a man does with what happens to him.' I could have done without the Disney experience.

Along Main Street the tempo of the piped music has picked up in a last attempt to lighten both our step and our wallets. There are still Bug Pops and Pooh musical watches to be sold. Since the park first opened, six hundred million people – the equivalent of every American and European – have walked past my bench.

'Take your picture, sir?'

Dean Gaschler has a kind mouth. His grey eyes crinkle. He is maybe fifty, with a nose like a small avocado pear. He is holding a green Goofy helium balloon.

'No, thank you. Not right now.'

'Certainly, sir.'

Then I see his badge.

After Mickey Mouse, Dean is the park resident that visitors most want to meet. Not because of his courteous – almost sycophantic – manner. But because he is in charge of choosing a Grand Marshal for each day's Magical Moments Parade. The wizard of schmaltz. I drag myself to my feet and hurry after him to ask about his role in this cyberEden. The sole of my holey sneakers flops off.

'It's wonderful,' he enthuses, bouncing his balloon. On his lapel are both 'Spirit of Disney' and 'Partners in Excellence' pins. 'Just wonderful.'

If enthusiasm is the key to a successful career at Disney, Dean is on the way to a seat on the board. Rebecca Grin-All-the-Time will be his deputy.

'Every morning I walk out into the park to find a family with the object to blow their socks off.'

A child in the crowd drops her Mouseketeer ears. Dean scoops them off the ground and returns them to her.

'The programme is developed as a random selection, but we do have some situations where we do requests.'

Dean picks up a discarded paper napkin then deadheads a hanging flower-basket, as houseproud as a Bavarian *Hausfrau*. I'm envious of his irrepressible energy.

'Last month I did a little twelve-year-old girl. When she was ten she fell off a boat. She was in the front of the boat. The boat dragged her underneath and pulled her face-first into the moving propeller. Then the water spun her around and caught her foot in the propeller. She was in a coma for five days. But she survived and came down on vacation to Disney.'

Dean stops at a Character Greeting queue to reassure the waiting parents. 'Sorry for the delay, folks,' he says. 'Minnie won't be too much longer.'

'And you made her a Grand Marshal?' I ask. All Disney's planning and strategies leave nothing, no single element, to chance. The message seems to be that a twelve-year-old is safer in the park than on the family boat.

'We start at 2 o'clock on the steps of City Hall,' he nods, explaining the Making of a Magic Moment. 'We get on the train and it takes us to a backstage area behind Splash Mountain. The announcement is made all over the loudspeaker system and the Grand Marshal rides in a little replica fire truck. They get a great seat for the parade and the people applaud and the kids wave and it is a marvellous situation. They're the star of the day.' Dean smiles with unquestioning joy. 'I've been here with Disney for seven years now.'

There are no serpents in Disney's Garden.

'I guess you don't have too many pessimists on the staff.'

'The job's not for everybody,' he admits. 'I don't want to get into the area of how hiring and firing work. But I tell the cast members who aren't willing or able to do the Disney thing, you know, to choose one of two options: either work backstage or eliminate yourselves. You have a certain percentage of people who aren't happy doing anything.'

I follow Dean as he helps a blind guest return a Personal Translator Unit, a rentable audio-cassette player which describes sights and smells. Then he directs another visitor to the Magic Kingdom kennel. I spot no employees eliminating themselves in Town Square.

'You know that Disney refers to "kids of all ages"?' he asks. 'Last week I selected two sisters – aged seventy-nine and eighty-three – to be Grand Marshals. At the end of the Meet-and-Greet the older sister grabbed my hand and said, "Dean, I've been looking at faces for all my life, and I see a true love of people in your face. Don't you ever lose that." Talk about something to carry with you.'

We stop at the exit. I need a drink. The nearest bar is a monorail-ride away at the Contemporary Resort. Above us flies the company flag: a golden globe mounted with black mouse-ears. As I try to reassemble my disintegrating shoes I notice that the cobblestones are embossed with names.

'Wally & Wanda Snedeker, Coral Springs, Fl.; Kou Dave Docwra and Family, London U.K.'

The Walk Around the World project enables fans to 'perpetuate their devotion to Disney' by sponsoring the laying of an inscribed stone.

'Alun, Helen, Matt & Rebecca Owens, Ponciau, Wales.'

A place in paradise is reserved.

'Ernst & Greta Westerman, Ulm, Germany.'

At a cost of a hundred dollars per cobblestone.

'Every day I stand on Main Street watching people turn into Town Square and see the Castle for the first time, and their enthusiasm's infectious,' says Dean.

His job is to ensure that guests have the ultimate Disney experience.

'I remember one day a gentleman walked in and enquired the price of a service that we offer. When I told him, he started throwing words a foot long at me. "I'm not about to pay that g.d. much money for no g.d. this." He cursed and swore and then walked outside of the location. Not fifteen seconds later he and his wife were sitting on a park bench, and they obviously wanted a photo of them together. I walked up to the gentleman and asked, "Can I help you?" You know those cartoons where the jaw drops and hits the floor? That's what his mouth did. I took his picture. I didn't want to do it, but it was *the* correct thing to do with the way my training here at Disney had taught me.'

Dean's dedication is absolute.

'I think there's a reason I'm out here,' he confesses. 'I'm blessed. I know I'm blessed having a position like this.'

Night falls. The Fantasy in the Sky fireworks light up the heavens. The Electrical Parade glitters along Main Street. A spotlit Tinkerbell launches herself off a Castle turret and glides through the air, suspended by a wire. Showers of pixie-dust sparkle down onto the applauding spectators. I call Katrin from a pay phone behind Peter Pan's Flight to Neverland.

'You sound exhausted,' she says.

'I nearly died today.'

'What?'

'In the Black Hole of Orlando.'

'Never heard of it.'

It's also called . . .' I pause as Simba the Lion King's son discovers his roar. '. . . Space Mountain.'

'The rollercoaster ride?'

'That's the one.'

'I rode it at Disneyland,' says Katrin. She once had a boy-friend in California. 'It was fantastic.'

12

Fearful in Orlando

A husband is sleeping with his wife's cousin. The wife is trying to break up the relationship while still living with the husband's father. Simply put, there are a dozen stories here.

JERRY SPRINGER SHOW, NBC

Yeehaw Junction, Sunday 30th – Forget Orwell's boot stamping on a human face forever. In *Brave New World* Huxley predicted that society will be tamed by desire and pleasure. Mass entertainment has eliminated the need for Thought Police.

I took in EPCOT this morning. The Experimental Prototype Community of Tomorrow had been conceived as a utopian city of 30,000 people. It was designed to solve the problems of urban living. But once Disney understood that Florida law would require its residents to have voting rights, and therefore be able to shape the community themselves, the park was redesigned as a trade fair. Adam and Eve never made it into this Eden.

I Journeyed into the Imagination with Kodak, travelled in Spaceship Earth compliments of AT&T, took in United Technologies' Living Seas and shared MetLife's Wonders of Life. A giant dog sneezed on me and I witnessed the miracle of conception, without the distraction of mucky fornication. I avoided extinction, piloted a submarine and was trapped – once again – in the mind of a twelve-year-old boy. 'Major corporations have combined their creative thinking with Walt Disney Imagineers to explore projections about the future.' At EPCOT Mickey acts as muse for allied multinationals.

While Future World sells tomorrow, the World Showcase packages eleven of today's cultures. Assembled around a forty-acre lagoon are pavilions from Britain, France, Germany, Italy, Norway, Morocco, Japan, China, Mexico and Canada, plus 'an old fashioned Fourth of July' American Adventure.

At the Rose and Crown I ordered a half pint. Then walked along the Great Wall and sailed with the Vikings. The smell of Beck's and *bockwurst* at *Der Biergarten* convinced me for a moment that my whole journey had been an illusion. I wasn't in the United States at all. I had really travelled to Europe. Until a beret-wearing Parisian was civil to me.

'Supercalifragilisticexpialidocious.'

A topiary Mary Poppins opened her umbrella above red telephone boxes in the United Kingdom Showcase. Anne Hathaway's cottage sat on the stubby High Street. Scottish pipers played beneath the towers of Hampton Court. Wales was represented by a shop.

I went back for the other half.

Sat in the Florida sun, listening to English voices, drinking Australian lager, looking across the lake towards the Doge's Palace and Marrakesh's Koutoubia minaret. A Japanese wedding party sailed by on the *Amazon Annie*. Chinese acrobats celebrated Carnivale. A Canadian couple at the next table decided to have lunch in Italy and dinner in Mexico. The

Latin motto on the pub sign – *Otium Cum Dignitate* – translated as Leisure with Dignity. I left.

Needed to sleep before my flight home and went looking for a motel. Found the cheapest on Highway 50. It was a low, single-storey corral of units, repainted baby-blue and white. Rotting. Uninviting. Inexpensive.

At reception I asked for the coupon rate.

'No more singles,' said the desk clerk behind the metal grille.

Took a double. An extra ten dollars. He handed me two keys. Didn't bother to look up from his TV.

'One's for your room, the other's for the security door to your floor.'

A dismal Lion supermarket lay in wait across the highway. In the parking lot black men hung around in their cars, doors open, engines off. White kids rode their bikes on the pavement. I parked as near as I could to the store's entrance. A dirty, blood-red Camaro idled up alongside me. *Whatever* was etched across its tinted windscreen.

I ran inside with my bag over my shoulder. My plan was to buy dinner and eat it in my room. Pre-cooked ribs, fruit and yoghurt. Maybe a sixpack too. Over the cucumbers a broad, muscular security guard approached me.

'You're not allowed to carry a bag around the store.' His biceps were like gammon joints. 'You gotta leave it at the desk.'

'My laptop is inside,' I explained. Plus all my notes.

'It's company policy. You can't shop with a bag.'

'Tell you what,' I suggested. 'I'll show you my bag when I'm through shopping.'

'I might have gone on my break.'

'In five minutes?'

'You'd be putting a burden on me. I don't need that. Hand in your bag at the desk or you can't shop.'

I put back the bananas. I thanked him and left the store. I returned to the baby-blue motel. I checked out. I escaped from Orlando.

I was in no real danger. The men in their cars were just hanging out. The boys on the bikes had no plans to run me down. I was simply tired, and dulled by Disney. I felt exposed. I was a stranger in a foreign place, conspicuous and vulnerable. It would just be bad luck if I was shot, robbed or beaten up.

On my drive out of town I saw no orange groves. Instead, in all directions, an asphalt skin seemed to have been laid on top of the dead-flat swamp. Yet another turtle lay squashed on the highway, the track of its entrails spread in a gory smear.

Once there were a hundred thousand acres of plantations around Orlando. Then Disney arrived. Farmers grubbed up their trees, or didn't replant after the 1984 freeze, sold out to developers and retired to the coast. The citrus industry moved to Latin America. Subdivisions made more money than frozen juice.

'The following advertisement is for post-menopausal women experiencing hot flushes,' announced Oldies Radio You 92. Then played 'Drive' by The Cars. Kool-aid Koolers were half-price at K-mart. 'Home is where the sweetness is,' purred the disc jockey. 'Your satisfaction is guaranteed.'

I switched off the radio and turned away from the curling ribbons of overpasses. To the north was Cassadaga, where windchimes tinkled in the breeze. In an hour I could be at Saint Leo. There would always be a welcome in Bristol. But I chose to move on, and headed south on SR 523.

At Yeehaw Junction two hefty blondes in a white pick-up check their lipstick in the mirror. Trucks thunder through the crossroads, between Highway 441 and SR 60, and onto the Florida Turnpike. Here there are great open trailers of oranges, low-loaders stacked with pine, and cattle transports. A gaunt vulture hovers above the intersection. Brackish drainage canals run away towards the horizon.

I pull into the empty parking lot. A cloud of dust settles onto the rambling, shingled Desert Inn, the only building in town. 'The present edifice,' declares the National Register of Historic Places' plaque, 'served as a supply and recreational center for cattle drovers, lumber men and tourists.' Fancy cockerels pick at the grass beside the road, the only males strutting their stuff today. It is an unlikely spot to be recommended by a monk.

Otium Sin Dignitate.

Inside, a dark clutter of relics surrounds the island of the bar. There are stuffed donkeys, mounted hare's heads and chrome sugar-shakers. Beyond the jukebox, two cigar-store Indian mannequins play cards at a corner table. On the wall are glazed trophy trout and pearls of wisdom: 'One man has enthusiasm for thirty minutes, another for thirty days, but it is the man who has it for thirty years who makes a success of his life (Edward B. Butler, American scientist).'

I sit on a leatherette stool at the counter.

'What'llyahave?' asks Cora.

Her eyes are pale blue, almost colourless. Her skin is sunburnt and lined. She too is a relic, of a life of hard work, of trying to satisfy appetites, of frying turtle-frog combos. Only her haircut looks young. A short teenager's bob.

The menu is written on paper plates pinned beneath winking coloured lights. Gator Burger at $3.99. The Sportsman's Special for $4.95. Hash browns topped with bell peppers and eggs. Texas toast and coleslaw are extra.

'Try our Hole in One' reads a sign above the kitchen hatch.

I ask Cora what she recommends.

'If you're from England, you won't like my chilli. It ain't wimpy.'

She serves it in a child's-size bowl. I burn the roof of my mouth.

'I had some Guatemalans come through this morning early,' she says, leaning back against the bottles of whisky and tequila. A reproduction thousand-dollar bill hangs above the bar. 'They ordered the chilli for breakfast. I thought it would finish them off, but they ate two bowls. I like men who ain't docile.' Pronounced *daw-sile*.

'You want my pretzels?' asks a sad soul on the next stool. She passes me a silver-foil pack of Summer Harvest Brand Low-Fat Mini-Pretzels. 'I can't eat no carbohydrates.'

'Thanks.'

'Any time.'

'Can't have no bourbon neither, huh Jo?' says Cora, lifting her chin to make the point.

'Nope,' says the woman, swallowing black coffee.

As I eat, Cora complains that her business has dropped off. A new law forbids truckers from stopping at restaurants that serve spirits.

'Drivers get just as drunk down the road on beer. But if they stop in here, their insurance is invalid.'

'You could give up your liquor licence,' I suggest.

'Can't do that. It's the third oldest in the county. Anyway, when folks come round, they like a drink. It helps them to relax at the end of the day. You want some pie?'

'It's home-made coconut cream,' says Jo.

'When it's warm, in the morning when it's first made, it's a sin.'

A handwritten sign by the till reads 'Museum Upstairs'. I finish the sickly pie and ask for a tour. Cora leads me up the creaking steps to the upper floor.

'The bordello's at the end of the hall; watch your step.'

The half-dozen board-and-batten rooms are filled with junk. A shapeless, threadbare dress is spread out on one bed. On the wall of another room are recipes for roast haunch of beaver and sweet-potato stew.

'Would they have been served here?' I ask.

'Could be.'

The front room is red: red carpet, red satin bedspread, red upholstered swing. There is a saddle, a railway lamp and a paint-by-numbers portrait of a girl. A pair of cowboy boots stand at the foot of the brass bed.

'The boots are a good touch,' I tell Cora.

'Someone loaned them to me,' she replies, giving nothing away. Then she glances out the window. 'Fucking birds,' she swears and bolts downstairs.

There was a brothel on the site for a century. First to serve the cowmen working cattle on the palmetto prairie. Then for railway workers building the Florida East Coast branch line from New Smyrna to Okeechobee Lake. Its doors were open to lumberjacks cutting timber in the adjacent pine lands. It accommodated the men who built the Interstate. African-Americans and Seminoles were also welcome, though they had separate dining facilities.

Yeehaw was the county's first pleasure destination. For men only. Marineland, Weeki Wachee and Disney World followed from this point. Its owners sold moonshine and package goods, jackasses and fantasy. Ox teams and cattle drives passed through town. Woodchoppers built rough cabins around the sawmill's cabbage-head smokestack.

In the thirties the roads were paved. US 441 ran past the front door on its way from Chicago to Miami. An owner named Dad Wilson fixed up the Inn. He erected a set of overnight cabins behind the original building. Tourists expanded the client base. Wilson added a gas station, the first between Kissimmee and Okeechobee, and his success attracted competition. Sol Padgett, a cattleman, opened his own gas bar across the road. The two men hated one another, as on most days only three or four cars came through town. They sat across the road from each other in their rocking chairs, smoking corncob pipes, shotguns across their laps.

At the start of the war there were eight gas stations, one garage, three restaurants, a motel and a grocery store in Yee-haw. As well as the Inn. Then in 1945 the railway tracks were ripped up. The Florida Turnpike opened and travellers bypassed the scarlet establishment on their way to the new fantasy sites on the coast. The Inn changed hands, lost money, hung on the edge of bankruptcy.

In the pitiful red room I try to imagine the women who once worked in the lonely outpost. I try to picture shouting, sunburnt labourers staggering down the hall, opening wrong doors, passing out on sweat-stained sheets. I see drunk travelling salesmen shouting evil profanities. Then a quiet, uniformed soldier sitting by the bedside remembering the face of the girl next-door. I hear a woman weeping too.

Through the window I watch Cora shoo a cockerel off the highway. She shambles back indoors. I go downstairs. She waits alone in her narrow office, counting pennies. I lean across the bar to say goodbye.

'We got rooms to rent,' she says without losing count.

I thank her.

'$33.50 a night.'

I drive on.

Gatwick, Monday 1st – Somewhere over the Atlantic I turn down the headphones and the plastic chicken breast. Lay the *Daily Mail* over my head. Fall asleep. Dream.

I am reading a newspaper. In it there is a photograph of the Magic Moments Parade. As I watch, the picture comes to life. It sweeps off Main Street and out of the page towards me. Adam and Eve are in the lead, wearing designer swim-suits. Ponce de León follows them down the aircraft aisle, slopping iron kettles of elixir from the Fountain of Youth. Rows of geriatrics drink down his tonic, then spring from their wheelchairs to dance the conga. Music is provided by a band of ebullient Honduran exiles. A phalanx of gorgeous gay alligators in tails serve finger-food. Monks feast on Devil Drops and Marshmallow Bunnies. Golfers hit birdies through the fuselage. Flamingos fly alongside the starboard wing. In the lavatory a real-estate huckster conjures skyscrapers out of the mangrove swamp.

'I feel *good*,' says Al Capone, waving from First Class. '*So good.*'

In my dream my fellow passengers become Disney charac-ters. Daisy Duck laughs at the antics of a pair of levitating spiritualists. Kanga and Roo applaud an evangelical preacher. Clarabelle drops her ice cream on the floor when Randall James Baker shoots the top off Robert Callihan's baseball cap and head.

'I'm forever reaching,' cries Virginia Blue from the African Pride hair-care float. She wears a sassy side-bang and ponytail. 'That's what I do. Forever reach.'

I look up and down the aisle for my mermaid but cannot see her. Instead Douglas Buchanan fries in the electric chair while a Citrus County woman douses herself with petrol and sets herself on fire.

'When you wish upon a star . . .'

Think I hear my mermaid singing, but realise it's Tanya the Miami redhead serenading me with a come-hither wink.

'. . . makes no difference who you are . . .'

'It's an old song,' explains the black-and-white cartoon character in the seat beside me. 'No school past grade eight, got into drugs, started selling to support my habit. Did four-to-nine cause they caught me with an ounce of cocaine. But I never hurt no one.'

'. . . up above the stars so high . . .'

It is then that I realise that I too am in the photograph, watching the parade, surrounded by animated idols. Snow White blows me a kiss, lifting her skirts to display her PVC knickers. Lady and the Tramp indulge in enthusiastic romping.

'Oh God,' despairs the sparky nine-year-old, rolling her eyes. 'Duh?'

I reach out to touch the illusion but find that my arm is in a sling. Space Mountain impingement syndrome. I unbuckle my safety belt with my good hand. Try to get up out of my seat. But the parade begins to shiver. It buckles along its length, as if again on a flat, printed surface. I lose sight of Virginia and Daisy Duck. I no longer hear Tanya's song. A crease runs down the aisle and up the middle of Main Street. With a final sharp shake, the sunny fantasy world closes in on itself.

I am no longer in the photograph. Wake up. The copy of the *Mail* has fallen into my lap.

I came to Florida by chance. Shut my front door, turned the key in the lock and cast myself adrift. Followed my instinct and learnt that intuition is a form of planning. Tried to recognise things of value in the arbitrary, to detect patterns where perhaps none exist. Then realised that no trip is random in itself. I chose my road, like so many travellers before me, hunting for the pure in a muddled world. I spent my days looking for a wholeness which isn't to be found, even in fanciful Florida. Took a small step towards the black void.

Now, here in this aircraft flying home, I feel not so much at the end as at a beginning. Ready to pause at the next crossroads and take the time to listen. A journey is not a linear thread, as the Cruel Fates would have it, with cause and effect tumbling over each other along its measured length. Rather it is an intricate spiral, fluid and unfixed, elegant and ephemeral, like the trail of a swallow's flight through the evening sky. Clouds may obscure its course. The wind may alter it. The bird may vanish in the twinkling of an eye. But for me the twists and turns will remain there to be traced on the air, ascending and descending, fated to end yet forever reaching. Perhaps pre-ordained. Never pre-known.

At Gatwick I call home. Last night the puppy pulled a plastic bag of glue out of the kitchen drawer. Chewed the Araldite. Spread Bostik all over her mat. There's a black patch of Superglue on her front left leg. At least Katrin didn't come down to find her nose stuck to the cupboard.

Next I call David.

'How was it?' he asks.

'I met a mermaid,' I tell him. 'I stayed in a monastery and went to the Garden of Eden. I saw utopia reduced to a trade fair and communed with my uncle's ghost. I tell you, Germany just wasn't meant to be. At least, it wasn't meant to be *yet*.'

The telephone line goes quiet. I wonder for a moment if David has heard me. Or if he has fallen asleep.

'That's great,' he says after a moment. 'But did you get laid?'

Acknowledgements

Thanks to Rosie Goldsmith and Max Easterman for their advice, guidance and expertise – on Germany.